ENCYCLOPEDIA
OF
WORLD
GEOGRAPHY

ENCYCLOPEDIA
OF
WORLD
GEOGRAPHY

VOLUME THREE
Canada and the Arctic

Marshall Cavendish
New York · Toronto · Sydney

Marshall Cavendish Corporation,
2415 Jerusalem Avenue,
P.O. Box 587,
North Bellmore,
N.Y. 11710,
U.S.A.

AN ANDROMEDA BOOK

Planned and produced by
Andromeda Oxford Ltd
11–15 The Vineyard, Abingdon,
Oxfordshire OX14 3PX, England

**Library of Congress
Cataloging-in-Publication Data
applied for**

ISBN 1 85435 631 3 (Set)
ISBN 1 85435 634 8 (Vol 3)

Origination: Scantrans, Singapore

Printed by:
L.E.G.O. S.p.A., Vicenza, Italy

This page: *Tracts of boreal forest in northern Canada*
Title page: *City highrise, Montreal*

CONTENTS

Introduction 294–295

Country Profiles

Canada 298–319

Dependencies in the Region

    Greenland 320–321

    St Pierre and Miquelon............................ 321

Regional Profiles

Physical Geography 324–333

Habitats and their Conservation 334–343

Animal Life...................................... 344–353

Plant Life.. 354–361

Agriculture 362–369

Industry 370–379

Economy 380–387

Peoples and Cultures......................... 388–397

Cities.. 398–407

Government 408–415

Environmental Issues 416–423

Glossary 424–427

Index... 428–431

Further reading & Acknowledgments...................... 432

INTRODUCTION

Canada and the Arctic

THIS VAST NORTHERN REGION CONTAINS JUST THREE countries; one an independent state and the other two dependencies of European nations. Canada is the world's second largest country after Russia. Greenland, a dependency of Denmark, is the world's largest island; and St Pierre and Miquelon (a dependency of France) is a tiny archipelago off Newfoundland. Extensive areas of the region are within the Arctic Circle. The surrounding seas are frequently ice-covered and treacherous to navigate, though international air routes cross the skies. The only international land boundary runs between the United States and Canada. The western boundary divides Canada from the 49th state, Alaska, and much of the southern part of the boundary follows the 49th parallel. The southern boundary also divides four of the Great Lakes – Lake Superior (the world's largest freshwater lake), Lake Huron, Lake Erie and Lake Ontario – and cuts across the Niagara Falls.

Most of the region is very sparsely populated. Greenland, for example, has only 53,000 inhabitants. Coniferous forests and thousands of lakes cover the ancient Canadian Shield, while north of the treeline, short summers and poor soils make agriculture impossible. Larger animals such as caribou, seals and polar bears adapt by making seasonal migrations in search of food, a practice also adopted by the Inuit peoples, some of whom still live in small settlements across the tundra. The potential for exploiting whales, furs and gold first attracted outsiders, and later the eastern frontier gained importance as a Cold War boundary between the West and the former Soviet Union. Although the region is rich in natural resources, efforts to exploit them are hampered by remoteness, the harsh climate, the unresolved land claims of native peoples and environmentalist concerns.

The majority of the region's inhabitants are found within 320 km (200 mi) of the southern border with the United States. This lateral population distribution accounts for two of Canada's significant features. Government has operated within a decentralized and federal system since independence in 1867, though the division between the English- and French-speaking communities continues to strain the political compromise. Secondly, much of Canada is economically and culturally closer to the United States than to the northern part of the region. The Free Trade Agreement made with the United States in 1988 recognizes this fact but also raises fears that the United States will wield economic and cultural dominance over Canada.

North America

Central and South America

A   ANDORRA
AL   ALBANIA
AR   ARMENIA
AU   AUSTRIA
AZ   AZERBAIJAN
BEL BELGIUM
B   BOSNIA AND HERCEGOVINA
BU   BURUNDI
CR   CROATIA
CZ   CZECH REPUBLIC
DEN DENMARK
DOM DOMINICAN REPUBLIC
EQ   EQUATORIAL GUINEA
HUN HUNGARY

L   LEBANON
LITH LITHUANIA
LUX LUXEMBOURG
M   MACEDONIA
NETH NETHERLANDS
R   RUSSIA
RW   RWANDA
SL   SLOVAKIA
S   SLOVENIA
SW   SWITZERLAND
T   TOGO
UAE UNITED ARAB EMIRATES
YU   YUGOSLAVIA

Europe

Asia

GREENLAND
(Den)

ICELAND

NORWAY
SWEDEN
FINLAND

RUSSIA

UNITED
KINGDOM
IRELAND
DEN
NETH
BEL
LUX
GERMANY
FRANCE
SW
A
ITALY
PORTUGAL
SPAIN
Gibraltar (UK)

ESTONIA
LATVIA
LITH
R
POLAND
BELORUSSIA
CZ
SL
AU HUN
S CR
B YU
AL M
ROMANIA
MOLDAVIA
BULGARIA
GREECE

UKRAINE

GEORGIA
AR AZ

KAZAKHSTAN

MONGOLIA

NORTH
KOREA
SOUTH
KOREA

JAPAN

ores
ort)

TURKEY

UZBEKISTAN
TURKMENISTAN
TAJIKISTAN
KIRGHIZIA

CHINA

MOROCCO

Canary Is
(Sp)

WESTERN
SAHARA
(Morocco)

MAURITANIA

TUNISIA

MALTA
CYPRUS L
ISRAEL
SYRIA
IRAQ
JORDAN
IRAN
KUWAIT
BAHRAIN
QATAR
UAE

AFGHANISTAN

PAKISTAN

NEPAL

BHUTAN

TAIWAN
Hong Kong (UK)
Macao
(Port)

ALGERIA
LIBYA
EGYPT

SAUDI
ARABIA
OMAN

INDIA

BANGLADESH

BURMA

LAOS

PE
RDE
SENEGAL
GAMBIA
GUINEA-
BISSAU
GUINEA
SIERRA
LEONE
LIBERIA

MALI
NIGER
CHAD
BURKINA
BENIN
IVORY
COAST
GHANA
NIGERIA
CAMEROON
SAO TOME &
PRINCIPE
Annobon
(Eq)

SUDAN

ERITREA

YEMEN

DJIBOUTI

Socotra (Yem)

SRI
LANKA

MALDIVES

THAILAND
CAMBODIA
VIETNAM

PHILIPPINES

BRUNEI
MALAYSIA
SINGAPORE

NAURU

CENTRAL
AFRICAN REPUBLIC
EQ
GABON
CONGO
UGANDA
RW
BU
ZAIRE
KENYA
ETHIOPIA
SOMALIA

SEYCHELLES

INDONESIA

PAPUA
NEW GUINEA

SOLOMON IS

Ascension
(UK)

Cabinda
(Ang)

TANZANIA

COMOROS

VANUATU

St Helena
(UK)

ANGOLA
ZAMBIA
MALAWI

MADAGASCAR

MAURITIUS
Réunion (Fr)

New Caledonia
(Fr)

Tristan da Cunha
(UK)

NAMIBIA
ZIMBABWE
BOTSWANA
MOZAMBIQUE
SWAZILAND
SOUTH
AFRICA
LESOTHO

AUSTRALIA

Georgia

Kerguelen
(Fr)

NEW
ZEALAND

Africa

Australasia, Oceania and Antarctica

Antarctica

Canada and the Arctic

COUNTRIES IN THE REGION

CANADA

DEPENDENCIES IN THE REGION

GREENLAND · ST PIERRE AND MIQUELON

The maple leaf, Canada's national symbol, emblazoned on garage doors in Saskatchewan. The maple leaf's official status was only confirmed in 1965, when it was added to the center of the national flag. Syrup is made from the sweet sap of the sugar maples that are native to the deciduous forests of the eastern part of the country, and whose leaves in fall turn a brilliant red.

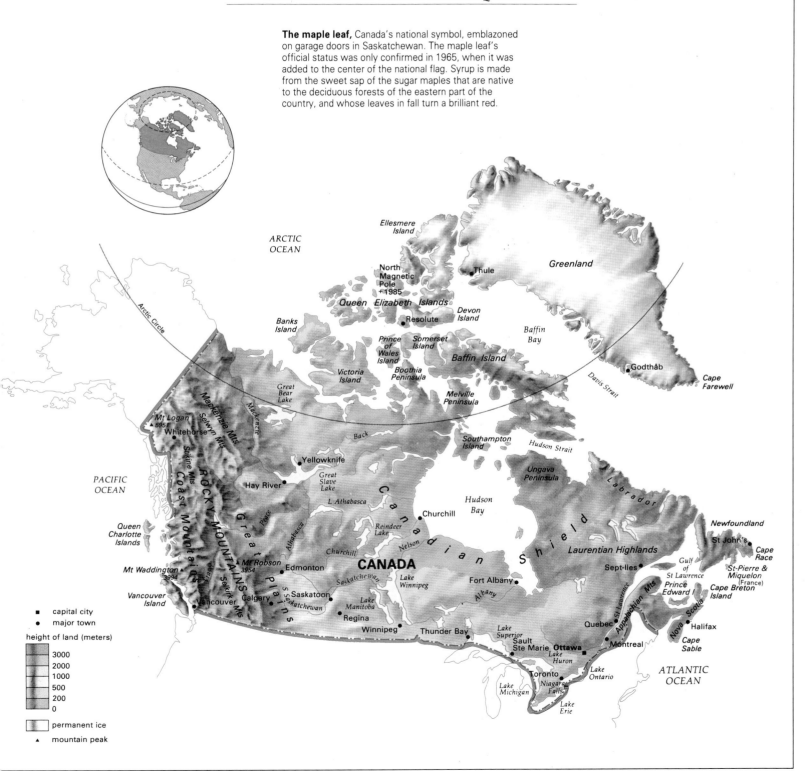

capital city
major town

height of land (meters)

3000
2000
1000
500
200
0

permanent ice

mountain peak

Canada

C ANADA OCCUPIES MOST OF THE NORTHERN half of the North American continent. Its economy and culture show many similarities with the United States – so much so that some outsiders tend to think of it as no more than a satellite. However, nothing could be farther from the truth: for Canada has its own distinct character and rich ethnic mix. Its unique bilingual and bicultural society can be traced back to the nation's French and British origins.

NATIONAL DATA

Land area 9,215,430 sq km (3,558,096 sq mi)

Climate	Altitude m (ft)	Temperatures January °C(°F)	July °C(°F)	Annual precipitation mm (in)
Resolute	64 (200)	−32 (−26)	4 (39)	136 (5.3)
Vancouver	0 (0)	2 (36)	17 (63)	1,068 (42.0)
Montreal	30 (98)	−9 (16)	22 (72)	999 (39.3)

Major physical features highest point: Mount Logan 5,951 m (19,524 ft); longest river: Mackenzie 4,240 m (2,635 mi); largest lake: Lake Superior (part) 83,270 sq km (32,150 sq mi)

Population (1990) 26,521,000

Form of government federal multiparty parliamentary monarchy with two legislative houses

Armed forces army 23,500; navy 17,100; air force 24,200; others 25,200

Largest cities Toronto (3,427,000); Montreal (2,921,000); Vancouver (1,381,000); Ottawa (capital – 819,000); Edmonton (785,000); Calgary (671,000); Winnipeg (623,000); Quebec (603,000)

Official languages English, French

Ethnic composition British 34.4%; French 25.7%; German 3.6%; Italian 2.8%; Ukrainian 1.7%; Amerindian and Inuit 1.5%; Chinese 1.4%; Dutch 1.4%; multiple origin and/or others 27.5%

Religious affiliations Roman Catholic 46.5%; Protestant 41%; Eastern Orthodox 1.5%; Jewish 1.2%; Muslim 0.4%; Hindu 0.3%; Sikh 0.3%; nonreligious 7.4%; others 1.4%

Currency 1 Canadian dollar (Can $) = 100 cents

Gross national product (1989) US $500,337 million

Gross domestic product (per person 1990) US $19,650

Life expectancy at birth male 74.0 yr; female 81.0 yr

Major resources agriculture and fisheries: 2.6% GNP; mining and primary industries: 3.9% GNP; manufacturing 18.8% GNP; finance 15.7% GNP; services 22.4% GNP

ENVIRONMENT

Canada covers a much greater expanse than the United States. This vast and often mountainous country is second only in land area to the former Soviet Union, although its population is much smaller.

The land

Canada as a nation has been shaped by its landscape. There are mountains to east and west, and it slopes down toward Hudson Bay, the sea gulf at its heart. These natural barriers have restricted settlement and preserved some of the wildest country remaining in the world.

The land can be divided into several geographical areas, of which the largest is the so-called Canadian Shield, occupying almost half the country. This bowl-shaped area centered on Hudson Bay consists of ancient rocks that were once raised into mountainous forms. Parts of its northern rim are still high enough to create fjords along the coast of the Hudson Strait and Labrador. Farther south it has been worn away by erosion, then ground down by ice age glaciers to become a landscape of low rocky hills and shallow lakes, sloping down to the deep depression of Hudson Bay itself. The Shield is strewn with boulders and rocky debris left behind by the glaciers. It

The Kicking Horse river (*above*) A canoe follows the path of early explorers through the Rocky Mountains in British Columbia. Today five of Canada's national parks lie within the spectacular scenery of the Rockies.

The Klondike highway (*left*) cuts through a forested landscape of snow-clad mountains that captures the romantic image of Canada's far north. In the two years between 1897 and 1899, some 30,000 people came this way in search of gold.

extends as far east as the Gulf of St Lawrence, and west as far as the lowlands around Great Bear Lake and Great Slave Lake in the northwest.

Southeast of the Shield lie the lowlands of the Great Lakes–St Lawrence river area, occupying southern Ontario and southwestern Quebec. This much smaller area is the most densely populated part of Canada. The gently rolling country of the Bruce Peninsula is bounded by Lake Huron and Georgian Bay, Lake Erie and Lake Ontario. It is traversed by the Niagara Escarpment over which the Niagara Falls cascade, and is host to a thick blanket of varied glacial and post-glacial materials. The Ontario Lowlands

to the northeast of the escarpment are an ancient glacial plain covered in drumlins – low ridges of rocky debris left by the retreating glaciers. These are bounded to the east by a ridge of ancient rock, an arm of the Canadian Shield known as the Frontenac Axis. Beyond this lie the lowlands of the Ottawa Valley and southern Quebec, which are covered in sediments left by the sea that flooded them during the ice ages. The level plain is broken only by ancient rocky outcrops, and by the eight Monteregian Hills east of Montreal – isolated peaks that were left behind following volcanic activity.

East of Quebec is the region known as Appalachian Canada, which includes the

Atlantic provinces of New Brunswick, Prince Edward Island, Nova Scotia and the island of Newfoundland. Here ancient rocks have been folded and reshaped over time into craggy, mountainous country, now much eroded by weather and glaciers. There are deep valleys, and some of the softer rocks have eroded faster to create several broad lowland areas, mostly around the Gulf of St Lawrence. Among the highest of the mountain chains are the Notre Dame Mountains that run northeast from Quebec, and the Long Range Mountains of Newfoundland.

Southwest of the Shield and Hudson Bay is the Great Plains area of Canada – a vast triangular expanse of more level country covering about one-fifth of the land area. The Manitoba Lowlands are seamed with a network of lakes, most of them remnants of one immense lake that covered the whole area during the last glacial retreat. The deep sediments that it left behind have turned this into rich farming country.

Westward, the land rises over the dissected edge of the Manitoba Escarpment, beyond which are found the rolling plateaus of the Saskatchewan Plain.

A park for dinosaurs

Humans may have inhabited Canada for only a relatively short period, but for millions of years the unspoiled wilderness has supported great numbers of animals. It boasts fossil remains that date back as far as the Mesozoic Era – the age of the dinosaurs – which began some 225 million years ago and ended only 65 million years ago. This was an era when Canada was teeming with animal life.

In the badlands of Alberta, north and west of Calgary, the country has been greatly eroded by rivers into deep, barren valleys with bizarre rock formations – an uninviting prospect to settlers in the Great Plains area. However, this deep channeling of the landscape has exposed an incredible wealth of fossilized dinosaur remains. One pioneering dinosaur-hunter of the 1900s, the American paleontologist Barnum Brown (1873–1963), was able to make many discoveries by floating down the wide badlands rivers on a

A Centrosaurus bone bed The paleontologists investigating the bones will eventually take their finds to the nearby Tyrrell Museum of Paleontology at Drumheller, Alberta, for study and possible reconstruction.

raft, stopping when he spotted bones exposed in the steep banks. He then had to haul his huge but fragile specimens out of the district by horse-drawn wagons over rough country to the nearest railhead.

Today the badlands have proved to be so rich a source of knowledge about this vanished phase of life on earth that a large area west of Calgary has been declared a Dinosaur Provincial Park, restricting all other exploitation. Farther north, near the small town of Drumheller, the new Tyrrell Museum of Paleontology has been constructed. From this relatively local base, teams of scientists can set out to carry on the painstaking and often exhausting task of recovering the bones from the park and the surrounding country. The bones are brought back to Drumheller, where they are carefully studied. The dinosaurs are then mounted for display, often against reconstructions of the landscape they would have lived in, which had a very different climate from that of today.

A smaller field station is being built within the park itself, offering both laboratory facilities and public displays. Others may follow, as Canada draws on a new and unusual natural resource, and extends its pioneering spirit deeper into its astonishing past.

Down river by dog sled (*above*) From October to June the Yukon river is frozen, but for the summer months and into the early fall it offers a navigable river highway 2,000 km (1,250 mi) long that goes deep into the heart of Alaska.

Again, this is lake-studded, ice-carved country, marked by fertile soils and ranges of low rolling hills. Torrential meltwaters from the ice-age glaciers have carved wide, steep-banked river channels through the countryside. Westward through Alberta the land continues to rise. It has been severely eroded since the glaciers last retreated to form a rough plateau area, cut across by the same glacial rivers into even deeper valleys.

Farther north the land falls away to the lowlands beyond the great Mackenzie River, which flows northward into the Arctic Ocean.

West of the Great Plains is the Canadian Cordillera – the mountainous area that borders Canada's Pacific coast. A great mountain belt some 800 km (500 mi) wide extends from Alaska through the Yukon Territory, western Alberta and British Columbia. The western spine of the Cordillera is formed by the Coast Mountains. Smaller ranges such as the British Mountains run along the northern coast from the Alaskan border. The range then turns south, interrupted by plateaus,

to form the Mackenzie Range and eventually the Rocky Mountains that form the eastern spine of the Cordillera. These mighty peaks of relatively young rock rise to heights of more than 3,000 m (10,000 ft), with craggy, uneroded profiles and few passes. This wild and beautiful landscape includes five of Canada's national parks. The Rockies overlook the foothills and Great Plains on the east and the spectacular Rocky Mountain Trench on the west, beyond which are lesser ranges and valleys as well as the interior plateau country of British Columbia.

Along the western seaboard lies a parallel and even higher chain. The St

Elias Mountains to the north include Mount Logan, which at nearly 6,000 m (20,000 ft) is Canada's highest peak. The Coast Mountains run southward along the coast, cut by deep fjords or inlets of the sea. Offshore, Vancouver Island and the Queen Charlotte Islands are the peaks of yet another parallel mountain range.

North of the Shield lies the Arctic. Although the term properly refers to that part of the Earth's surface north of the Arctic Circle (latitude 66° 30'N), in practice the characteristic Arctic environment often extends much farther south, and can be said to include all areas to the north of the northernmost treeline.

To the northwest the broad archipelago of the Arctic islands border the permanent ice of the Arctic Ocean. Much of the ocean's surface is covered throughout the year by a layer of ice at least 3 m (10 ft) thick, yet less than half the surrounding land is ice-covered. The islands rise toward the northeast, becoming mountainous in Ellesmere Island and along the east coast of Baffin Island. Their barren, rocky terrain is largely covered with permanent or semipermanent fields of snow and ice, and around the mountain peaks there is extensive glaciation. Even where some soil is exposed, it is usually underlaid with a permanent ice layer known as permafrost. In some permafrost areas the surface melts a little during the summer, creating an "active zone" where water is free to move. When the temperature falls again, this water may refreeze to form swellings known as pingos, which can be up to 60 m (200 ft) high.

Climate
Such a large area as Canada naturally shows wide variations in climate. More than half the country has a subarctic climate, with cool summers and extremely cold winters – often colder than in the Arctic itself, where great extremes of temperature are moderated by the waters of the Arctic Ocean just below the ice. In the polar regions winter begins in August. Temperatures drop rapidly until December, then remain low until March. The more equable waters of the Atlantic Ocean also moderate the climate where they flow into the Arctic, producing warmer winters, colder summers and higher precipitation. Summer temperatures are usually more uniform throughout the Arctic, though some continental areas may enjoy short periods of almost Mediterranean warmth.

In many areas, especially in northeastern Canada, the windchill factor makes a considerable difference to the perceived temperature. Moreover, visibility is often affected by windblown snow or drifting fog.

Farther south the climate is typically continental, with hot summers and cold winters. Southern Ontario, among the Great Lakes, has the warmest summers. The southeast coast and especially the west coast enjoy the mildest winters. However, the extent of the maritime influence is limited by prevailing westerlies in the southeast and by the mountain barrier in the west.

Precipitation is also affected by the mountains. Onshore winds bring heavy rain and snow to the Coast Mountains, but the air over the interior is dry, especially in winter. In the summer, the famous prairie thunderstorms help to redistribute moisture across the Great Plains. Farther east the Great Lakes provide some moisture, while moist Atlantic air supplies ample rainfall to the Atlantic seaboard, where the winter snowfall is particularly heavy.

In the late 1980s a hole was discovered in the atmospheric ozone layer above the North Pole. This layer shields the earth's surface from harmful solar radiation. The Arctic ice has been slowly retreating since the 1930s, and some scientists think that

The icy grip of winter blankets Montreal in snow. Although lying in the same latitude as Florence in Italy, Montreal has bitter winters with temperatures falling below zero for more than 150 days each year.

damage to the ozone layer may help to accelerate this process, with incalculable effects on the rest of the world.

Vegetation
The treeline in northern Canada arches northward from Labrador on Canada's east coast across the Ungava Peninsula, then down the east side of Hudson Bay. Across this bay it sweeps sinuously northwest to the lower Mackenzie Valley and Alaska. North of it there is little or no fertile soil, and most of the country, known as the Barren Grounds, is tundra. The few plant species that thrive here show remarkable adaptations to permafrost, high winds, low temperatures and continuous summer daylight.

Farthest from the pole the tundra vegetation includes low shrubs, grasses

and sedges. These plants can produce amazingly colorful summer displays. Farther north the plants become fewer and smaller. In the most northerly lands, the cushion plants of the polar desert cover less than one-tenth of the ground surface. Specialized plants such as purple saxifrage survive in rock crevices, with mosses and lichen, often brightly colored, growing on the rock surfaces.

South of the treeline, a vast mass of forest carpets most of the remainder of the country. The boreal region forms one of the world's largest coniferous forests, stretching from Alaska to Newfoundland. Growing on acid and infertile soils, it consists largely of white and black spruce. Other trees include the balsam fir and jack pine, and some hardy broadleaf trees such as white birch and poplar.

Robert Peary and the race for the North Pole

For 300 years the North Pole remained unconquered; it was to become the dangerous goal in a long and bitterly cold race by British and American explorers. As early as 1607 Henry Hudson (c.1565–1611) set out by ship in search of a route across the North Pole to China. He started by sailing northward near the east coast of Greenland, but turned east when he encountered the Arctic pack ice. Later British attempts in 1773 and 1818 fared

Robert Peary's 1905 expedition
(*above*) This contemporary artist's impression shows the team that penetrated as far north as 87° 6′ N. Another three years were to pass before he reached his goal.

Nansen's ship, the *Fram* (*left*), as shown on a Wills' cigarette card. The *Fram* was specially constructed to withstand the pressure of Arctic ice.

no better. Many further attempts were made, several with sledges. The earliest of these, in 1827, reached 82° 45′ N. In 1879 the American *Jeannette* expedition met with disaster, and the wreckage of the ship was carried right across the Arctic Ocean. In 1895–96 the Norwegian explorer Fridtjof Nansen (1861–1930) followed the route of the *Jeannette* in a specially constructed vessel, the *Fram*. He proved for the first time that the polar seas were entirely covered in ice; but his attempt to reach the pole by sledge failed.

Even before Nansen made his epic voyage across the Arctic, an American naval officer named Robert Edwin Peary (1856–1920) had already begun his own preparations for a sledge journey to the pole. He used a "pyramid" approach similar to that adopted on British expeditions to climb Mount Everest in Nepal in the 1950s: beginning with a large group, he would set up a chain of depots, sending back some of the support sledges each time. Between 1891 and 1895 he surveyed northern Greenland as a starting point for his run to the north, but his experiences suggested

that Ellesmere Island would be a better starting place. His next expedition (1898–1902) reached 84° 17′ N. In 1905 he tried again, using the *Roosevelt* – a ship built to his own specifications. This time he reached 87° 6′ N – a new record. In 1908 he finally succeeded; his expedition took him from Ellesmere Island's Cape Columbia all the way to the North Pole. There were five people on the final run: Peary himself, three Inuit, and his dog-driver Matthew Henson (1866–1955).

Peary's was by no means the only attempt. Three American polar expeditions (1898–99, 1901–2 and 1903–6) and an Italian expedition in 1900 had already failed. But on his return in 1909, Peary was astonished to learn that his former companion Frederick Albert Cook (1865–1940) was claiming to have reached the pole before him. Cook's proof was far from satisfactory, but the evidence is hard to judge, and the debate continues even today. Peary's claim seems the more valid, but the bitter arguments left him little opportunity to enjoy his achievement. He retired with the rank of rear admiral in 1911, and died in 1920.

Rough and tumble (*above*) Young adult male Polar bears engage in aggressive play-fights. Once fully grown the bears will lead solitary lives, and encounters between males – especially during the breeding season – can result in serious fights.

A prairie landscape in Manitoba (*right*), at the heart of Canada's prime wheat-growing country. The state capital, Winnipeg, is Canada's leading grain market. The rich soils of this area support dairy cattle as well as wheat, oats and barley.

The eastern forests, from the Great Lakes to the coasts, are mostly mixed, with sugar maple, beech, birch, pine and hemlock. But the lowland plains of the far south are covered with broadleaf woodland: hickory, oak and elm flourish here, along with chestnut, maple and walnut. In the western mountains spruce, Douglas fir and lodgepole pine are the commonest, with aspen and yellow pine in plateau areas. On the Pacific coast, with its high rainfall, are some of the world's most imposing forests – dense, towering ranks of Douglas fir, western red cedar and hemlock, some growing to 60 m (200 ft) or higher.

The prairie country is too dry for more than a scattering of tree cover and was originally wide rolling grassland. Today little of this remains, the rich black soils having been plowed up and turned into the famous wheat-growing country. What is left is mostly the drier shortgrass of the more arid southwestern prairie, often termed Palliser's Triangle.

Wildlife

Canada's wilderness is still relatively unspoilt, and its variety of climate and terrain makes it a rich haven for wildlife. The Arctic waters support whales, walruses and seals, along with the semi-aquatic Polar bear. On the tundra there are Musk oxen, caribou, wolves, Arctic foxes and lemmings; many migratory birds also spend the summer here, including auks, sea ducks, gulls, terns and shorebirds. Caribou flourish in the northern forests, along with moose (known as elk in Europe), lynx, and Black and Brown bears. Beavers, martens, muskrats, mink and other fur animals were once, and to a degree remain, the basis of the fur trade.

Farther south the White-tailed deer is common, while the more settled country harbors mostly smaller mammals such as Gray and Red squirrels, chipmunks, weasels and otters. Among the varied and noisy bird life are cardinals, wood warblers, Baltimore orioles and catbirds. European birds such as sparrows and starlings have been introduced, often competing with the native species.

The prairies, today robbed of their former vast bison herds, still support smaller creatures such as jackrabbits, gophers and Sharptailed grouse. Some bison and Pronghorn antelopes have been preserved, but the Wild turkey and the Passenger pigeon, whose flocks used to darken the skies, have been hunted to extinction. The western mountains support highly adapted species such as the Bighorn sheep and the Mountain goat.

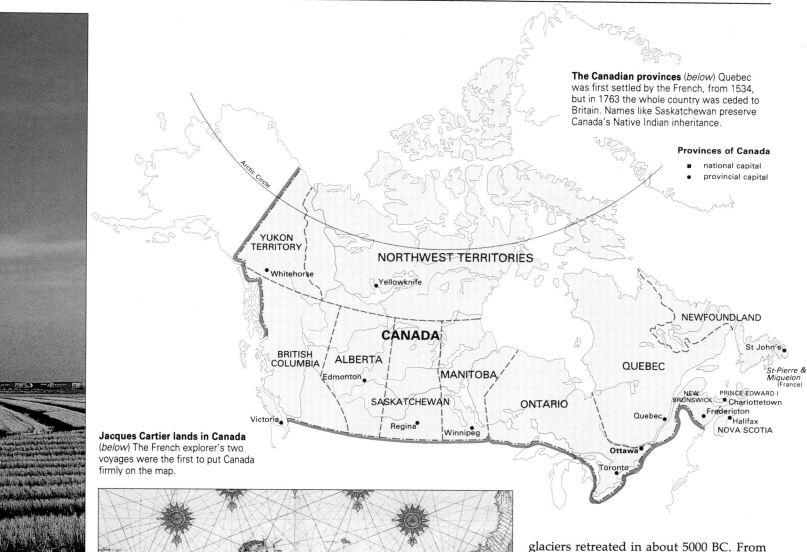

Provinces of Canada

■ national capital
● provincial capital

YUKON TERRITORY
• Whitehorse

NORTHWEST TERRITORIES

• Yellowknife

NEWFOUNDLAND

CANADA

St John's

BRITISH COLUMBIA   ALBERTA

MANITOBA

QUEBEC

St-Pierre & Miquelon (France)

• Edmonton

NEW BRUNSWICK   PRINCE EDWARD I
• Charlottetown

SASKATCHEWAN

ONTARIO

Quebec ●   • Fredericton
• Halifax
NOVA SCOTIA

Victoria •

• Regina   • Winnipeg

■ Ottawa

• Toronto

Jacques Cartier lands in Canada
(*below*) The French explorer's two voyages were the first to put Canada firmly on the map.

Hunting for sport is a popular Canadian pastime; conservation measures to protect species from overhunting have been in force for years.

SOCIETY

Canada's democratic government derives from that of Britain, of which it was once a colony. It has also retained elements of its French heritage, such as the civil law of Quebec. It is a country that has come increasingly to accept its obligations toward its indigenous peoples. After centuries of immigration, its population has great diversity. This has sometimes caused division and has left unsolved problems, but Canada's history has been remarkably peaceful.

History

The first peoples to enter the Americas almost certainly came from Siberia via the Bering Strait and Alaska as the ice age glaciers retreated in about 5000 BC. From about 2000 BC successive waves of Mongoloid hunter–gatherers moved eastward from Siberia across the Canadian Arctic toward Greenland.

These ancestors of today's Inuit and Native Indians spread rapidly throughout the rich, uninhabited land. In the western Arctic the traditional Inuit culture, based on hunting for food in small family groups, still survives, but old patterns are changing: snowmobiles have replaced dog teams, while guns and whaling bombs have replaced harpoons, and today's Inuit boats are driven by outboard motors. Their underground sod-walled houses or their summer tents and winter igloos have been replaced by modern buildings, and many have relocated to large settlements. The Canadian government has launched programs to settle northern aboriginal land claims; these efforts aim to bring new economic security and political self-determination to the Inuit populations.

Europe's first definite contact with Canada came with the arrival of Viking adventurers such as the Norse explorer Leif Eriksson (originally from Greenland) and the Icelander Thorfinn Karlsefni in about 1000 AD. Archaeological evidence

The quest for the Northwest Passage

Early European explorers of the Americas drove themselves to despair and death in their search for fabled prizes such as the Fountain of Youth and El Dorado – a mysterious city of gold that was believed by Spaniards in the 16th century to exist somewhere in the Americas. To some explorers the Northwest Passage – a navigable route between the Atlantic and the Pacific across the north coast of Canada – seemed a much more realistic and attainable goal. Yet in the end it was to betray them just as savagely.

Immense riches awaited whoever could discover a western trade route between Europe and Asia. Small wonder, then, that European nations sent their earliest expeditions to Canada, not for what the land might offer, but in search of the Northwest Passage. The Italian-born English commander, John Cabot (1450–98), first reached Newfoundland in 1497. Believing that China lay beyond, he repeated the journey from England in 1498 with a large expedition, but was never seen again. The Passage had already claimed its first victims.

The first explorer to brave the Arctic was the English mariner Martin Frobisher (1535–94). In 1576 he reached Labrador and Baffin Island, but his search for the Passage was diverted by the discovery of "gold" ore, which eventually turned out to be nothing more than worthless mica. John Davis (1550–1605), an English pioneer of navigational instruments, made three voyages between 1585 and 1587; he used his ship's musicians to establish friendly relations with the local Inuit. Davis sailed northward, deep into the strait that runs between Baffin Island and Greenland and now bears his name, but like Frobisher he missed the much larger bay beyond.

In 1610 the great English navigator Henry Hudson (b.c.1565–1611) sailed west and south through the strait and the bay that were later named after him. During the winter of 1610 his ship was frozen into the ice, and when spring came his lieutenant and crew mutinied. Hudson and a few others, including his young son, were set adrift in a small boat and were never seen again. All but a few of the mutineers were later killed – very unusually – by Inuit, and when the survivors reached England they were imprisoned. However, despite Hudson's fate, explorers flocked to follow him. In 1616 the English pilot William Baffin (1584–1622) guided Hudson's old ship *Discovery* through the Davis Strait into what is now Baffin Bay. He came nearer to finding the Passage than any of his successors – who largely discounted his discoveries – until the 19th century.

During the 19th century the British navy made a series of expeditions, of which the most successful were led by the naval explorer John Franklin (1786–1847). In 1845 he launched a last expedition, which apparently vanished without trace. A 12-year search followed, largely financed by his widow, and this contributed significantly to existing knowledge of the Passage.

In 1850, during the course of this search, the British explorer Robert Mc-Clure (1807–73) reached Mercy Bay on Banks Island via a western route from the Pacific. He was forced to abandon his ice-bound ships, and was rescued by another expedition in 1852, but by

Francis McClintock's Arctic expedition (*above*) in 1859 cuts roads for sledges through heavy snow hummocks in Queen's Channel in Canada's far northwest. McClintock's expedition found the logbook of an earlier British explorer, John Franklin, detailing the illnesses that fatally overwhelmed his expedition in 1845.

The Inuit seen through European eyes (*below*) A print of 1675 shows the traditional hunting skills still used by many Inuit today – but the pattern has already begun to change. Where their ancestors hunted for whales, seals, walrus and fish from kayaks, using spears and bows, today's Inuit are equally likely to use power boats and hunting rifles.

returning eastward he was the first to pass through the Passage and live. In 1859 the British naval explorer Francis McClintock (1819–1907) found Franklin's logbook. This proved that Franklin had in fact reached King William Island, another westward point, but had then been forced to abandon his ships. Plagued by illness, he and all his men had perished.

After World War II powerful ice-breakers were developed that were at last able to smash a channel through the deadly pack ice. However, the Panama Canal had been opened since 1914, linking the Pacific and the Atlantic across the narrow isthmus of Panama in Central America; and, moreover, good land and air links made a sea route less vital.

Efforts were continued to open up the Northwest Passage, including the experimental passage of the reinforced American tanker called the *Manhattan*. They were successful, but made no economic sense and posed a possible danger to the environment. In short, the Northwest Passage has proven possible at last, but it is no longer either necessary or desirable.

has confirmed the existence of brief Viking settlements at L'Anse-aux-Meadows on Newfoundland at about this time. The Vikings did not stay, however, perhaps because of the hostility of the local Native Indian peoples.

In 1497 an Italian navigator called John Cabot (1450–98) led an English expedition to discover unknown lands, and arrived at Newfoundland. English and Welsh fishermen may already have been fishing the nearby Grand Banks in summer, and French and Portuguese fishermen soon followed. In the 16th century explorers began to penetrate the interior. Among them were Henry Hudson (c.1550–1611) from England, Jacques Cartier (1491–1557), who is supposed to have given Canada its name, and his fellow-Frenchman Samuel de Champlain (1567–1635), who is known as the Father of New France for his work in founding the colony that grew along the St Lawrence river from Quebec to Montreal.

French influence and colonization also invaded the Maritime Provinces, and from its St Lawrence core spread with the fur trade across the Great Lakes to the Mississippi and Saskatchewan river watersheds. However, French northern and western fur interests came increasingly to be rivaled by those of the British Hudson's Bay Company, founded in 1670. During the next century there was a gradual erosion of French control following the expansion of British interest and that of her American colonies. Growing friction culminated in the capture of Quebec and Montreal by the British, led

by General James Wolfe (1727–59) in 1759. This was followed by the Treaty of Paris in 1763, by which New France was ceded to Britain as the colony of Quebec, along with its Maritime territory. However, the tiny islands of St Pierre and Miquelon off Newfoundland have remained French territory to the present day.

Britain guaranteed the religious and political rights of the French settlers, thus maintaining their loyalty throughout the American War of Independence (1775–83), when North American colonies revolted against British rule. During and after this conflict, several thousand British loyalists fled to Canada, especially to Nova Scotia and Quebec. In 1791 the separate colonies of Upper Canada (Ontario) and Lower Canada (Quebec) were created by the Constitutional Act of 1791. This enactment also granted limited self-government to the Canada colonies as well as to New Brunswick, Nova Scotia, Prince Edward Island and Newfoundland. Immigration from the United States, as well as from England, Scotland and Ireland, added large numbers to their growing populations.

During this colonial era, the Hudson's Bay Company remained a powerful territorial force in British North America, both north and west of the Canadas. Indeed, the Company often acted as a surrogate for British administrative

The capture of Quebec in 1759, as shown in an 18th-century lithograph. British forces under General Wolfe scaled the Heights of Abraham west of the city, and drove out the French with a surprise attack, in which General Wolfe was killed.

A Scots immigrant family support Canadian government publicity – but their "dream of happiness" was only to be achieved at the price of hardship, loneliness and unremitting toil in a country with a harsh winter climate.

authority in this huge territory. As its roving personnel spread westward they came into fierce competition with their numerous fur rivals, of which the largest were the North West Company from Montreal and the American Fur Company from Detroit. By 1793 they had reached the Pacific coast, and not until about 1850 did the rivalry cease.

In 1837 dissatisfaction in both Upper and Lower Canada with British economic policy, along with the continuing tight constraints on self-government, brought open revolt. The uprising failed, but it did bring about political reform and the reunification of the two Canadas. In 1849 the tiny colony of Victoria was created on Vancouver Island in the far southwest of the region (off the coast of present-day British Colombia). Following the subsequent gold rush in the Fraser Valley in the southwest, the colony of British Columbia was born in 1858, and Victoria became its capital.

In 1867 the British North America Act created the Dominion of Canada, comprising the provinces of Quebec, Ontario, Nova Scotia and New Brunswick. The Dominion Government bought the Hudson's Bay Company lands, which became the Northwest Territories. In 1870 Manitoba joined the Dominion, followed in 1871 by British Columbia (encouraged by the promise of a great transcontinental railroad). Prince Edward Island followed in 1873, the Yukon Territory in 1898 and Saskatchewan and Alberta in 1905, establishing a transcontinental dominion stretching from the Atlantic to the Pacific. Newfoundland remained nominally independent until 1949. Canada today is composed of ten provinces and two national territories.

Meanwhile, Canada's prosperity had risen, swelled by the enormous grain production across the recently settled

The Hudson's Bay Company

For two centuries of its early history Canada was not so much a country as a commercial venture. Its pioneering explorers and settlers were sent out not by ambitious governments but by firms in the fur trade, of which the Hudson's Bay Company was perhaps the most important.

The company was founded in England in 1670 by the distinguished soldier and admiral Prince Rupert of the Rhine (1619–82), a cousin of King Charles II of England (1630–85). The Company's chief object was to continue the search for the fabled Northwest Passage, which would link the Pacific and the Atlantic across the north of Canada; but it was also granted territorial rights to all watersheds draining into Hudson Bay, with freedom to develop or exploit whatever might be found there. This huge area, christened Rupert's Land after Prince Rupert, its first governor, covered most of northcentral Canada and areas west as far as the Rockies – a vast tract of land that was still largely unknown to European settlers.

The most obvious commercial opportunity was the fur trade; the Company opened a network of trading posts on the shores of Hudson Bay for trading with the Native Indian population – in competition with the already established French fur trade out of Montreal. All but one of these posts were seized or destroyed by the French in the 1690s, but those that survived were returned to the Company by the Treaty of Utrecht in 1713. As the British grip on Canada tightened and settlements spread westward, so the Company faced increasingly strong competition from first French and then British traders with headquarters on the St Lawrence. This pressure forced the Company to set up tributary trading posts in the hinterland behind their coastal "factories".

By 1783, the rivals (now Scottish) in Montreal began to associate together in a loose and ever-changing stock association called the North West Company. This soon transferred much of the field administration and logistical operation to its new base at Fort William (present-day Thunder Bay) on Lake Superior. From here, it drove

rapidly westward into Rupert's Land. Its competing posts often gave rise to open conflict between rival traders, sometimes resulting in loss of life. Such intercompany rivalry culminated in the Seven Oaks Massacre of 1816 in the Red River Settlement (around present-day Winnipeg). In retaliation for these actions by the North West Company, the Hudson's Bay Company men destroyed a post at Lake Gibraltar, and troops in the employ of a major stockholder, Lord Selkirk (1771–1820), captured Fort William.

The British government eventually forced the two companies to merge in 1821 under the name Hudson's Bay Company. The Company now had an exclusive license to trade over almost all of British North America, save settled colonial areas such as the Atlantic provinces and Quebec. In 1859, however, when the license came up for renewal, it was not extended, and in 1870 the Company was forced to sell most of its enormous holdings; these lands were then molded into a major part of the new Dominion of Canada.

From then on, although the Company still owned lucrative property, principally in tracts around its former trading posts (some of which have now become cities), its influence declined. It remained a major fur trade organization, but in this century it has increasingly branched into Arctic posts. It has also developed a more orthodox retailing firm in northern centers, to which southern department stores have been appended in traditional old post cities

Fur traders at Upper Fort Garry, an outpost of the Hudson's Bay Company established in 1822 close to the site of Winnipeg.

such as Winnipeg and Calgary. In the 1970s it even generated a chain of modern mall outlets. However, in 1931 its management passed largely from British into Canadian hands, though it remained under British ownership until it was sold to the Thomson family group in 1979.

The Company has a checkered history. The fur trade on which it thrived, like that of the Nor'westers and the French before them, brought animals such as the beaver near to extinction (the beaver fell victim to the fashion in Europe for beaverskin top hats). But to set against this, the Company, like its historical competitors, made real contributions to the exploration of British North America.

Early pioneers such as Henry Kelsey (c.1667–1724), who explored Lake Winnipeg in the 1690s, and Samuel Hearne (1745–92), who reached the Coppermine river in the far north of the Northwest Territories in 1771, were sent out by the Company. Hudson's Bay men accompanied later explorers such as Sir John Franklin (1786–1847), and forestalled Russian competitors reaching down from Alaska into the Yukon. But it was the lesser-known men – the trappers and traders who carried out the day-to-day business of the Company facing the numerous hazards of what was uncharted and often hostile country – who made the greatest contribution of all.

prairies, by the exploitation of northern forests for lumber and pulp, and also by the development of a range of other nonmineral and mineral resources. The most famous were the gold deposits along Klondike Creek in the Yukon, the discovery of which in 1896 precipitated the famous Gold Rush. Vast deposits of nickel were discovered at Sudbury, Ontario, during the building of the Canadian Pacific Railway: the first of three transcontinental lines that were to cross Canada by World War I. Copper, silver, gold, iron and base metal deposits in the Canadian Shield have all seen increasing exploitation over the last century.

All these developments disrupted the way of life of the indigenous population. Disturbance of their traditional activity went far deeper than the impact on their fragile economy of the withdrawal of the fur trade or the destruction of the bison. The armed uprising among the *Métis* – a rural people of mixed French and Native Indian descent – led by Louis Riel (1844–85) was related to these changes. It attracted little support among the French Canadians at the time, but when Riel was hanged in 1885 their growing nationalist movement adopted him as a martyr.

Canada's vigorous support of the Allies (Britain, France, Italy, Russia and the United States) during World War I, and especially the prowess in combat shown by the Canadian Corps, gave the Dominion the status and confidence to pursue a more independent identity. This was recognized by Britain in 1931, when the Statute of Westminster gave all the British dominions greater autonomy. However, not until 1982 did Canada gain full control of its own constitution.

During World War II Canada again supported Britain and the United States. It joined the North Atlantic Treaty Organization (NATO) in 1949, and assisted the United States in the Korean War of 1950–53. Economically Canada now has much closer ties with its southern neighbor than with Britain (in 1988 Canada and

Panning for gold on the Klondike (*above*) The first prospectors of the 1896 gold rush were men like this, but by 1900 gold worth $22 million was being panned every year. The accessible creeks were soon worked out, and the last gold was taken in 1966.

Dawson City at the time of the Gold Rush (*below*) This community arose almost overnight on the banks of the Yukon river, and at one time had 25,000 inhabitants. Today it has dwindled to a small supply town with a population of a few hundred.

the United States agreed a major new freetrade agreement), but it has maintained a consistently independent line with regard to international affairs.

Throughout the 1960s and the 1970s, French-Canadian nationalists in Quebec campaigned vigorously for independence from Canada. In 1967 the nationalist movement received encouragement from the president of France, Charles de Gaulle (1890–1970), and in 1976 the Parti Québecois won control of the provincial government. In 1980, however, Quebec voters decisively rejected nationalist independence proposals in a referendum. Despite this, nationalists have continued to press for independence. They have considerable influence on the policies of the provincial government, particularly in matters of language and education.

The resort town of Banff (*above*) is dominated by the spectacular Rocky Mountains. The town lies in a deep valley in southwestern Alberta at the heart of Canada's first national park, and caters almost exclusively for the thousands of tourists that visit each year. Founded in 1885, the Banff National Park offers magnificent landscapes, sulfur springs and a rich diversity of wildlife.

Bright lights of the city (*right*) The parliament building in Victoria, capital of British Columbia, situated at the southeastern tip of Vancouver Island overlooking the strait of Juan de Fuca. Victoria is a center for salmon fishing, shipbuilding and ship repair, and is also the Pacific headquarters of the Canadian Navy. The city was founded in 1843, and became a provincial capital in 1868 after Vancouver Island had been united with British Columbia.

Government

Essentially Canada still remains the federation of states set up by the 1867 British North America Act. Although it now controls its own constitution, much of this remains embodied in British laws, which, as in Britain, are not set down in any single document. As a constitutional monarchy, Canada is headed by a sovereign, now specifically the sovereign of Canada and not the sovereign of the British Isles; the titles are vested in the same person, but independently.

In practice the sovereign's power is exercised by a governor-general, usually appointed for a six-year term on the advice of the current prime minister. The governor-general formally summons and dissolves federal parliaments, and after a general election calls upon the leader of

The scarlet-coated crimefighters

On 23 May 1873 an enabling bill set up a police force known as the North West Mounted Rifles. One hundred and fifty men of good character between the ages of 18 and 40 were enlisted to patrol the vast plains of northwestern Canada, clearing the area of American whisky traders, collecting customs dues, and preparing the way for settlement. They were the first of the red-coated riders that were to become known as the Mounties.

The men did their job well: the whisky traders had aroused the hostility of local Native Indians, but the even-handed dealings of the Mounties defused a potentially explosive situation. During the Riel Rebellion of 1885, the Mounties joined forces with the Canadian militia, and had their first taste of armed conflict. The rebels were defeated, and the role of the Mounties continued to grow. Their jurisdiction was extended westward into the Yukon and into other northern parts of Canada, where they once again paved the way for new settlement. They rescued many new arrivals who had underestimated the dangers of the wilderness, and earned a reputation for dogged persistence in the pursuit of criminals.

The British king, Edward VII (1841–1910), gave the force royal recognition in 1904, and in 1920 it joined forces with the Dominion Police to become the Royal Canadian Mounted Police (RCMP). With its headquarters in Ottawa, it was now a federal force covering the entire country. It remains the only police authority in the Yukon and Northwest Territories, and also operates provincial police services in all the provinces except Ontario and Quebec. It has a marine division (with 12 vessels) and an air division (with about 30 aircraft), and also controls three major crime-detection units – the Canadian Security Service, the Canadian Police Information Center (CPIC) and the Identification Branch.

The Mounties' enormous area of jurisdiction is unique, and the force is not without its critics. During the 1970s the Canadian Security Service

The popular image of the Mounties – a still from the musical film *Rose Marie*. Today's Royal Canadian Mounted Police are a sophisticated modern force with an unusually large area of jurisdiction extending across the region.

was investigating domestic terrorism, and became involved in a series of break-ins and thefts that then led to a federal investigation. Resignations and jail sentences followed.

Today all applicants for the RCMP must be Canadian subjects or British citizens aged between 19 and 30, normally single, and of good character, with no criminal record. They should be able to speak, read and write English or French; a growing number of bilingual recruits are being taken to meet new government guidelines. Basic training lasts for 26 weeks, followed by six months' further training on the job. Only members of the world-famous Musical Ride are required to spend time in the saddle – and in the far north, power toboggans replaced the last dog teams in 1969. Yet in most people's minds the words "Royal Canadian Mounted Police" still conjure up the image of a scarlet-coated rider who would "always get his man".

the majority party to become prime minister and form a government. The governor-general's other main function is to give the royal assent to new legislation, without which it cannot become law.

To receive assent, legislation must first pass both houses of the federal parliament. The Senate (upper house) has 104 members, appointed to represent the provinces on a permanent basis until the age of 75. The House of Commons has 282 members, elected for a maximum term of five years. The prime minister generally selects his ministers from among the elected members, or occasionally from the Senate, because holders of ministerial responsibility must be personally answerable to parliament. Most ministers, however, also head executive departments of public servants. Both houses can introduce legislation, but only the Commons can introduce new taxation or expenditure bills.

The federal parliament has authority over all international affairs and all major domestic ones, including defense, the criminal law, financial affairs, regulation of trade and commerce, postal and telecommunications services, and transportation. In theory it also retains a residual authority over the provincial governments and can disallow any of their enactments. In practice, however, provincial governments enjoy a quite considerable degree of independence, especially in Quebec.

Provincial governments
Each of Canada's ten provinces has a governmental structure mirroring that of the nation. A lieutenant-governor appointed by the governor-general summons a single-chamber elected legislative assembly, in which the majority leader becomes premier and appoints a cabinet. Provincial governments are responsible for local concerns such as civil law, local taxation, land management, local trade and commerce, hospitals, health, welfare and education.

In the province of Quebec, however, nationalist governments elected by the Frenchspeaking majority have extended this authority in recent years, seeking to protect and promote the French language and culture, and often demanding constitutional reform or outright secession.

The huge but very sparsely populated Yukon and Northwest Territories are administered directly by the federal government, but have representatives in parliament and elected councils headed by appointed commissioners.

People

The Canadians as a people are as much a product of immigration as their neighbors in the United States. Canadians of British descent (primarily Scottish in Nova Scotia and Prince Edward Island) form the largest group, accounting for somewhat less than half the total. French Canadians form about one-fourth of the national population and some four-fifths of Quebec's. A further one-tenth of Canadians are of mixed origin, the largest group being the *Métis* (mixed Native Indian and French). Most of the rest are descended from other Europeans, especially German, Italian, Ukrainian and Dutch. Native Indians and Inuit, the original inhabitants, now account for less than one-fiftieth of the population.

Most Canadians speak English as their first language. The exception is in Quebec, which has a French majority – rigorous laws here protect and encourage French language and culture. Elsewhere, however, English and French enjoy equal status as the official languages of the country, and an increasing proportion of the English-speaking population are attempting to become bilingual. Roman Catholics slightly outnumber Protestants in Canada's current Christian population – the vast majority of French Canadians are Roman Catholic. However, heavy immigration from Asia in recent decades has greatly increased the variety of religions practiced in the country.

Downtown Toronto (*left*), and the CN tower. Modern buildings in the lower part of the city have replaced those that were destroyed by fire in 1904.

A baseball player slides into base (*right*) Baseball is one of the less controversial imports from the United States, whose economic domination is still sometimes seen as a threat in Canada.

French influence (*below*) in Montreal, the main commercial center in Quebec province, where French language and culture are protected and encouraged by law.

ECONOMY

Canada is rich in resources, with massive mineral deposits, enormous areas of commercial-grade timber and vast areas under cultivation. The resulting prosperity has created one of the highest standards of living in the world. Yet this prosperity all too often depends on the export of resources in a raw or unfinished state of manufacture, and this costs the country dearly in potential employment, profits and productivity.

Agriculture

Agriculture is one of Canada's major industries, though today it employs only one-twentieth of the labor force on one-twentieth of the total land area. Most agricultural land lies in the south; in more northerly latitudes the growing season is too short.

British Columbia's extensively irrigated southern plateau and Fraser delta lands are almost entirely given over to fruit growing, while cattle and sheep ranching prevail farther north in parts of the interior. Almost four-fifths of Canada's farmland lies between the Rocky Mountains and the Great Lakes. Limited irrigation is needed here, despite the often unreliable annual rainfall, because of reliance on dry farming methods to retain soil moisture. In the prairie provinces hard wheat remains the dominant crop, though there is increased competition from other grains and also from rapeseed (canola).

In Alberta, cattle, pigs and sheep are raised, principally in dryer areas and in the foothills. Similar livestock emphasis is characteristic of the more marginal parts of Manitoba. Southwestern Ontario is Canada's corn and soybean belt, but it also produces most of the country's tobacco and much of its fruit and vegetables. Dairying and livestock rearing are also important throughout southern Ontario, across the St Lawrence Lowlands and into the Maritime Provinces. The exception is Prince Edward Island, where the economy is largely dependent on tobacco, vegetables and seed potatoes. There is usually a large surplus of wheat available for export. Other agricultural export crops include feed grains, oilseeds, apples, potatoes and maple syrup.

Forestry

Canada is the world's leading exporter of wood products. Sawn timber, plywood and pulp for newsprint account for more

Calgary, Alberta (*above*) stands at the heart of a rich farming and cattle-ranching area. The city can trace its origins to a fort built in 1875 by the North West Mounted Police – the original Mounties. The famous Calgary Stampede rodeo, celebrating the mythology of the old frontier, is an annual event lasting for 10 days. Calgary today is also a major center for the petroleum and gas industries.

A logging mill in British Columbia (*left*), Canada's most productive timber-growing area and (since 1871) its most westerly province. Canada leads the world in timber production, which provides more than one-tenth of all the country's exports. Tourism is another important industry, and the rugged, mountainous landscapes of British Columbia are being carefully conserved: the province has four national parks and some 250 provincial parks that offer a wide range of recreational activities.

than one-tenth of exports, and there is potential for even higher production levels. Forestry is an important industry across Canada, except in the Yukon and the Northwest Territories, where timber of commercial quality is rare.

The most productive area is British Columbia, the majority of which is covered by forests that are largely exploited by major multinational companies. In the prairie provinces forestry is small scale by comparison, taking second place to agriculture. Quebec's massive forests are not fully exploited, though there are many small operations. Much of Ontario's forest cover was taken for lumber in the 19th century, but wood products from the north are still a significant source of income. Most of the Atlantic provinces have a well-developed woodland industry.

Fishing and the fur trade

Historically, the Canadian fishing industry centered on Newfoundland; indeed, it was coastal fishing that brought this province into being. Today's catches are taken principally by large trawlers fishing the banks out to the extended 400 km (250 mi) limit set by the Canadian government in 1977. Ashore, fish are frozen or canned for export. These limits and subsequent quota regulations have brought sharp disputes with France over fishing rights around the islands of St Pierre and Miquelon on the east coast, but have helped to revive the ailing Pacific fisheries, famous for their salmon. Canada's extensive freshwater lakes are also exploited for both commercial and sport fishing.

Furs remain an important export, notably from Quebec, Saskatchewan, the Northwest Territories and the Yukon. While some of this export is derived from modern fur farms, most is the product of northern trap lines, and provides Native Indian communities with a significant element of their income.

Industry

Canada's mineral wealth is very considerable and makes a major contribution to its exports. In the Arctic the Canadian–Greenland Shield contains extensive mineral deposits. The shield is flanked by sedimentary rocks which contain large reserves of coal, oil and gas. Exploitation of these potentially massive resources is very difficult. Transportation and labor costs are high, environmental damage is considerable, and special techniques are needed to build houses, facilities and pipelines on the fragile permafrost. Overland links with the developed south are few, and costs are increased by long-distance transportation.

The western provinces, particularly Alberta, have the greatest part of Canada's known fossil fuel deposits, including oil, gas and coal. Gas and oil have also attracted much recent attention in the Mackenzie Valley and under the Beaufort Sea. Northern Ontario and Quebec have rich iron mines exploited in the past, and they contain some of the largest untapped low-grade iron-ore deposits in the world. Other important minerals include zinc (notably in New Brunswick), nickel, copper, lead, uranium (in the north of Quebec, Ontario and Manitoba), potash (in Saskatchewan) and molybdenum (in British Columbia).

To a great extent Canadian industry is financed and controlled by multinational

The fishing village of Peggy's Cove on the coast of eastern Canada. It was to exploit the yearlong coastal fishing, notably around Newfoundland, that Europeans first settled permanently in Canada.

and foreign interests. To counteract this, the federal government has invested heavily in major industries such as oil and gas. Recent new projects include the Hibernia offshore oilfield southeast of Newfoundland.

Hydroelectricity remains the most important source of power, but there are thermal and nuclear power stations as well. In Ontario, for instance, the supply is shared about equally between the three types of generation.

Manufacturing accounts for nearly one-fifth of Canada's gross national product and about one-sixth of the workforce. The most important industries are petroleum refining and automobile production. Apart from pulp and paper production, other significant activities include meat-packing and iron and steel production. Ontario is the country's most important industrial area. Here the traditional milling, farm-equipment and furniture-making industries have been overtaken by modern manufacturing and chemical industries. This shift Ontario shares with the cities of Quebec's St Lawrence Lowland. The prairie provinces produce food, beverages, petroleum and chemicals. British Columbia produces machinery

and chemicals. In the future, petroleum refining may become a major industry in the Yukon and Northwest Territories, and could prove to be an enormous opportunity for the Native Indian peoples of these areas.

Trade and commerce

In the past Canada's broad range of exports tended to guarantee economic stability. Falling prices in one area were likely to be offset by rising prices in another. However, the economy is heavily dependent on trade, and some two-thirds of all Canada's trade is with the United States. This dependency, along with worldwide recession and internal problems such as inflation and high unemployment, led to persistent difficulties throughout the 1980s. A slump in the prices of oil, gas and wheat diminished their value as important exports, and the production of wheat was affected by periods of drought in the late 1980s. Even so, Canada remains one of the world's most affluent countries.

Transportation and communications

Many northern communities are accessible only to all-terrain vehicles, tractor-drawn sled trains or aircraft; a multitude of so-called bush pilots operate in these areas. Air Canada and Canadian Airlines provide both domestic and international

An engineering triumph

The great Saint Lawrence river has been a trade route since the earliest days of settlement. Today ocean-going cargo vessels ply the waters where once the fur-trappers paddled their canoes. Flowing 1,200 km (750 mi) from Lake Ontario to the sea, the Saint Lawrence travels through the attractive Thousand Islands area before narrowing as it passes over a series of turbulent rapids above Montreal. It widens beyond Montreal to form Lake Saint Francis and Lake Saint Louis, and flows into Lake Saint Pierre. The final section follows a gently meandering course, eventually broadening out at the Gaspé Peninsula to enter the Atlantic via the Gulf of Saint Lawrence.

Until the 1950s the rapids denied passage from the Great Lakes to the sea to all but smaller river craft. In 1954 the United States and Canada began an ambitious joint project to open the river to deep-sea vessels, at a total cost of over $340 million to the Canadians and over $130 million to the Americans. The project involved building a total of 16 locks and a complex of canals and deepened waterways. Far to the northwest of the Saint Lawrence itself, Lake Huron and Lake Superior are linked by the Sault Sainte Marie Canal and its single lock. The Welland Ship Canal between Lake Ontario and Lake Erie has eight locks, and bypasses the Niagara Falls. The main seaway has seven locks between Lake Ontario and Montreal, and was opened in 1959.

Tolls are levied on vessels passing through the system. These are intended to cover the building costs (which must be met by the year 2009), interest on the funds raised for construction, and the normal operating and maintenance costs of the system. The seaway can accommodate most ocean-going vessels apart from the very largest. This makes the whole stretch from Montreal to the Great Lakes accessible to about four-fifths of the world's merchant shipping.

The seaway is closed by ice from mid-December to early April – about 115 days a year – but at other times it provides passage to the Atlantic from numerous inland cities in both Canada and the United States. Altogether 66 American and 12 Canadian ports have access to the seaway. The routes from these ports to western Europe are shorter than the transatlantic routes from the United States' eastern seaboard. About nine-tenths of the cargoes carried on the seaway are bulk commodities such as

Crashing through frozen water, an icebreaker in the St Lawrence Seaway clears a passage for a merchant ship in early spring. The seaway is closed by ice from December until mid-April.

grain, iron ore and coal, but other vessels also use it to transport a great variety of general cargoes.

flights. In the Atlantic provinces the once strategic airfields now serve mostly local traffic. Canada's most important airports are at Toronto and Montreal.

There are two transcontinental railroad systems: the privately owned Canadian Pacific Railway and the Canadian National Railway. The British Columbia Railway, which is controlled by the provincial government, provides a vital link to the province's central and northern areas. A similar provincial railway links Moosonee on James Bay at the southern tip of Hudson Bay to southern Ontario. In the prairie provinces a network of increasingly unprofitable branch lines is under rationalization – a process that is reducing the viability of many small commercial centers as unneeded tracks are torn up. The hub of the whole system is Montreal, which connects not only with the Canadian West, but with the American Midwest as well as with New York, the seaboard cities and the ports of the Atlantic provinces.

In the Atlantic provinces ferries still provide essential road, rail and passenger links. The ports of Halifax and St John in Nova Scotia and Newfoundland respectively carry much of Canada's external Atlantic trade, especially in winter, while Vancouver and Prince Rupert on the west

coast are Canada's year-round Pacific outlets. The St Lawrence Seaway connects the Atlantic Ocean lanes directly with Great Lake ports such as Chicago and Thunder Bay in the heart of the continent. In summer, when Hudson Bay is free of ice, there is a shorter route to Europe from Churchill in Manitoba, but this route sees little modern use.

In British Columbia one of the largest ferry fleets in the world plies between Vancouver Island and the mainland, where Vancouver itself serves the northwestern coastal ports with freight and passengers. In the Northwest Territories the Mackenzie water system connects the Arctic Ocean with the Mackenzie river, the Great Slave Lake and Lake Athabasca; the Great Slave Lake Railway and the Mackenzie Highway connect with the south.

About half Canada's 885,000 km (550,000 mi) of roads are in the prairie provinces, though only four-fifths of these are surfaced. The more populous eastern provinces are better served by roads. The Trans-Canada Highway links the capitals of the four Atlantic provinces to Toronto, Montreal, the prairies and Vancouver, while superhighways serve the Windsor–Quebec City corridor and major western centers such as Calgary and Edmonton.

Canada is also linked by pipelines that transport its oil and gas. Some of these connect wellheads to regional facilities for refining or compression, but most are intended for the transfer of the product over long distances. They not only provide the link for western producing areas with central and eastern markets and refineries, but also transfer large quantities of petroleum for production, and particularly gas, into the United States.

The media
All Canadian newspapers are privately owned, mostly by three big chains. There is no media censorship, but broadcasting is controlled by a government body – the Canadian Radio-television and Telecommunications Commission. The Canadian Broadcasting Corporation (CBC) is modeled on the British Broadcasting Corporation (BBC). It is publicly owned and operates two national television networks, one broadcasting in English and the other in French. There are also many independent television and radio stations. Microwave telecommunications, fiber-optical systems and satellite transmission operate from coast to coast; the development of this technology is a particular benefit to the isolated northern and Arctic communities.

A railroad wagon loaded with grain rumbles past grain elevators at Thunder Bay, Ontario, on the northwestern shore of Lake Superior. The railroads provide a vital transportation link for agriculture in the prairie provinces.

Health and welfare

Federal government provides pensions, unemployment insurance and family allowances, while the provinces provide everything else. Most people belong to the federal medical insurance program, and are covered by provincial hospital insurance schemes. Health services are good, and life expectancy is high. Tuberculosis among the indigenous people of the Arctic has been largely eradicated.

Each province has its own education system, reflecting local needs. Children usually attend pre-school classes, then elementary and secondary education leading to college or one of 60 or so universities. Most education is free and compulsory from the age of six to secondary level. In Quebec most schools are Roman Catholic and most teaching is in French. There are normally separate schools for minority groups; in Newfoundland education is administered on denominational lines. The federal government organizes Native Indian and Inuit education, and controls or subsidizes education in the Territories.

John Grierson and the National Film Board

John Grierson (seated on the right) in his studio, discussing the design of a film poster with one of his clients.

In 1939, at the outbreak of World War II, the Canadian federal government set up the National Film Board of Canada. Its brief was to produce films, filmstrips and still photography that reflected the lifestyle and thinking of the Canadian people, and to distribute them both in Canada and abroad. One of the Board's founding fathers was a Scotsman by the name of John Grierson (1898–1972), the man who had, himself, effectively created the British documentary film.

Grierson was the personal choice of the Canadian Liberal prime minister, Mackenzie King (1874–1950), who was much impressed by his "brightness and dedication to public service". The two men had much in common: both came from radical political backgrounds, both had studied the social sciences, and both had also attended graduate school at the University of Chicago. King gave Grierson his full backing and an almost unlimited budget. The results of so doing more than justified his confidence.

In 1940 two landmark documentary series – *The World in Action* and *Canada Carries On* – were released internationally. At the time, the Board had only 12 full-time employees. There was little equipment or time; a four-reel review of the war's second year was produced in little over a week. In 1942 the British-born animator Norman McLaren (1914–87) set up an Animation Unit, and his own cartoons, drawn directly onto the film, soon became well known. In all some 500 films were released in the five years of the war.

By 1945 the Board employed 785

people. Many had been hand-picked by Grierson, who had a remarkable ability to spot native talent. The result was a distinctively Canadian style of "lyrical documentary". After the war Grierson resigned, and the Board went through a troubled period of conflict and suspicion. But its revival in the 1950s coincided with the arrival of television and a remarkable "golden age". In 1952 its productions won a crop of international awards, including British Film Academy Award Best Documentary for *Royal Journey*, Cannes Best Animated Short for *Romance of Transportation in Canada* and an Oscar for *Neighbours*. Between 1950 and 1964 the films of the Board's tight-knit Unit B continued to win critical acclaim, and in 1979 *Going the Distance* was nominated for an Oscar. However, *The Kid Who Couldn't Miss*, a controversial 1982 film about World War I air ace Billy Bishop (1894–1956), provoked a senate enquiry.

Canada's National Film Board has been much flattered by imitation – for example, in Australia – but its unique ability to capture the spirit of a nation, and the sheer quality, variety and volume of its output, will be difficult to equal. Moreover, its finest achievements will always be coupled with the name of John Grierson.

The spirit of a nation A still from *Romance of Transportation in Canada*, which took the award for the Best Animated Short at the Cannes Film Festival in 1952. It was one of many award-winners in a vintage year for the National Film Board.

Dependencies in the region

GREENLAND
DENMARK

Greenland, the world's largest island, lies largely within the Arctic Circle. Some 85 percent of the land area is covered by the northern hemisphere's biggest ice cap. Near its center it is over 3,000 m (10,000 ft) thick and its base is about 300 m (1,000 ft) below sea level. At its edges, along the coast, glaciers have created a complex landscape of deep fjords and offshore islands. The ice sheet is partly enclosed by mountains to the west and east, where they rise to Greenland's highest peak, Mount Gunnbjørn.

The climate is arctic, but precipitation is noticeably higher in the south, which is warmed by the North Atlantic Drift. The east coast is cooled by the Labrador Current, which flows from the Arctic Ocean to the Atlantic. Wildlife and vegetation in the ice-free areas are characteristic of the Arctic tundra. There are salmon and trout in rivers and streams, while cod, salmon, halibut, flounder and capelin are found offshore.

A series of Inuit migrations probably reached Greenland between 4000 BC and 1000 AD, and Inuit have lived here ever since. In the 10th century Viking settlers from Norway established two colonies, but contact with Scandinavia was lost some 500 years later. Colonization was only resumed in 1721, when Greenland became a Danish colony. Hans Egede, a missionary from Norway, founded a trading post – with Danish permission – near Godthåb (now the capital). In 1776 the Danes assumed a trade monopoly (free trade was not reestablished until 1951). During World War II, while Denmark was under Nazi German occupation (1940–45), the United States protected Danish interests in Greenland. After the war Denmark met local demands for extensive reform, and in 1953 Greenland became part of the Kingdom of Denmark, no longer a colony.

Home rule was instituted in 1979. However, Denmark retains control of foreign affairs, and Greenlanders are Danish citizens. The 21-member Landsting (parliament) is elected by all adults aged 18 or over, and is chaired by the leader of the majority party. Greenland also elects two members of the Danish parliament. Today more than four-fifths of the population are native Greenlanders, mostly descended from Inuit with an admixture of early European settlers. The remainder are largely Danes. The official languages are Greenlandic (Eskimo) and Danish, and most people belong to the Danish Lutheran church.

Settlement is effectively limited to the coastal fringe. Sheep and reindeer are raised in the extreme south, where hay is grown for fodder. Vegetables are cultivated in the south and along the warmer west coast. Fishing has displaced seal-hunting as the leading industry. It is largely state-financed, as are the onshore canning and freezing plants. Hunting in the north produces pelts for export.

Greenland's mineral resources are large but difficult to exploit. Mining of the world's largest cryolite deposits was abandoned as uneconomic in 1963. Exploration has revealed valuable metal deposits, of which zinc and lead are now being mined. Electricity, from thermal

The colorful corrugated houses of Jakobshavn (*above*) on the west coast of Greenland. Fishing is the main occupation, and there is a large processing and canning plant beside the bay.

The frozen sea (*below*) at the Ammassalik trading post on Greenland's eastern coast, just south of the Arctic Circle, prevents the movement of cargo.

has its own hospital. Nine years of elementary education are free and compulsory; four years of secondary education are optional. Both vocational and university education are available for Greenlanders in Denmark.

ST PIERRE AND MIQUELON
FRANCE

This tiny archipelago lies off the south coast of Newfoundland on Canada's eastern seaboard. The largest island, Miquelon, consists of two islands linked by a narrow isthmus. St Pierre to the southeast is smaller, but accommodates most of the islands' small population. The scenery is barren, with few trees and extensive peat bogs. The tall cliffs and rocky islets are home to many sea birds.

The islands were first settled by fishermen from western France in the 17th century, and the population has remained staunchly French ever since. The islands became a French overseas *département* in 1976, but in 1985 they were promoted to the status of a *collectivité territoriale*. The people vote both in local and in French national elections; the governor is appointed from France.

There is little agriculture apart from the growing of a few vegetables for local consumption, and the economy depends primarily on fishing from the rich waters nearby. Most food is imported from Canada and France, with which good transportation links are maintained. The islanders enjoy the benefits of French citizenship, including free education and good health and welfare provisions.

stations, relies on imported fuels. Other major imports include machinery and transportation equipment, manufactured goods and food.

Greenland has no railroads. The small road network is well used, but dog sleds remain the chief form of surface transportation. Most freight arrives by sea, but there is a well-developed internal and external air service. A sophisticated telecommunications network is available to most of the population. Radio and television broadcasts, like Godthåb's one newspaper, *Atuagagdliutit*, are in both Greenlandic and Danish.

A full range of welfare services is funded by the Danish government. Free health care is available to everyone, and each of the three administrative districts

Erik the Red - Viking explorer

In about 982 AD a man called Erik the Red set out from Iceland on a dangerous voyage into the Atlantic. According to a 13th-century saga Erik was a violent man who had been sentenced to three years' exile for "some killings" – but he was also a brave man. His target was a little-known island far to the west of Iceland – a place that had brought disaster and death to a group of Icelandic colonists only a few years before.

Sailing due west, Erik made landfall near a massive glacier. However, re-calling an earlier ill-fated expedition by another explorer, he decided to sail southward. After rounding the cape, he discovered fertile valleys hidden among the glaciers on the western coast, and called the place Greenland – believing "people would be much more interested in going there if it had a pleasant name".

Some four years after his first voyage he set sail again from Iceland with 300 prospective colonists in 25 ships. Just 14 of these vessels reached the fjord that Erik had named for himself – present-day Tunugdliarfik. On a steep, grassy hillside he founded his Eastern Settlement, where the site of his house can still be seen. A breakaway group then founded a Western Settlement farther up the coast.

Greenland in the 10th century was appreciably warmer than it is today. The Vikings raised cattle and sheep in the south, but also ventured north to hunt caribou, whales, seals and bears; Polar bears were much prized as curiosities at European courts. For a while the colony flourished. About 280 farms are recorded in written sources, and archaeologists believe there were many more. Christianity reached Greenland in about 1000 AD, brought by the Norse explorer Leif Eriksson on his return from the recently Christianized Norway, and over the next 200 years nearly 20 churches were built, along with a convent and a monastery. The remains of a 12th-century cathedral at Gardar still survive.

In 1261 Greenland, like Iceland, came under Norwegian rule, but within a century the Western Settlement had been abandoned, and the Eastern Settlement went into a long decline. No one knows exactly why this happened, but it is known that in the late Middle Ages the climate changed for the worse, and this may have had a serious impact on the settlers. Inuit stories also suggest battles between their ancestors and Viking settlers. Animals and people would certainly have died in the bitter cold of the Arctic winter. The last recorded contact was in 1406. After that, the last Viking settlement on Greenland vanished into the cold and darkness of the Arctic night.

REGIONAL PROFILES

Canada and the Arctic

Physical Geography........................ 324–333

Habitats and their Conservation......... 334–343

Animal Life.................................... 344–353

Plant Life...................................... 354–361

Agriculture 362–369

Industry 370–379

Economy 380–387

Peoples and Cultures 388–397

Cities 398–407

Government 408–415

Environmental Issues 416–423

Harvesting wheat, Canada

PHYSICAL GEOGRAPHY

Some of the world's largest landscape features can be found in Canada and the Arctic islands to the north. Canada has more lakes than any other country and shares the world's greatest expanse of fresh water, Lake Superior, with the United States. The region contains four of the world's largest islands including Greenland, the world's largest, which has the biggest ice sheet in the northern hemisphere. There are also massive mountain ranges with forests, swift rivers and snowy peaks. The Rocky Mountains run parallel to the Pacific coast and the older Appalachian Mountains border the Atlantic. Between these ranges lie the farmlands of the vast prairies and, centered on Hudson Bay, the ancient and bleak Canadian Shield with its lakes, formed by the movement of the retreating ice sheet.

COUNTRIES IN THE REGION

Canada, Greenland (dependency of Denmark)

LAND

Area 12,151,739 sq km (4,691,791 sq mi)
Highest point Mount Logan, 5,951 m (19,524 ft)
Lowest point sea level
Major features Rocky Mountains, Canadian Shield, Arctic islands, Greenland, world's largest island

WATER

Longest river Mackenzie, 4,240 km (2,635 mi)
Largest basin Mackenzie, 1,764,000 sq km (681,000 sq mi)
Highest average flow Saint Lawrence, 13,030 cu m/sec (460,000 cu ft/sec)
Largest lake Superior, 83,270 sq km (32,150 sq mi), world's largest freshwater lake

CLIMATE

	Temperature °C (°F) January	July	Altitude m (ft)
Resolute	−32 (−26)	4 (39)	64 (200)
Vancouver	2 (36)	17 (63)	0 (0)
Winnipeg	−18 (0)	20 (68)	248 (813)
Montreal	−9 (16)	22 (72)	30 (98)
Halifax	−4 (25)	18 (64)	30 (98)

	Precipitation mm (in) January	July	Year
Resolute	3 (0.1)	21 (0.8)	136 (5.3)
Vancouver	139 (5.5)	26 (1.0)	1,068 (42.0)
Winnipeg	26 (1.0)	69 (2.7)	535 (21.0)
Montreal	83 (3.3)	89 (3.5)	999 (39.3)
Halifax	137 (5.4)	96 (3.8)	1,381 (54.4)

World's highest recorded snowfall in 24 hours, 1,180 mm (46 in), Lake Lakelse, British Columbia

NATURAL HAZARDS

Cold and snowstorms, drought, gales, avalanches, rockfalls and landslides

---

MOUNTAINS, LAKES AND PLAINS

Canada can be divided into four broad physical areas: the western mountain system, the central lowlands, the Canadian Shield north of the five Great Lakes and the Appalachian Mountains in the east. Each of these main physical divisions has different geological origins, but climatic change was responsible for shaping the varied landscapes of today.

Changes in the climate affected the movement of ice sheets, which at their farthest advance covered the whole of Canada. The most recent advance, known in North America as the Wisconsin glaciation, lasted until 10,000 years ago. As the climate fluctuated, the ice sheets advanced and retreated. Glacial erosion flattened and scoured the landscape and redirected rivers; debris deposited by the ice formed landscape features such as moraines and provided the basis for the fertile soils of the central lowlands.

Rockies and prairies

The western mountain system or cordillera stretches some 800 km (500 mi) from the islands and the coast mountains along the Pacific seaboard to the eastern slopes of the Rocky Mountains. Between the Pacific ranges and the Rockies lies a high plateau region. The Rocky Mountains and neighboring areas are relatively recent. They were created some 80–40 million years ago when the Pacific Ocean crust was forced under the westward-moving North American plate. The area is still undergoing change, as the 1980 eruption of Mount Saint Helens in the northern United States showed. In the Rocky Mountains peaks 4,000–6,000 m (13,000–19,000 ft) high alternate with deep and frequently U-shaped valleys carved out by glaciers. The slopes are steep, and avalanches and rockfalls are common.

The central lowlands, also known as the Great Plains, offer a landscape of wide horizons. They are a continuation of the Great Plains of the United States, and taper northward from a width of about 1,500 km (900 mi) at the United States border, to the Mackenzie delta in the Arctic. The prairies in the south are Canada's main farmland area. Spread across the Great Plains are beds of rock of great thickness, evenly deposited on the floor of a former sea. Overlying this are softer materials, produced by erosion and deposited by rivers and glaciers. The relief is varied by some hilly areas and by long lines of steep slopes (escarpments), such as that between lowlands near Lake Winnipeg and the Great Plains to the west. These features are often concealed by glacial and postglacial lakes. Bitterly cold winters give way in the south to burning summers, which produce semi-arid or near-desert conditions in some places. By contrast, on the Pacific coast temperatures vary less, and moist air from the sea gives the Coast Mountains the highest rainfall in Canada.

The Shield, south and east

The vast semicircle of the Canadian Shield extends north from the Great Lakes, encompassing Hudson Bay. The shield is a plateau of much-eroded granite rocks, over 600 million years old. It has thin soils, yet the area is not barren but covered by forests. The mixed forest of the south gives way to a coniferous belt that thins to true tundra in the north.

South of the Canadian Shield there is an abrupt change. Here there is rolling

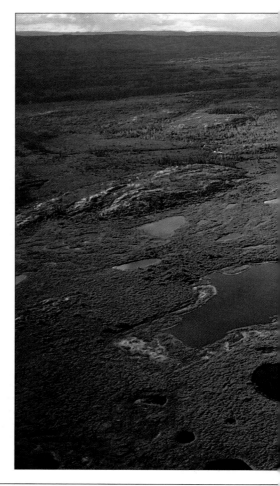

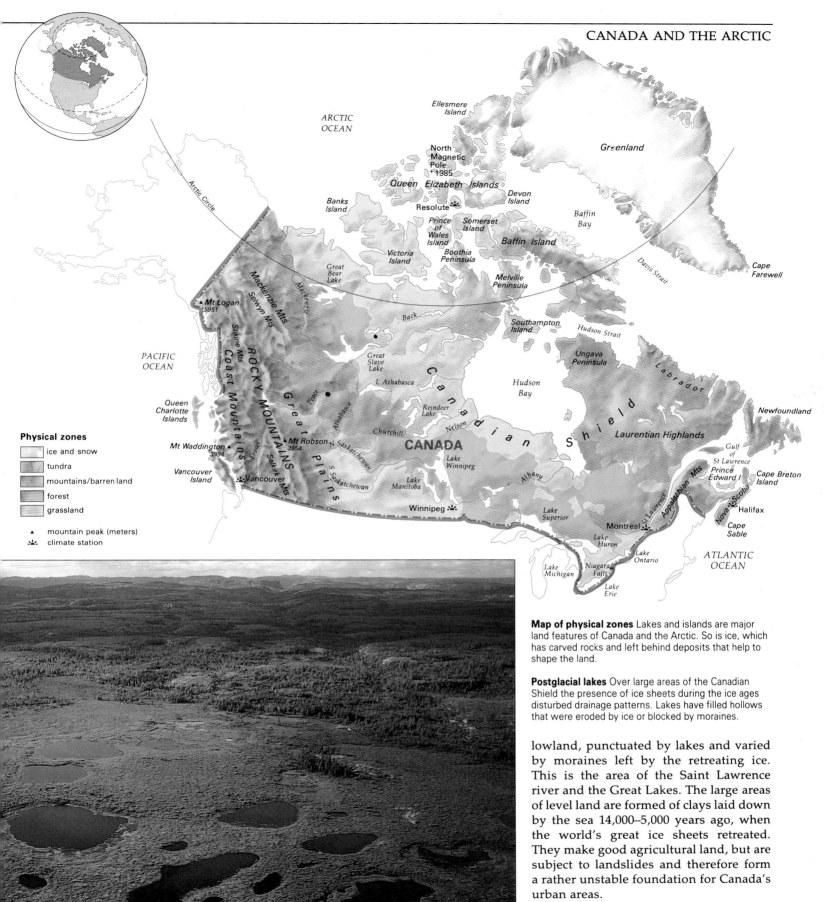

ARCTIC OCEAN

Ellesmere Island

North Magnetic Pole +1985

Greenland

Queen Elizabeth Islands

Resolute

Devon Island

Banks Island

Baffin Bay

Prince of Wales Island

Somerset Island

Victoria Island

Boothia Peninsula

Baffin Island

Davis Strait

Cape Farewell

Great Bear Lake

Melville Peninsula

PACIFIC OCEAN

Mackenzie Mts

Selwyn Mts

Mackenzie

Back

Southampton Island

Hudson Strait

Stikine Mts

▲ Mt Logan 5951

Great Slave Lake

Ungava Peninsula

Labrador

ROCKY MOUNTAINS

L Athabasca

Hudson Bay

Queen Charlotte Islands

Coast Mountains

Great Plains

Peace

Athabasca

Reindeer Lake

Canadian Shield

Newfoundland

Mt Waddington ▲ 3994

▲ Mt Robson 3954

N Saskatchewan

Churchill

Nelson

CANADA

Laurentian Highlands

Gulf of St Lawrence

Fraser

Selkirk Mts

S Saskatchewan

Lake Winnipeg

Albany

Prince Edward I

Cape Breton Island

Vancouver Island

Vancouver

Lake Manitoba

Appalachian Mts

Nova Scotia

Halifax

Winnipeg

Lake Superior

St Lawrence

Montreal

Cape Sable

Lake Michigan

Niagara Falls

Lake Huron

Lake Ontario

ATLANTIC OCEAN

Lake Erie

Arctic Circle

Physical zones

☐	ice and snow
☐	tundra
☐	mountains/barren land
☐	forest
☐	grassland

▲ mountain peak (meters)
☼ climate station

Map of physical zones Lakes and islands are major land features of Canada and the Arctic. So is ice, which has carved rocks and left behind deposits that help to shape the land.

Postglacial lakes Over large areas of the Canadian Shield the presence of ice sheets during the ice ages disturbed drainage patterns. Lakes have filled hollows that were eroded by ice or blocked by moraines.

lowland, punctuated by lakes and varied by moraines left by the retreating ice. This is the area of the Saint Lawrence river and the Great Lakes. The large areas of level land are formed of clays laid down by the sea 14,000–5,000 years ago, when the world's great ice sheets retreated. They make good agricultural land, but are subject to landslides and therefore form a rather unstable foundation for Canada's urban areas.

The Appalachians form a mountain system raised between about 400 and 225 million years ago as the North American plate met the African plate. The gently rolling uplands are separated by deep valleys, fringed by the rugged, indented coasts and islands of the Gulf of Saint Lawrence and the Atlantic Ocean.

THE FROZEN NORTH

The two-fifths of Canada lying to the north of the 60th parallel are a continuation of the mountains, plains and shield to the south. However, the climate, vegetation and detailed landforms are all so overwhelmed by the extremes and duration of cold that Canadians regard this as a separate area. The frozen, barren and largely treeless landscapes extend from the precipitous peaks of the Yukon Territory and the delta of the Mackenzie river in the west to the arc of Baffin Island in the east. A narrow strait separates Ellesmere Island from the great ice sheet and bare coasts of Greenland.

The islands of the Arctic Archipelago cover an area of about 1,300,000 sq km (500,000 sq mi) and make up one-seventh of the land of Canada. They range over 2,200 km (1,400 mi) from the southern tip

of Baffin Island to the northern tip of Ellesmere Island. Two-fifths of the Arctic is affected by ice, and on the islands the highland areas are covered by glaciers. The Arctic holds just one-eighth of the world's glacial ice; most of this is found in Greenland's huge ice cap.

Greenland is the world's largest island. At 2,175,600 sq km (840,000 sq mi) it is four times the size of France, and shares with Antarctica the distinction of preserving a major remnant of the ice sheets that covered much of the Earth in the high latitudes until about 10,000 years ago. The thick central ice dome is fringed by coastal mountain ranges rising to 3,700 m (12,000 ft). The ice sheet reaches the sea at about a hundred places.

A narrow and broken strip along the coasts, amounting to about a seventh of Greenland's area, is free of ice. The coasts have many raised beaches and terraces. They are very indented, with many deep

The pingo is a striking feature in the Arctic tundra landscape. Pingos, named from the Inuit people's word for a mound, are formed by water under the ground expanding when it freezes. As the ice core grows it pushes up the surface of the land.

fjords, so the coastline is some 40,000 km (25,000 mi) long. The climate is milder along the more populated south and west coasts, which are warmed by sea currents from the south. The west coast is enclosed by pack ice for fewer months of the year than the east coast.

To the west of Greenland, across Baffin Bay and the Davis Strait, is Baffin Island – the fifth largest island in the world. In the north is Ellesmere Island, another of the world's ten largest islands. At its closest it is only 25 km (15.5 mi) from Greenland. Ellesmere Island has an unusual climate: with only 65 mm (2.6 in) of precipitation each year, it is far drier than much of the Sahara desert. Most of the islands receive only 130–250 mm (5–10 in) each year.

Clues to a rising land: a series of old raised beaches in northern Baffin Island. The beaches are a legacy of the ice sheets of the last ice age. About 20,000 years ago ice extended as far south as the Great Lakes. The weight of the ice depressed the Earth's crust. The world's climate subsequently became warmer and the ice melted. As the ice sheet retreated the land began to rise again (isostasy). Pauses in this recovery are marked by landforms associated with coastlines, such as beaches, cliffs and wave-cut platforms. These shorelines have been abandoned by the sea as the land has risen still further. Raised beaches can also be formed by changes in sea level rather than land level, a process known as eustasy.

However, if the Arctic islands qualify as desert, much of the land is "wet desert" in the short summer as the surface of the land thaws.

Baffin, Ellesmere and the smaller Devon Island are all mountainous, like Greenland. The islands lying further west are much flatter, their tundra landscapes contrasting with those of their neighbors.

The tundra

The northern region of Canada has a tundra landscape. The key feature of this treeless zone is the permanently frozen ground beneath the land surface. This layer may be hundreds of meters thick and can represent tens of thousands of years of cooling. Across much of the Arctic tundra the top 20–100 cm (8–40 in) of the surface will thaw out each summer. The water is not able to flow into the underlying layer of permafrost; nor can it evaporate, because the air is usually too

cold, so the landscape becomes waterlogged with many bogs and lakes. During the long winter the water refreezes and the land surface contracts, cracking into polygonal patterns 10 m (40 ft) or more across. The cracks fill with ice each year and in time grow to become buried wedges of ice.

In some places the process of expansion and contraction linked to freezing and thawing produces patterns of stones. The slow churning of the ground separates large stones from the surrounding soil, moving them into polygonal and striped arrangements.

Tundra mounds, or pingos, are another feature of this landscape. Water trapped underground that is frozen during the

winter expands to produce mounds filled with ice. Where the underground water supply is abundant (as beneath an old lake bed) progressive growth of this ice core over long periods can produce a pingo up to 60 m (200 ft) high.

Not surprisingly, the tundra environment is one in which few plants and animals can survive. Much of the landscape is bare rock and ice. Vegetation is sparse, with lichens and mosses, tussock and sedge grass and dwarf shrubs and trees. Apart from polar bears, which feed on the abundant fish and seals, most large creatures forage over larger areas. They include Musk ox and caribou, the Arctic fox and hare, and game birds including grouse, partridge and duck.

THE ARCTIC GREENHOUSE

Some predictions of the greenhouse effect, which results from increased quantities of carbon dioxide and other compounds in the atmosphere, suggest a global warming of 3°C (5.4°F) in the next 50–100 years, with temperatures rising about 1°C (2°F) in the tropics, but by up to 12°C (22°F) in the Arctic.

In the Arctic the changes would be dramatic. The delicate balance of the tundra environment would be upset. When permafrost melts, the surface degenerates into a jumble of hummocks, hollows, lakes and mudflows. These features are called thermokarst,

because the scenery resembles the karst features found in limestone country. At present the short tundra vegetation helps to insulate the soil from much of the warmth of the brief summers. However, if temperatures rise as predicted, thermokarst is likely to spread widely over the now frozen north, covering both empty wilderness and human settlement areas. Trees and shrubs would spread farther north, as would grazing animals. More snow would fall, so most of the Arctic Archipelago would cease to be the cold desert it is today.

THE PAST IN TODAY'S LANDSCAPE

Canada has only recently emerged from a tumultuous past, the geological history of which is imprinted on the landscape. The mountains, plains and coasts, which are subject to sea-level changes, all carry clear indications of having origins in conditions very different from those of today. However, there are also processes – such as glaciation and erosion – that have been at work for millions of years and are still going on.

Prairie badlands to the southwest

At first sight the prairies, or Great Plains, of southern Alberta give an impression of a barely undulating landscape clothed in wheat. On closer inspection, they reveal a dramatic past. Complex patterns of deposits left 10,000–5,000 years ago by retreating ice sheets show that this area had an unusually varied ice-age history, dominated by the ice sheets centered on the shield and the Rocky Mountains. Since then rivers flowing eastward from the Rocky Mountains and swollen by melt waters have carved deep, wide canyons (as much as 100 by 1,500 m/330 by 5,000 ft) through the nearly horizontal, multicolored sand stones and shales, producing a spectacular eroded and barren landscape often known as badlands.

Badlands are formed in arid and semi-arid regions and are areas of deep winding gullies divided by steep ridges. The differences in rock type can produce stepped landforms, and the joining and separating of the gullies creates rock-spires, earth pillars (known as hoodoos) and flat-topped, steep-sided plateaus called mesas. The detail of the badlands has been formed as a result of recent intense summer rainstorms, but the canyon walls reveal rocks 80 million years old and are

Fantastic hoodoos on the Red Deer river. Here in the rain shadow of the Rocky Mountains the climate is semiarid; further west rainfall is heavy. The hoodoos are pillars formed by erosion caused by flash floods and wind-blown particles.

Banff National Park in the Canadian Rockes includes mountains, glaciers and lakes. Millions of years ago the walls of rock enclosing this ice-sculpted valley were deposits beneath the seas. Debris falls from the frost-shattered peaks, forming scree slopes.

famous for the dinosaur fossils that can still be found there today.

A changing landscape

Present landscapes in many parts of the world owe much to the last period of glaciation and its aftermath. Canada is

one of the few places where the evolving environment can still be found by those who visit the mountains of the north.

The glacial landscapes of today include the Columbia icefield in the Rocky Mountains. It is small by global standards, only covering an area of 310 sq km (120 sq mi)

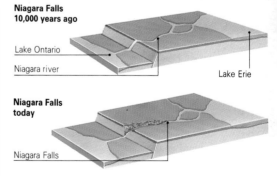

Niagara Falls 10,000 years ago

Lake Ontario

Niagara river

Lake Erie

Niagara Falls today

Niagara Falls

The dramatic landscape of the Niagara Falls and gorge on Canada's southern border owes its origins to the meltwaters of the retreating ice sheet some 10,000 years ago. Water from this part of North America once flowed to the sea through the Mississippi river. With the land to the north sagging under the weight of the ice sheet, water overflowed from Lake Erie to Lake Ontario and then into the North Atlantic. On the way the Niagara river crossed an escarpment whose capping of dolomite (a hard limestone) gave some protection to the softer sandstone and shale beneath. The plunging waters of the river

gradually undermined the dolomite, and the waterfall slowly retreated upstream at approximately 90 cm (3 ft) a year, cutting a gorge some 60 m (200 ft) deep and 11 km (7 mi) long. At this rate the falls will reach Lake Erie in 25,000 years' time.

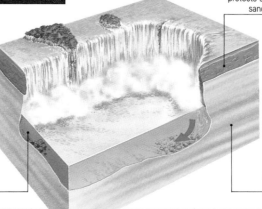

Hard dolomite rock layer protects softer shale and sandstone beneath

Plunging waters undermine dolomite, eroding softer rock, and waterfall gradually retreats upstream

Sandstone and shale

and 1,000 m (3,300 ft) thick, but unique in its accessibility to thousands of visitors to the Rocky Mountains' national parks. Although only 10 km (6 mi) long, the Athabasca glacier tongue in the Columbia icefield perfectly demonstrates the change that has dominated Canada's landscapes. Parallel to its tip, or snout, lie concentric rubble ridges (moraines) produced every year or two by debris dumped by the retreating ice margin. So regular has this landscape change been that the path leading to the snout is marked with signboards that date the positions occupied by the ice front as it has retreated over the last few decades.

THE HILL THAT DISAPPEARED

Late in the evening of 4 May 1971, in the village of Saint-Jean-Vianney just north of the Saint Lawrence, a Mme Laforge telephoned a friend to say she could see the lights of the neighboring town, Chicoutimi. Her surprised call was prompted by the fact that this view was usually obscured by a hill. In fact the hill and its surrounds had turned to liquid clay and started to flow downhill.

Clay was laid down here when the sea inundated areas around the retreating ice sheet some 14,000 to 5,000 years ago. These marine clays can become fluid if the amount of water that is retained in the soil increases.

On a slope, the increased weight of the waterlogged clay overcomes the cohesion between soil particles, and the earth starts to move. Such flows often come after heavy rains, and in some parts of the world are triggered by earthquake shocks.

At Saint-Jean-Vianney a towering wall of liquid clay 20 m (66 ft) high flowed 3 km (1.9 mi) down the valley at 25 km/h (15.5 mph) to the Saguenay river, carrying with it a bridge, a bus, 40 houses and 31 people. Mme Laforge was among the victims.

Icesheets, glaciers and icebergs

The Greenland ice sheet is the largest in the northern hemisphere and the second largest in the world, after Antarctica. Measuring 2,600 by 1,200 km (1,600 by 750 mi) at its greatest extent, the ice sheet is on average some 2,000–3,000 m (6,500–10,000 ft) thick. This volume adds up to about a tenth of the world's ice.

Ice in the form of glaciers and ice sheets now covers some 10 percent of the world's land area. During the last glacial period, between about 110,000 and 10,000 years ago, ice sheets covered up to 30 percent of the land. On the North American continent the Laurentide ice sheet extended over an area that was nearly as large as Antarctica's ice cap today and as far south as parts of the United States. Further ice sheets developed in the Rocky Mountains and on Greenland.

Since this last (Wisconsin) glaciation the ice has been in retreat, though there have been occasional readvances, such as the so-called Little Ice Age, which lasted several hundred years and ended about a hundred years ago. Mounds of rocky debris (moraines) that were left by the retreating glaciers can still be seen, for example in Glacier National Park in the Selkirk Mountains in the Rockies.

The ice sheet is at present very stable. The central dome thickens by 3–10 cm (1–4 in) a year because of snowfall, while the margins become 20–50 cm (8–20 in) thinner. Every year snow accumulates to an equivalent of an estimated 500 cu km (120 cu mi) of water. This is balanced by the melting of ice equivalent to 295 cu km (71 cu mi) of water, together with the separation of icebergs equivalent to a further 205 cu km (49 cu mi) as they break off the ice sheet into the sea.

Icebergs and sea ice

Continued pressure from the great weight of ice and snow inland forces the ice sheet to flow outward to the sea. In the northern hemisphere both ice sheets and glaciers usually meet the sea at deep inlets or fjords. Here they produce large numbers of tall, jagged icebergs. Most Antarctic icebergs, by comparison, are broad and flat, as they break away from ice shelves, floating sheets of ice, rather than glaciers.

Sea ice is formed when the sea freezes. Most of the Arctic Ocean, with the North Pole at its center, is permanently frozen. During the summer some of the ice melts, releasing large blocks of ice known as pack ice that drift into the northern oceans. About a quarter of the world's oceans at any one time are affected by pack ice, the area remaining more or less constant because of the alternating Arctic and Antarctic winters.

The future of glaciers and ice sheets is closely linked to that of the global climate. We are most probably living in a period between glaciations: the ice could return. However, predictions of rising temperatures as a result of the greenhouse effect open up the possibility of major and irreversible change to the normal pattern of ice ages. If global temperatures rise, more ice would probably melt, tending to raise world sea levels. At the same time there might also be increased snowfall, as the climate is likely to become generally wetter. Would the balance be one of growth or shrinkage in the world's great concentrations of ice, and for how long? Such questions are of particular interest to the many people who live on low-lying land in the world's coastal cities, which may become flooded.

ICE SHEETS AND GLACIERS

Ice sheets and glaciers account for three-quarters of the world's fresh water. Most permanent ice lies in the polar regions, but altitude is also important. There are several small glaciers in mountains near the Equator.

Landmass	Ice area	
	sq km	sq mi
Antarctic including ice sheets, glaciers and islands	12,588,000	4,860,250
North America including Greenland ice sheet and glaciers, Canadian Arctic islands and Alaska	2,032,649	784,810
South America	26,500	10,232
Europe including Svalbard, Iceland, Scandinavia, Alps, Caucasus	79,465	30,682
Asia including Arctic islands, Himalayas, Kunlun and Karakoram mountains	170,679	65,899
Africa	12	5
Oceania including New Zealand	1,015	392
World total	14,898,320	5,752,270

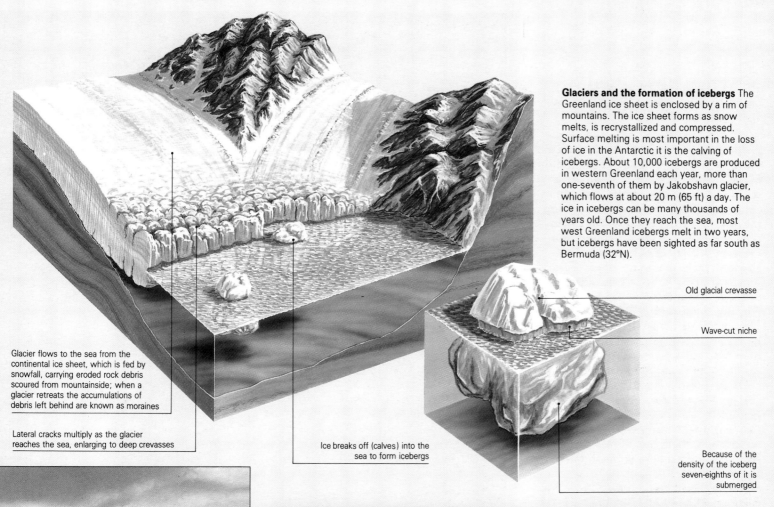

Glaciers and the formation of icebergs The Greenland ice sheet is enclosed by a rim of mountains. The ice sheet forms as snow melts, is recrystallized and compressed. Surface melting is most important in the loss of ice in the Antarctic it is the calving of icebergs. About 10,000 icebergs are produced in western Greenland each year, more than one-seventh of them by Jakobshavn glacier, which flows at about 20 m (65 ft) a day. The ice in icebergs can be many thousands of years old. Once they reach the sea, most west Greenland icebergs melt in two years, but icebergs have been sighted as far south as Bermuda (32°N).

Old glacial crevasse

Wave-cut niche

Glacier flows to the sea from the continental ice sheet, which is fed by snowfall, carrying eroded rock debris scoured from mountainside; when a glacier retreats the accumulations of debris left behind are known as moraines

Lateral cracks multiply as the glacier reaches the sea, enlarging to deep crevasses

Ice breaks off (calves) into the sea to form icebergs

Because of the density of the iceberg seven-eighths of it is submerged

A tongue of ice marks the end of a glacier fed by Greenland's ice sheet. The barren glacial valley in the foreground shows that the glacier extended along the valley until quite recently. The end or snout of the glacier has receded because rising temperatures since the last glaciation caused glaciers like this to melt faster than they can move down the valley. This broad U-shaped valley is in Stauning's Alps, east Greenland.

Icebergs in the midnight sun On the west coast of Greenland the Jakobshavn glacier receives about a tenth of the Greenland ice sheet's total flow. When the glacier meets the sea, huge chunks of ice break off, forming icebergs. The glacier produces many of the 15,000 icebergs that Greenland releases into the ocean each year. It was one of these that sank the passenger liner *Titanic* on 15 April 1912.

The ultimate light show

The greenish-blue glow on the horizon forms an arc across the sky. The bottom of the arc brightens and streamers are sent out toward the zenith, sometimes converging. The arc slowly transforms into shining curtains of white, green, blue and occasionally pink light, the brilliant display of patterns slowly changing as if blown by a heavenly wind. After perhaps an hour the curtains dissolve into luminous patches, then fade away altogether.

Such light shows take place in the high latitudes. In the northern hemisphere they are known as the aurora borealis or northern lights, in the south as the aurora australis or southern lights. They are named after Aurora, the Roman goddess of dawn. The show can recur on many nights in succession. Within the atmosphere the lights stretch from several hundred kilometers down to about 100 km (60 mi) above the surface and are seen from points on the ground several thousand kilometers apart. Yet they are less than 1 km (0.6 mi) in depth and the stars can shine through to add to the splendor.

Auroras are most brilliant when there is intense activity in the Sun, indicated by the presence of sunspots. Electrically charged particles emitted by the Sun (the solar wind) are drawn to the Earth's magnetic poles, where they bombard molecules and atoms in the ionosphere. As the atoms become excited they emit radiation: oxygen atoms emit greenish light, nitrogen atoms pink light.

The aurora borealis or northern lights over Canada
The North Magnetic Pole, focus in the northern hemisphere of the magnetic activity that produces the aurora, is situated in the islands of the Canadian Arctic.

HABITATS AND THEIR CONSERVATION

The vast tracts of Canada and Greenland extend from a narrow, urbanized zone bordering the United States to within a few hundred kilometers of the North Pole. They encompass a wide range of habitats from temperate rainforest to Arctic tundra, and from prairie grassland to dense coniferous forest. Most of their huge open spaces are sparsely inhabited, or not at all, and are likely to remain wilderness areas because of their harsh climate and inhospitable terrain. The region marks the furthermost limit for many American plants and animals that traveled northward at the end of the most recent ice age. It also shares many species with Europe and Asia that migrated across the Bering Strait over the land bridge formed by the advance of glaciers and changing sea levels many thousands of years ago.

COUNTRIES IN THE REGION	
Canada	
Major protected area	**Hectares**
Algonquin PP	765,345
Banff NP	664,106
Bruce Peninsula NP	27,000
Fathom Five NMP	147,000
Gros Morne NP WH	194,240
Jasper NP	1,087,800
Kejimkujik NP	38,151
Kluane NP WH	2,201,500
Kootenay NP	137,788
Laurentides/Charlevoix PP BR	966,300
Melville Bay NR (Greenland)	1,050,000
Mont St Hilaire BS BR	5,550
Mont Tremblant PP	124,800
Mount Revelstoke NP	26,263
Nahanni NP WH	476,560
Northeast Greenland NP BR	70,000,000
Ellesmere Island NP	3,950,000
Northern Yukon NP	1,016,865
Pacific Rim NP	147,000
Point Pelee/Long Point PP BR	27,000
Polar Bear PP	2,410,000
Polar Bear Pass NWA	81,000
Quetico PP	475,819
Riding Mountain NP BR	297,591
South Moresby NP	147,000
Waterton Lakes NP BR	52,597
Wood Buffalo NP WH	4,480,700
Yoho NP	131,313

BR=Biosphere Reserve; NMP=National Marine Park; NP=National Park; NWA=National Wildlife Area; NR=Nature Reserve; PP=Provincial Park; WH=World Heritage site

Prairie wetlands, or sloughs, are valuable habitats for waterfowl and waders. The typical vegetation includes sedges, reeds, horsetails, bulrushes and floating duckweeds and water lilies. Most of the prairie grasslands have now vanished beneath the plow.

NORTHERN HABITATS

Canada contains large areas of relatively flat land that are dominated by mountains in the west; these form the northern end of the Cordillera belt, which extends southward through the United States to Central and South America. To the west of these mountains, the land is deluged in rain coming in from the Pacific. This supports a belt of temperate rainforest of huge, ancient evergreens.

To the east, in the rain shadow of the mountains, lie stretches of treeless grassland. This is the prairie zone, which experiences extremes of temperature in the annual alternation of airmasses flowing up from the subtropical south and down from the Arctic north. The prairie grassland ecosystem is maintained by drought, fire and grazing. Most of it has been destroyed by plowing and cultivation. Only a pitiful remnant is left among the vast fields of crops as a reminder of what was once a paradise of colorful flowers and rich animal life. The landscape is studded and pocked with dry sandhills and many pools shaped by the retreating glaciers of the last ice age.

Forest zones
Forests cover a great swathe of Canada from the Yukon in the northwest to Newfoundland off the eastern coast. They form part of the taiga zone of coniferous forest that extends across northern Europe and Asia. The taiga is dominated by spruces, with pines, tamarack and fir, and intrusions of hemlock, deciduous aspen, beech and maple. Large areas consist of muskeg, a quaking, waterlogged peatland where tree cover is patchy. The

Biomes

- subtropical and temperate rainforest
- coniferous forest
- temperate broadleaf forest
- arctic desert and tundra
- temperate grassland
- mountain and highland system
- lake system

- ◆ major protected area
- ○ Biosphere Reserve
- × World Heritage site

Virgin temperate rainforest is found on the islands off the Pacific coast of Canada. The mild climate and high rainfall combine to give a long growing season that allows this luxuriant vegetation to thrive. The forest is characterized by sitka spruce, western red cedar, western hemlock and Douglas fir.

forests are rich in animal species. Among the large mammals are moose, caribou, beavers, lynx and bears.

To the north of the forests, and merging with them in a ragged boundary, are the treeless expanses of the tundra, which stretches from the western shore of Hudson Bay to the tip of Labrador and the Arctic archipelago. The feature most striking to the human visitor is the summer plagues of mosquitoes and blackflies that breed in the many ponds. These support large populations of wildfowl and waders that migrate to the tundra to breed in summer. Caribou also visit the tundra for summer grazing. The nutrient-rich coastal waters support populations of seals, whales and seabirds, especially where currents maintain stretches of open water throughout the year.

In the southeast corner of Canada the climate becomes more moderate under the influence of the Great Lakes and the Atlantic. It was the first area to be settled by Europeans, who found its deciduous

forests of oak, beech, sugar maple and basswood very similar to those of their home countries. Little of the original forest cover has survived the encroachment of agriculture, industry and urbanization in this densely populated area of the country.

A northern wilderness

Greenland has much in common with the Canadian Arctic. Only the coastal fringe is clear of permanent ice and supports a tundra vegetation with sparse populations of musk oxen, caribou, Arctic hares, lemmings, Arctic foxes and polar bears, together with visiting birds. The southwestern coast of Greenland, coming under the influence of the North Atlantic Drift, is relatively mild; stands of juniper, birch and rowan grow in sheltered valleys and sheep herding is practiced on a modest scale. The human population is only 53,000 and exploitation of mineral and oil resources in this wilderness area has barely started.

A NETWORK OF PARKS AND RESERVES

The preservation of Canada's wilderness started in November 1885 when 260 ha (643 acres) of country around Banff's Cave and Basin Hot Springs were set aside for public use. In the next decade more reserves were created: these were eventually to become the Yoho, Kootenay, Mount Revelstoke and Waterton Lakes National Parks. The creation of the Canadian Parks Branch in 1911 provided the impetus for many new national parks over the next 25 years, but changes in federal legislation concerning the transfer of land caused a lull after that. However, since the 1960s there has been renewed activity in park creation, especially in the empty west and north.

Today Canada has 36 national parks and national park reserves, comprising over 182,000 sq km (72,250 sq mi). The largest, Wood Buffalo National Park, covers an area greater than Switzerland. At the present time, nearly 2 percent of Canada's land area is within the national park network.

The primary aim of the national parks is to protect representative examples of the Canadian landscape. The latest addition, albeit not yet fully established, is Saskatchewan's grasslands national park, which has been set up to protect the nation's most endangered ecosystem. The idea of a "magnificent park" for the grasslands was first suggested by the explorer George Catlin in 1832 when he predicted the demise of the prairie, along with the plains Indians and the bison herds that roamed the grasslands.

A second category of parks – the provincial parks – has the wider goal of catering for tourism and recreation. The first of these, the Algonquin Provincial Park, was established in Ontario in 1893. Provincial parks now range from the 24,100 sq km (9,300 sq mi) Polar Bear Provincial Park on Hudson Bay to tiny urban sites scattered throughout the populated parts of Canada.

Other protected areas

There are a multiplicity of other protected areas in Canada, covering a wide range of functions, including critical wildlife habitats, ecological reserves, refuges for migratory birds and wilderness areas. Some areas are under provincial authority; others are federally administered. In July 1987 Ontario's Fathom Five Provincial Park off the Bruce Peninsula became the country's first marine park, and there is a growing system of Canadian Heritage Rivers.

Canada's protected areas occupy a significant place within the international framework of reserves. As well as 17 wetlands considered to be of international importance (Ramsar sites), it has 6 Biosphere Reserves and 6 World Heritage sites. Waterton Lakes National Park is linked with the contiguous Glacier National Park on the other side of the border with the United States and together they have been given the status of the world's first International Peace Park.

Components of the ecosystem
1 Heather family plants
2 Mosses and lichens
3 Marsh grass
4 Cotton grass
5 Peat
6 Permafrost
7 Caribou
8 Arctic hare
9 Ptarmigan
10 Arctic lemming
11 Snowy owl
12 Wolf
13 Arctic fox

Energy flow
⇨ primary producer/primary consumer
➡ primary/secondary consumer

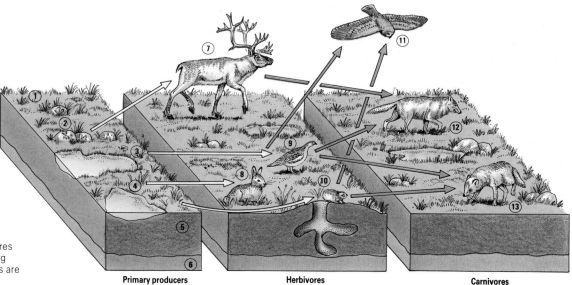

A tundra ecosystem Freezing temperatures slow down the decomposition and growing rates of plants. Lichens and cushion plants are vital components in the food chain.

Primary producers   Herbivores   Carnivores

Snow and ice cloak the land during the long winters in the Northwest Territories of Canada. The spring thaw brings flowering plants, such as this yellow poppy, along with swarms of insects. Migrating birds and mammals move north as the short summer begins.

Taiga forest on the mountains of the Kluane National Park in Yukon Territory. These coniferous forests of spruce, pine and fir provide a habitat for large mammals such as bears, moose, caribou and lynx.

Ecological reserves are a new and important form of protection. They are set aside either for ecological monitoring or to protect unique and endangered species and habitats. Many sites in Canada were identified by the International Biological Program in the 1960s. One, Polar Bear Pass on Bathurst Island, has become a national wildlife area; it is an "oasis" inhabited by 11 land and marine mammals, including polar bears, musk ox and caribou, and 42 bird species, one of the largest known concentrations of animals in the Arctic. Protection was opposed by the mining, oil and gas industries who feared it would lead to widespread restrictions on economic development in the Arctic. Similar controversy confronts other Arctic wildernesses.

The world's largest park

The population of Greenland is dependent on fishing and hunting, and conservation of natural resources is vital. Consequently egg collecting and other forms of harvesting are forbidden on certain cliffs and islands; in an area of Melville Bay on the west coast, where both hunting and motorboats have been banned, there is a reserve for polar bears and ringed seals. The most extensive protected area is the Greenland National Park: the largest in the world, and the emptiest. Most of it is polar desert, but it includes important wildlife habitats in the north.

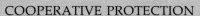

COOPERATIVE PROTECTION

The federal government of Canada is increasingly keen to gain the cooperation of private individuals and organizations in protecting isolated sites in urbanized and farmed areas. While such sites frequently contain reduced populations of species, they are often all that is left and their protection is consequently vital if Canada is to look to the future and prevent its natural heritage from being completely destroyed.

The Ontario Natural Heritage League (ONHL) was founded in 1982, and is now a coalition of 28 public and private organizations. Its guiding principle is cooperation; by securing support in both the private and public sectors and by encouraging private landowners to act as stewards of the countryside, the

ONHL has attained goals that other, individual efforts have not.

Among its successes the ONHL has helped to establish cooperative protection for more than 20 provincial ecological and geological sites. It was instrumental in obtaining final provincial government approval for a comprehensive land-use plan for the 300 km (186 mi) Niagara Escarpment and helped, with others, in preparing a conservation strategy and trust fund to protect the remnants of the Carolinian forest in southwestern Ontario between lakes Huron, Erie and Ontario. In cooperation with the Ontario government it has worked to set up a Natural Heritage Tax Rebate to help owners of important natural areas.

CONFLICT OF INTERESTS

There is no shortage of threats to protected areas in Canada. To people living in more crowded parts of the globe it may seem incredible that the Canadian wilderness is under pressure from such a sparse population, especially in the remote areas of the north and west. However, one threat comes from powerful forestry interests, especially in British Columbia and Ontario, which question proposals to preserve forest land. The widespread practice of clear-felling often destroys the environment, and has adverse effects that spread far beyond the cleared area through, for example, the disruption of rivers and streams.

Balancing resource use
Mineral extraction, with its associated pipelines, hydroelectric schemes and settlements, probably presents the greatest threat of all to the environment. The building of access roads endangers wildlife: in the areas bordering Waterton Lakes National Park, for example, roads to natural gas drilling rigs have enabled hunters to come within range of bighorn sheep, whose winter migrations lead them out of the park.

Longstanding mining claims may have to be resolved before a protected area can be established. In British Columbia mining interests have succeeded in opening up some provincial parks for exploration and development, despite protests from local people and conservationists. Such experiences show that in Canada, as elsewhere in the world, legal declaration of a protected area is not always sufficient to ensure its preservation. Developments for hydroelectricity or oil in the Canadian Arctic affect huge areas of wilderness. With the degree of commercial investment involved, it is often hard to gain a hearing for the priceless value of wildland and wildlife conservation.

The increased demands of visitors for greater access to the wilderness areas are being felt in many areas. In the Rocky Mountains the Trans-Canada highway, which runs through Banff National Park, has been widened to four lanes. Visitors to parks pollute water supplies, trample

On the rocks in the Jasper National Park. The mountain goat is a rock climbing specialist; it lives on rock faces and in alpine meadows where it is safe from predators.

vegetation and start fires. The dilemma facing conservationists is that tourism is often cited as the means of bringing employment to a local community as an argument against allowing more damaging forms of development.

The threats to protected areas are not diminished by the attitude of federal and provincial governments. Not only can they hamper proposals for protected areas, but they can pass legislation to alter existing parks. Banff National Park's boundaries have changed ten times since 1885. Over half the area of Waterton Lakes National Park was removed by the government in 1921, so it no longer conserves an entire plant and animal community. More recently, however, Waterton has been designated a Biosphere Reserve which has led to greater co-operation over activities that may affect it.

Even where the federal government is willing to establish a national park, the provincial government may be reluctant

SOUTH MORESBY NATIONAL PARK

Rainforests are so linked in most people's minds with the tropics that it comes as a surprise to many to find that they exist on the western seaboard of North America. Giant, ancient evergreen trees thrive in the high rainfall of the Pacific coast and support a varied wildlife that has led to the islands of British Columbia being called the "Canadian Galapagos". But, just like the rainforests of the tropics, these temperate rainforests are coveted for their timber.

The story is familiar: new techniques have allowed logging operations to speed the destruction of the forests. It is estimated that at the present rate of felling the forests of British Columbia will be exhausted in the first decade of the next century.

In 1985, a group of Haida people, who have lived in the forest for generations, were arrested for blockading a logging road. The logging continued but the blockade helped to unite the opposition mounted by the Haida and a local group, the Islands Protection Society. As a result of their campaign, an agreement was made two years later between the federal and provincial governments to create the South Moresby National Park at the southern end of the Queen Charlotte Islands. Felling was stopped, though there were reports that the loggers had worked double shifts while negotiations were going on in order to remove as many trees as possible. The price exacted by the logging companies and provincial government in compensation was in excess of $100 million.

to cooperate in implementing it, and control of the land and natural resources lies with the provincial rather than federal authorities. Local communities may oppose protection of land out of fear that it will curb their activities.

Indigenous land claims
Matters are most complicated in cases

Canadian rainforests suffer from the worldwide demand for timber. This interior hemlock forest, however, is protected as part of the South Moresby National Park. These isolated forests have given rise to endemic species such as the Columbian blacktail deer.

Harp seal pups bask in the winter sun on the frozen Gulf of St Lawrence. The Gulf's populations of seals and whales are increasingly threatened by pollution from the chemicals that are dumped into the waters by the many industries in this highly-populated area.

where indigenous peoples have land claims. These have assumed an increasing importance in Canada with the growth of oil and mineral extraction. Most claims are recognized by the federal government but not necessarily by the relevant provincial government. Since 1976 national parks in such areas are established as "national park reserves" pending final settlement of the land claim. The Inuit and other indigenous peoples regard the land not as wilderness but as homeland and habitat. Thus, while they may not want development of their land, they may also not want protective measures that would restrict their hunting.

However, land claims in northern and western Canada are proving to be a significant force for national park establishment. It is recognized that an area can be protected from resource development and opened for tourist use, while still being used by indigenous peoples for hunting and harvesting game. The Northern Yukon, Northern Ellesmere Island and South Moresby National Parks owe their existence at least in part to indigenous land claims.

The Northern Yukon

The Canadian Arctic is one of the empty parts of the world. Its hostile climate of dark, freezing winters and short, cool summers that barely thaw the soil has kept human settlement to a minimum. The wildlife that evolved to withstand and thrive in these conditions has provided food, clothing and shelter for the scattered nomadic bands of people who also adapted to this harsh but incredibly beautiful environment.

The success of these people is seen at the Engigstciak archeological site on the Firth river in the Northern Yukon National Park. It provides evidence of more than 5,000 years of occupation by many different people. Other archeological sites show the arrival of Arctic whalers, of trappers and hunters from the Hudson Bay Company and of the Royal Canadian Mounted Police. The last twenty years have seen the Arctic wilderness brought into the 20th century. Improved technology now enables the quest for oil and

minerals to take place where once it would have been impossible, so that even the most remote wilderness stands in need of protection. One way is through the involvement of those people who have traditionally been part of this wilderness habitat.

The 10,168 sq km (3,925 sq mi) that make up the Northern Yukon National Park rise gently from the Beaufort Sea and reach a peak in the 1,800 m (5,900 ft) British Mountains close to the Alaska border. Near the southern edge the tundra is replaced by taiga, with open stands of stunted white spruce and balsam poplar marking the transition zone.

The park is home to one of North America's highest concentrations of large birds of prey and to large numbers of grizzly bears. The coastal plain of lagoons, spits, islands and river deltas makes an important corridor for millions of waterfowl, birds of prey, guillemots and shorebirds. But the park is best known as the

Fall in the north brings color to the alpine tundra in the Northern Yukon National Park. Above the treeline is tundra vegetation of low shrubs, grasses and lichens. The flush of growth in the spring and summer creates lush meadows that attract insects, birds and mammals. To cope with the harsh winters, many small mammals hibernate while the larger mammals and birds migrate down the mountains or to warmer habitats.

Remote wilderness The remote location and harsh climate of the Northern Yukon National Park means that it is wilderness territory. There are a few settlements of the indigenous peoples who have adapted to these severe conditions over the centuries. They have been instrumental in ensuring that the area remains protected and have negotiated exclusive rights to hunting game.

On the southern edges of the park taiga takes over from Arctic tundra. The freezing winters, short growing season and poor acidic soils produce a vegetation of coniferous trees, with deciduous trees such as birch, poplar and aspen in clearings. It forms the largest ecological zone in Canada, stretching from the Yukon to Newfoundland.

home of a 150,000-strong caribou herd. Their summer calving grounds lie along the coastal tundra and foothills; the animals move north in summer to graze on the tundra, and then travel southward to spend the winter feeding on caribou moss in the more protected forest.

Local involvement

The park is closely involved with the local Inuvialuit people. It came into being through agreement between the Inuit Committee for Original People's Entitlement (COPE) and the federal government, and was formally designated in 1984 as part of the settlement of the Inuvialuit land claim. The agreement gives the Inuvialuit certain rights in the park. These include exclusive rights to harvest game, preferential rights to employment and economic opportunities within the park, and the right to be involved in planning and management.

Wilderness of ice

Although much of the Arctic Ocean is permanently frozen it supports a surprisingly rich food chain. Light fliltering through the ice supplies energy to a film of algae on the undersurface. Shrimp-like crustaceans graze the algae, and are food for fish and migratory whales. The fish are eaten by marine mammals such as seals and walruses, and by a host of migratory birds that breed on the tundra.

In places, the water is kept ice-free by ocean currents. These oases of open water, or polynias, are important feeding grounds for marine mammals and seabirds. They also attract unwelcome human activity in the form of oil and gas extraction along the coast of North America. There are proposals to cut a channel through the ice to take tankers from the oilfields to the ports around Hudson Bay. In the event of a spill, oil would spread for hundreds of kilometers under the ice, destroying the algae – the basis of the Arctic food chain – and blocking the oxygen supply to the animals living in the waters below.

Polar bears on the frozen Arctic. In winter the sea ice is so extensive that it is possible for these animals to walk all the way from Greenland to the Svalbard Islands off the coast of Norway – a distance of almost 1,000 km (620 mi).

ANIMAL LIFE

THE ARCTIC CHALLENGE · SECRETS OF SURVIVAL · BACK FROM THE BRINK

The varied animal life of Canada reflects its vast wildernesses, the seasonal contrasts of its extreme continental climate, and its diverse habitats. Rattlesnakes live in the most arid areas, great herds of caribou cross the tundra, and countless migrant birds visit the region for part of the year. Many of the species that live in the endless tracts of tundra and the boreal forest are common to the European landmass: they crossed into Canada during the last ice age over a land bridge where the Bering Strait now exists. Seals, walruses and Polar bears inhabit the offshore islands, and whales swim off the northern seaboard, feeding on the rich fish stocks of the Arctic Ocean. With its low human population density, Canada remains one of the last reserves capable of supporting large and healthy populations of wildlife.

COUNTRIES IN THE REGION

Canada

ENDEMISM AND DIVERSITY

Diversity Low
Endemism Low

SPECIES

	Total	Threatened	Extinct†
Mammals	136	15	0
Birds	450*	5	2
Others	unknown	28	2

† *species extinct since 1600 - Great auk (Alca impennis),*
Labrador duck (Camptorhynchus labradorius)
* *breeding and regular non-breeding species*

NOTABLE THREATENED ENDEMIC SPECIES

Mammals Vancouver Island marmot (*Marmota vancouverensis*)
Birds None
Others Lake lamprey (*Lampetra macrostoma*), Copper redhorse fish (*Moxostoma hubbsi*), Periodical cicaca (*Magicicauda septendecim*)

NOTABLE THREATENED NON-ENDEMIC SPECIES

Mammals Gray wolf (*Canis lupus*), wolverine (*Gulo gulo*), Polar bear (*Ursus maritimus*), Bowhead whale (*Balaena mysticetus*), Northern right whale (*Eubalaena glacialis*)
Birds Whooping crane (*Grus americanus*), Piping plover (*Charadrius melodius*), Eskimo curlew (*Numenius borealis*), Spotted owl (*Strix occidentalis*), Kirtland's warbler (*Dendroica kirtlandii*)
Others Shortnose sturgeon (*Accipenser brevirostris*), Atlantic whitefish (*Coregonus canadensis*), Dakota skipper (*Hesperia dacotae*)

DOMESTICATED ANIMALS (originating in region)

Well concealed The Ruddy turnstone migrates from the sea shore to the tundra to nest and rear its young. The tundra is an exposed habitat that lacks cover, so the bird is well camouflaged to protect it from predators such as falcons, jaegers and Arctic foxes.

THE ARCTIC CHALLENGE

An animal must possess special qualities to withstand the extreme weather conditions of the Arctic: an area that encompasses about one-third of Canada, almost all of Greenland and the whole of the Arctic Ocean. There are far fewer permanent inhabitants than in more temperate areas: resident species include Arctic lemmings and Arctic foxes. Many of the region's animals are also found in northern North America, northern Europe and the north of the Soviet Union. This is because until relatively recent times the Eurasian and American landmasses were connected by land bridges.

After the spring melt, when the climate is more hospitable to wildlife, many species of animals are attracted to the Arctic tundra to give birth and feed their young on the abundant supply of food. Thousands upon thousands of birds migrate north every year to find nesting sites and mates, and to take advantage of the bountiful food supply provided by the grasses and wild flowers that carpet the tundra in summer, and the insects that breed among the foliage and in the pools that dot the landscape. The visitors include many of the world's long-distance migrants: Canada geese fly in from the southern United States, Ruddy turnstones arrive from Argentina, and for the Arctic tern the summer visit is just a brief pause on its year-round migration between the Arctic shores and the edge of the Antarctic pack ice. Lesser golden plovers come from South America and Northern wheatears migrate here from Africa.

The empty north

The majority of Canadians live within 160 km (100 mi) of the United States border, leaving the north relatively empty of people. Although pressure from the south – in the form of mining, damming and forestry – competes with the animals for use of the land, a great deal of the north is inaccessible to, or free from, industry. This leaves ample space for events such as the annual mass migration of caribou from their winter refuge in the coniferous forests to their summer home in the Arctic tundra. Herds of tens of thousands of animals migrate northward to their traditional calving grounds. Groups of females and yearlings arrive first and give birth in the spring: the males then join them to spend the summer grazing. In September, thousands of closely spaced bands return across ice fields, mountains and marshes to their wintering grounds. Many will have done over a thousand kilometers in their annual circuit.

The Arctic seaboard also supports a great number of migrants. In summer plankton thrive in the surface waters, supporting dense shoals of shrimplike invertebrates. These in turn are preyed on by fish, which attract seabirds and Harp, Ringed and Harbor seals. The seals are preyed on not only by Polar bears, but also by people; they are an important food source for the few remaining Canadian and Greenland Inuit who still live by hunting: the pelts of the seals are an important part of their livelihood.

There has been worldwide controversy over the commercial hunting of Harp seal pups in Canada. Annually every February and March female Harp seals gather on the ice to give birth and then mate: the perfect opportunity for hunters to harvest large numbers of newborn pups. Now, after 200 years, the clubbing has finally been brought to an end and the Harp seal population continues to thrive.

Teeming seas

The northern Atlantic and Pacific oceans support a very large quantity of marine life. For centuries fishermen from Europe, and more recently from Canada, have exploited the huge shoals of cod found along the Grand Banks of Newfoundland ·in the Atlantic. Lobster were also so abundant here a century ago that they were considered a "poor man's dish". The Pacific is the ocean of the giants: the Giant octopus, whose outstretched arms may reach 2 m (6 ft) across; the goeduck (pronounced gooweyduck), a clam that has a feeding siphon over 1 m (3 ft) long; and the halibut, a flat fish that can easily weigh as much as 150 kg (330 lb).

The world's largest carnivore A Polar bear roams the sea ice in search of seals. Superbly adapted to Arctic conditions, Polar bears have been known to reach Iceland and Norway over the ice. Canada has several important denning areas for Polar bears, who give birth in snow holes in midwinter.

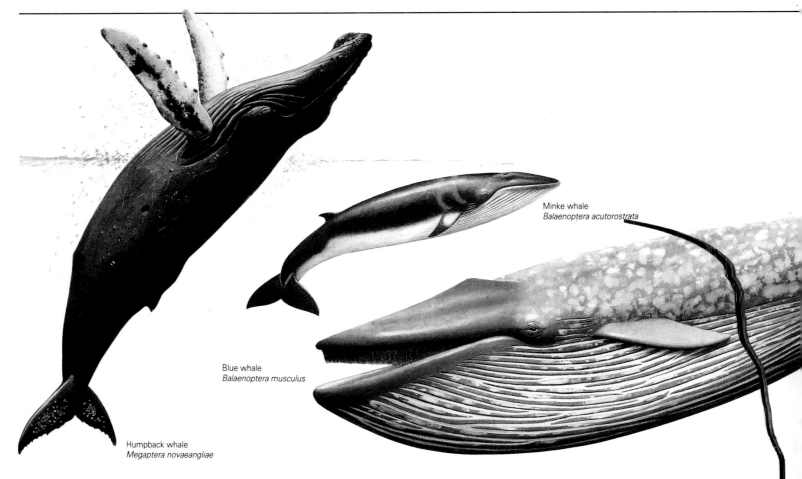

Minke whale
Balaenoptera acutorostrata

Blue whale
Balaenoptera musculus

Humpback whale
Megaptera novaeangliae

SECRETS OF SURVIVAL

The animals of the Arctic have had to adapt to withstand the severest of winter weather conditions. Insulation is an essential means of heat conservation. The Polar bear, the Arctic fox and caribou, for example, have a thick fur coat and dense underfur to keep them warm and protect them from the penetrating winds. Animals with a low surface area to volume ratio are able to conserve heat for longer; short, thick limbs and small ears, such as those of the Arctic fox, are adaptations for reducing heat loss.

Coping with snow

A typical adaptation of animals in the Arctic is the matching of coat color to the seasonal changes that affect the landscape. Camouflage aids both the hunter and the hunted on the bare tundra. The Rock ptarmigan, for example, has mottled brown plumage in summer that blends with the foliage. As winter approaches this is replaced by dense white feathers that provide insulation as well as camouflage. In severe weather it burrows in the snow for warmth. However, despite its protective coloring, it often falls prey to Arctic fox and ermine, both of which also turn white in winter.

Snow poses problems for forest species too: both the Snowshoe hare and its main predator, the lynx, have broad feet that

enable them to walk on snow. The moose (elk) has another approach; its long legs and high-stepping gait enable it to move swiftly through deep snow to escape from pursuing wolves, which must plow their way through.

One way in which animals deal with cold conditions is to avoid them by hibernating. An animal in hibernation becomes completely inactive; it enters a prolonged period during which its body temperature and metabolic rate are reduced. Torpor is akin to short-term hibernation; the animal's body temperature is not reduced to the same extent, and the animal may become active at frequent intervals so that it can feed. Hibernation and torpor are both means of conserving energy when food is scarce and when conditions are too severe for normal activity. Northern bears usually enter a state of torpor and are easily wakened; chipmunks, by contrast, enter a deep and prolonged sleep.

Seals are well adapted to the cold waters in which they live for much of the time. They have developed various adaptations that enable them to swim efficiently, and to conserve heat in the cold, heat-draining waters. These include a torpedolike body shape to improve streamlining, the modification of limbs into flippers and the ability to hold their breath for long periods while diving for food. Adaptations to minimize heat loss include a thick layer of blubber, which

SCOURGE OF THE SEA LAMPREY

The Sea lamprey is a primitive eel-like fish that spends much of its adult life at sea, living as a parasite on other fish. Clinging to its host with a suckerlike mouth armed with sharp, horny teeth, it feeds on the host's blood. This seriously weakens the fish, especially if several lampreys attach themselves. The lamprey's skin has glands that secrete a poisonous mucus, which is thought to deter predatory fish. Lampreys travel hundreds of kilometers upriver in order to spawn. The males build nests for the eggs by making a shallow depression in the gravel. After the eggs have hatched the strange filter-feeding larvae remain in fresh water for several years.

The American Sea lamprey used to migrate along the St. Lawrence seaway to Lake Ontario to spawn, but was prevented by the Niagara Falls from reaching the other Great Lakes. In 1828, however, the building of the Welland Canal, which links Lake Ontario to Lake Erie, let in the Sea lamprey. The lamprey modified its ways to spend its whole life in fresh water. Its depredations devastated a once thriving fishing industry; on Lake Michigan the catch of lake trout fell from 3,000 tonnes (3,000 tons), in 1944 to 16 kg (35 lb) in 1955. There have been many attempts to get rid of the lamprey, ranging from traps to electrical barriers and poison, but despite all the money spent, it still survives – at the expense of the trout.

Gray whale
Eschrichtius robustus

Fin whale
Balaenoptera physalus

Whales of the far north (*left*) The Humpback whale is renowned for the variety of its underwater calls. The Minke whale is one of the smallest, but has been extensively hunted since stocks of the larger species were depleted. The Blue whale is the largest living creature on earth, up to 27 m (88 ft) long. Despite the worldwide ban on whaling, native Arctic peoples are still allowed to hunt the Fin whale. The Gray whale is confined to the Pacific Ocean, where it is often seen near the coast.

acts as insulation, shortened limbs – to reduce surface area – and an efficient circulation system that can reduce blood flow to the flippers while redirecting blood from the body surface to the core of the animal's body in order to conserve heat. It also directs oxygenated blood to vital organs such as the brain. In the case of the fur seal, further insulation against the cold is provided by the animal's dense pelt with its thick layer of softer underfur.

Life on the open plains
On the open Canadian prairies the lack of cover can pose problems for both predators and prey. A social organization is one adaptation to these conditions: wolves, for example, live in packs, allowing them to hunt large prey and to defend kills from other wolves and predators. In response to such pack hunters, and to being easily spotted on the grasslands, prey such as bison and Pronghorn antelopes live in large herds. This may offer advantages to the individual as a herd is more likely to detect the approach of a predator than a single grazing animal.

In addition to living in herds, the Pronghorn antelope exhibits other antipredator adaptations. For its size, the Pronghorn has relatively large eyes that probably enable it to see predators at great distances. Pronghorns also react to predators by raising two white patches of hair on their rump, signaling danger to the rest of the herd. The herd then flees as one, which reduces the danger to individual animals as they make their dash for safety. These small antelopes can attain a speed of 86 kph (53 mph), comparable to that of the cheetah, which is reputed to be the fastest land animal in the world.

Dolphins of cool waters (*below*) The Bottle-nosed dolphin is a common coastal species. The beluga or White whale has the popular name "the canary of the sea" because of its wide repertoire of underwater calls. The male narwhal has a single tusk up to 1 m (3 ft) long; its function is unknown.

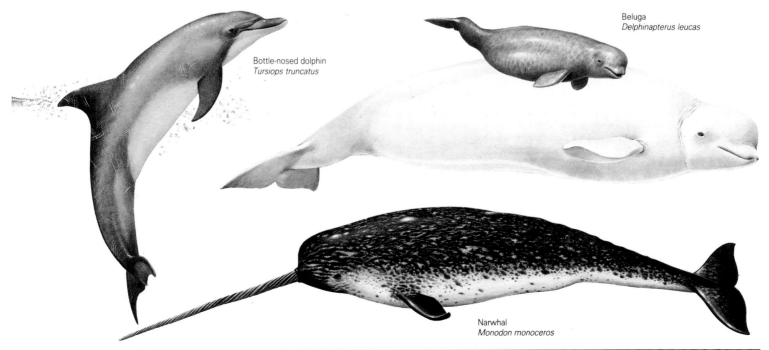

Bottle-nosed dolphin
Tursiops truncatus

Beluga
Delphinapterus leucas

Narwhal
Monodon monoceros

BACK FROM THE BRINK

Canada's prosperity was founded on the fur trade of the early 17th century, and the tradition of hunting continues to this day. Hares, lynx, beavers and raccoons were trapped for their pelts, and wolves were killed because they, like humans, were deer hunters. A bounty was imposed on wolves to reduce their numbers, thus preserving larger deer populations for the human hunters. The irony is that humans are far more likely than wolves to be the cause of low deer numbers. The best catch for a hunter is the largest buck with the biggest antlers: a mature breeding male. This leaves younger or less healthy males to do the breeding, which may weaken the deer population. Wolves, on the other hand, tend to hunt old or sick animals (those easiest to capture), thus removing from the population individuals that are likely to die from starvation or exposure to the elements anyway.

Rescue and reintroduction

One of the best-known stories of near-extinction is that of the North American bison or buffalo. The ancestor of the two subspecies (the Plains and the Wood bison) moved into the region approximately 100,000 years ago across the land bridge that once joined North America to the Eurasian landmass. Bison spread throughout the continent wherever grasslands produced the food they required, reaching a population of 60 million or more. When European settlers reached the prairies the animals were slaughtered indiscriminately for their meat and hides, and by 1900 were practically extinct. In the safety of government reserves, however, the remaining animals survived and bred, and they are now numbered in their thousands.

The North American bison is extremely large, its massive head and shoulders indicating its great strength. The bulls can be very dangerous during the rut, when they compete with aggression to establish dominance. Ranchers have considered raising bison and selling the meat for profit, but the animal does not take well to captivity and can jump over 2 m (6 ft) fences. They have had greater success with a hybrid between beef cattle and buffalo, the "beefalo".

The stately Whooping crane has made an even more remarkable recovery than the bison. In 1941 there were only 23 Whooping cranes left in the world, two of which were being kept in captivity. Their decrease in numbers was perhaps not unexpected, considering what an easy target for hunters the great white birds made flying over the prairie: they stand close to 2 m (6 ft) tall and have a 2.5 m (7 ft) wing span. The Whooping crane migrates from the Northwest Territories (its breeding grounds are in Wood Buffalo National Park) to its wintering grounds in Texas on the coast of the Gulf of Mexico. Once it was recognized as being close to extinction public concern was quickly aroused, and publicity campaigns to save the bird were mounted along its migration route.

Whooping cranes usually lay two eggs, but raise only one young to fledgling age. In an attempt to boost the present population of about 200 birds in Canada, conservationists are using fostering techniques. One egg will be taken from a Whooping crane nest in Wood Buffalo National Park and placed in the nest of a pair whose own eggs have been lost through accident or predation. Another method is to fly the egg to Grays Lake National Park in Idaho in the northwest of the United States, where it is placed in the nest of a Sandhill crane (a closely related species). It was hoped that this would extend the range of the bird in North America as well as increase its numbers, but though the 16 Idaho-raised Whooping cranes migrate regularly, not one has so far reproduced.

The gregarious walrus (*above*) Ungainly on land, in the sea the walruses' fat provides buoyancy and streamlining. They feed on clams and other invertebrates on the seabed, squirting high pressure jets of water to uncover them. Their sensitive whiskers help them locate their food in murky waters during winter or at depths where light barely penetrates. The powerful tusks are mainly for display, but are occasionally used when hauling themselves onto the ice or for defending their young.

Exposed to danger (*left*) A vulnerable female Long-tailed duck incubates her eggs alone on the tundra for 23 days: duck eggs are a favorite prey of Arctic foxes. These ducks migrate from the open sea to the tundra to take advantage of the long summer days for feeding their young on the abundant mollusks and crustaceans in the Arctic lakes. The ducklings are well developed by the time they hatch, and are able to fly within 5 or 6 weeks.

Snow geese (*above*) migrate in their thousands to the tundra to breed in spring. They feed only on plant life, taking advantage of the flush of new growth prompted by the melting snow. The goslings are much better camouflaged than their parents.

Public awareness has not produced such successful results with other species, such as the Swift fox, whose population was greatly reduced by hunting and poisoning, and became extinct in Canada. A breeding program in Alberta has led to the reintroduction of the Swift fox into parts of its former range in the dry areas of the southern prairie, but its numbers are still extremely low.

The Vancouver Island marmot has a little-known history, perhaps because its numbers have never been high. It survives only in an alpine habitat, and is a slow breeder; the young remain with their parents for three years. These two circumstances are often related to species' extinction. However, if its habitat is preserved, and if there is minimal interference from humans, it should continue to survive and perhaps even gradually increase its numbers.

The threat from humans

A grave threat to many of Canada's animals comes from habitat loss and pollution. The unique temperate rain-forests of the Pacific coast – home of the Bald eagle, the Grizzly bear and Pacific salmon – are being felled at an alarming rate, and the Great Lakes are so polluted that in many places the fish are unsafe for human consumption. Dam projects threaten many wetland bird refuges, including part of Wood Buffalo National Park, home to North America's northern-most pelican colony; and moose, musk-rats and many other species face the inundation of meadows and muskegs.

LIFE UNDER THE ICE: THE HARP SEAL'S SONG

Female Harp seals congregate on sea ice in February and have their pups in late February or early March. Mating, which takes place underwater, follows in about mid-March. Much of what is known about the behavior of these seals under the ice comes from studies of their underwater calls: eerie chirping and clicking sounds comprising sixteen call types. An increase in calling in mid-March coincides with the onset of courtship and mating. It is thought that the calls have two main functions: to draw other seals to the breeding herd, and to attract mates. Natural selection may favor females that produce loud calls, which attract more males to the breeding area. This results in a larger pool of suitors from which a female can choose a mate. Quieter calls may be made by males that are trying to attract

a female or to establish territory by warning other males to stay away from a breeding hole in the ice.

Harp seals sing in dialects. Although the calls of the seals that live in the Gulf of St. Lawrence have not changed for over 15 years, their calls are noticeably different from those of Harp seals breeding off the coast of Norway. In this respect Harp seals resemble birds, which are well known to have different song dialects in different locations. The song dialects of Harp seals may reflect their dependence on a vocal means of communication. The visual and chemical signals used by many land mammals would be ineffective under-water because they do not carry over even moderate distances: sound, on the other hand, travels considerable distances through water.

Hunted for their fur

Since earliest human times people have hunted animals not only for food but also for their fur, to make clothes for warmth and adornment. Until the comparatively recent development of artificial fibers that provide thermal insulation, people commonly wore animal skins to protect them from the snow and bitter winds. Animal furs have also long been valued for the status of wealth, and sometimes dignity, they confer upon the wearer. This is exemplified by the symbolic importance given to the wearing of ermine (the white winter coat of the stoat) in the courts of medieval and renaissance Europe. Ermine was originally used to border the hems and cuffs of costly robes, and came to signify royal or noble birth. It is still used on some ceremonial occasions. The coronation in 1937 of Britain's King George VI (1895–1952) is said to have accounted for 50,000 ermine, needed to trim the robes of the British peerage.

So great was the appetite of 17th century Europe for furs (particularly beaver fur, which was used to make men's hats) that the fur trade was one of the main forces in the opening up of Canada, with its vast wealth of fur-bearing mammals of all sizes. In 1670 a British trading organization, the Hudson's Bay Company, was formed so that the British could trade with the Amerindians for furs. Trading posts gradually spread across the country.

Even today, although it has many other interests, furs remain an important part of the company's activities.

The colder the conditions in which an animal lives, the greater is its need for insulation, and the denser the fur it grows. The many fine hairs of its pelt enable it to retain body heat by trapping air in a layer next to the skin. Arctic foxes have such thick winter coats that they are able to sleep on the snow at temperatures of −40°C (−40°F) without coming to harm.

Grooming fur is essential for maintaining its insulatory capacity. The beaver has a unique split toenail used specifically for cleaning and oiling its fur: it spends much of its time in the water, and has developed a waterproof inner coat of short fur. The mink, another water-loving species, has one of the thickest and most luxurious furs. Fur seals, which spend even more time underwater, also have a thick layer of fat (blubber) below the skin for insulation.

Victims of fashion

Over the centuries many millions of animals in Canada have died in traps and snares set by humans, originally to provide the necessities for survival in a harsh environment, more recently to supply the

The coat of Arctic foxes occurs in two color forms, each with a different winter and summer coloration. A White, or Polar, form in winter coat attacks a ptarmigan. A Blue form, really a gray to brown color, looks for carrion in winter. A Blue fox vixen "helper" in brown summer coat with her year-younger siblings: the light gray cubs have the summer coat of the Polar form, while the dark gray cub is a variant of the Blue's summer coat. The extent of snow cover influences the predominant color form of the population.

whims of fashion. As an example of the numbers involved, one winter's total taking in North America might include 400,000 Red foxes, 250,000 Gray foxes and 37,000 Arctic foxes.

A few fur-bearing animals, such as Polar bears, are now protected, but many more are vulnerable to hunters who can trap them for their fur without legal restriction. Wolverines, martens, fishers, Arctic foxes, bobcats and lynx all have desirable coats. Among the sea mammals, both Harp seals and Hooded seals are still widely hunted for their fur. Beavers and wild mink are trapped in or near their freshwater habitats.

Since at least the turn of the century the market for fur has been met partly by fur farms, which raise animals such as mink

Alone on the ice (*above*) A Harp seal pup waits for its mother to nurse it. It will be weaned in only 10–12 days. The killing of Harp seal pups for their pelts by clubbing them to death in front of their mothers has caused international uproar.

Fierce carnivore (*right*) The fisher has a unique method of catching a porcupine, repeatedly darting in to bite its face until it rolls over and the fisher can attack its soft underbelly. On this occasion it has caught a less well-defended chipmunk.

and foxes. Although this reduces pressure on the wild populations, farmed furs rarely reach the quality of the best wild furs, and the latter are still sought by connoisseurs. Nevertheless, in recent years there has been a considerable shift away from the wearing of natural furs by many people – a result of international campaigning by animal protectionists.

Monarch of the forests

The moose is the largest member of the deer family, found throughout the northern forests of North America, Europe and Asia. A mature bull stands some 2.13 m (7 ft) tall at the shoulder, and can weigh up to 816 kg (1,800 lb). The moose is a browser, feeding mainly on leaves, twigs and bark. In summer it can often be seen standing in water, feeding on water plants. Here it gains some respite from the flies and mosquitoes that pester it on land. The water plants are thought to supply it with minerals that have been lacking from its winter diet.

The moose is a powerful swimmer; the hollow hairs of its coat are filled with air, which improves its buoyancy. It can remain submerged for up to half a minute while feeding. It is also well adapted to walking on marshy ground or snow: its wide, split hooves spread its weight over soft ground, and its long legs keep its body above the wet snow. The massive antlers are grown only in the breeding season, when the bulls meet up with herds of females and compete for the right to mate.

A bull moose browses for food among snow-covered trees. A male of this size will eat vast quantities of vegetation (the equivalent of over 20,000 leaves) every day. During the warmer months they also eat a considerable quantity of sodium-rich aquatic plants.

PLANT LIFE

Canada's plants reflect the size of the country in their distribution and their variety. They have found ways to survive in the very different conditions of temperate and polar latitudes, humid coastal areas and the dry continental interior. Much about Canada is vast – the expanse of the central grasslands, the frozen stretches of the tundra, and the towering heights of stands of coniferous and deciduous forest. In the Arctic, tundra plants withstand icy temperatures, frozen soil and short summers. Farther south are forests of evergreen conifers and mixed forests, which cover about half the country. Deciduous forests in the southeast enjoy long, mild summers, and herald the cold winters with spectacular displays of color in the fall. Only grasslands survive the hot, dry summers and freezing winters of the arid interior.

COUNTRIES IN THE REGION

Canada

DIVERSITY

	Number of species	Endemism
Canada	4,000	low
Greenland	497	3%

PLANTS IN DANGER

	Threatened	Endangered	Extinct
Canada	8	7	–
Greenland	–	–	–

Examples *Armeria maritima* subsp. *interior*; *Cypripedium candidum* (small white lady's slipper); *Isotria medeoloides* (small whorled fogonia); *Limnanthes macounii*; *Pedicularis furbishiae* (Furbish's lousewort); *Phyllitis japonica* subsp. *americana*; *Plantago cordata*; *Salix planifolia* subsp. *tyrrellii*; *Salix silicicola*; *Senecio newcombei*

USEFUL AND DANGEROUS NATIVE PLANTS

Crop plants *Acer saccharum* (sugar maple), *Oxycoccus macrocarpus* (cranberry), *Vaccinium myrtilloides* (blueberry)
Garden plants *Hamamelis virginiana*, *Lilium canadense* (Canada or meadowlily), *Syringa reflexa*, *Syringa villosa*, *Tsuga canadensis*
Poisonous plants *Aconitum columbianum*; *Cicuta maculata* (water hemlock), *Robinia pseudacacia* (black locust); *Sanguinaria canadensis*; *Toxicodendron radicans* (poison ivy); *Veratrum viride* (false hellebore)

BOTANIC GARDENS

Montreal (20,000 taxa); Royal Botanic Gardens, Hamilton; University of Western Ontario (15,000 taxa)

Lowgrowing Arctic shrub Mountain avens is typical of many boreal plants, growing very slowly in the low temperatures and northern light. It may take up to a hundred years to spread 1 m (3 ft). The mosses and lichens grow even more slowly.

TUNDRA, FOREST AND PRAIRIE

About 40 million years ago the climate in Canada was warmer than it is now, and much of the land was covered with temperate mixed forest of both deciduous broadleaf trees and evergreen conifers. Gradually the climate in the north cooled, and the vegetation zones shifted southward. The deciduous species of the mixed forests were displaced farther than the conifers as they were less able to withstand cold conditions, leaving the northern zone inhabited only by pine (*Pinus*) and spruce (*Picea*).

As the Rocky Mountains formed they increasingly deprived the interior of rain. Grasslands developed in the dry areas lying in the rain shadow to the east of the mountains, and tundra plants evolved in the far north as forest and grassland species adapted to the extreme cold.

Plants of the north

The tundra plants of the Arctic and the coastal strip of Greenland consist mostly of grasses, sedges and rushes, and herbaceous species such as lousewort (*Pedicularis*) and yellow marsh saxifrage (*Saxifraga hirculus*). There are also lowgrowing shrubs such as Arctic white heather (*Cassiope tetragona*), cushion plants such as mountain avens (*Dryas integrifolia*) and purple saxifrage (*Saxifraga oppositifolia*), and plants with creeping woody stems such as the willow *Salix arctica*. Mosses and lichens are also widespread. Many flowering plants, such as *Ranunculus sulphureus*, are found only in the Arctic; some, like alpine sorrel (*Oxyria digyna*), extend southward to alpine habitats.

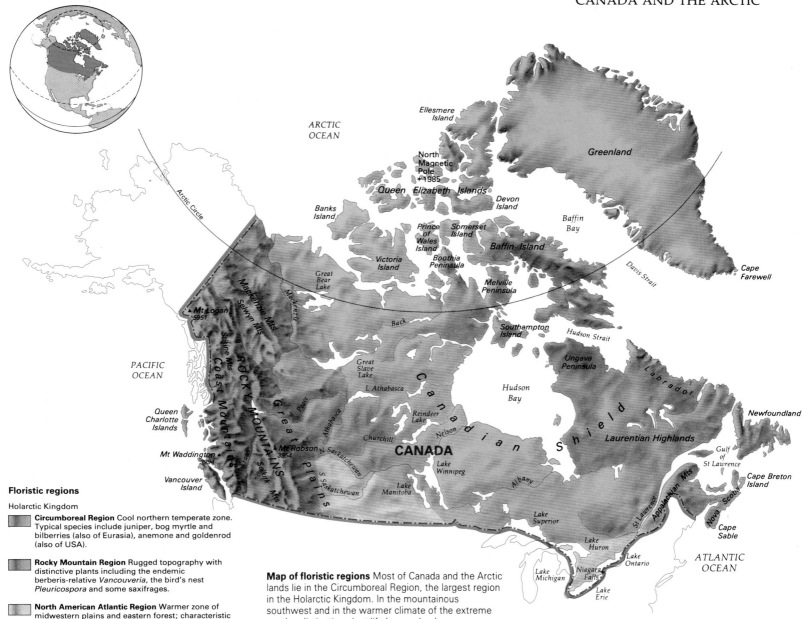

Floristic regions

Holarctic Kingdom

Circumboreal Region Cool northern temperate zone. Typical species include juniper, bog myrtle and bilberries (also of Eurasia), anemone and goldenrod (also of USA).

Rocky Mountain Region Rugged topography with distinctive plants including the endemic berberis-relative *Vancouveria*, the bird's nest *Pleuricospora* and some saxifrages.

North American Atlantic Region Warmer zone of midwestern plains and eastern forest; characteristic species include hemlock, snakeroot and squirrel corn.

Map of floristic regions Most of Canada and the Arctic lands lie in the Circumboreal Region, the largest region in the Holarctic Kingdom. In the mountainous southwest and in the warmer climate of the extreme south a distinctive plant life has evolved.

In the coniferous forests tree species such as black and white spruce (*Picea mariana* and *P. glauca*) and the one-flowered wintergreen (*Moneses uniflora*), range across the continent and into Eurasia. Other important trees include tamarack (*Larix laricina*) and jackpine (*Pinus banksiana*) in the east, and lodgepole pine (*Pinus contorta*) and alpine fir (*Abies lasiocarpa*) in the north and west. White birch (*Betula papyrifera*), aspen (*Populus tremuloides*) and other poplars are distributed throughout the region.

Temperate forests and grasslands

Temperate mixed forest covers much of the southeast, with conifers such as white pine (*Pinus strobus*) and eastern hemlock (*Tsuga canadensis*) growing together with deciduous trees such as sugar maple and red maple (*Acer saccharum* and *A. rubrum*), basswood (*Tilia americana*), white elm (*Ulmus americana*) and oaks (*Quercus*).

Other conifers, such as red spruce (*Picea rubens*), thrive in the wetter forest areas. Deciduous forests flourish in southern Ontario, in the southernmost part of the region; their range extends into the eastern United States.

The temperate forests of the west coast contain only a few deciduous species. They are dominated instead by conifers such as western hemlock (*Tsuga heterophylla*) and douglas fir (*Pseudotsuga menziesii*). These trees form towering evergreen rainforests along the coast and on the western slopes of the Coast Mountains. Similar species occupy the western slopes of the Rocky Mountains, giving way farther east to Engelmann spruce (*Picea engelmannii*) and eventually to alpine fir, lodgepole pine and white spruce, as the trees of the upland (montane) forests mingle with those of the far north.

Grassland and ponderosa pine (*Pinus ponderosa*) savanna have developed in the drier lands between the mountains. Alpine meadows rich in grasses and herbaceous perennials occupy the high summits throughout the western mountains.

In the arid south-central plains of Canada the temperate forests give way to grasslands that form part of the northern American prairies. In the driest areas, close to the Rocky Mountains, the most abundant species include blue grama grass (*Bouteloua gracilis*), which is short and densely tufted. It grows together with shrubs that have adapted to dry conditions, such as sage (*Artemisia*) and even cacti (*Opuntia*).

Farther east the mixed-grass prairies contain other short, tufted grasses, the taller wheat grass (*Agropyron*), sedges (*Carex*), shrubs and broadleaf herbs. Larger grasses, such as big bluestem (*Andropogon gerardi*), which grows to 2 m (6.5 ft), predominate in tall-grass prairie, which is found on heavy clay soils.

THE NORTHERN FORESTS

About half of Canada is covered with forests composed of species that have adapted to the long, cold winters and short, but relatively warm summers.

Black spruce is one of the most abundant trees, partly because it is evergreen and can withstand dry, cold conditions. It is one of the few trees able to survive in the waterlogged, oxygen-deficient soils of *Sphagnum* bogs. In the north it grows on drier soils, and it even persists in climates that are too severe to allow seed production. Instead, it reproduces vegetatively: the lowest branches grow close to the ground and become covered by moss and litter, in which they form roots and eventually give rise to new trees. Along the northern boundary of the forest black spruce survives in a shrublike form often less than 1 m (3 ft) high. Its low, compact shape and a blanket of snow protect it from the desiccating winter winds.

Lightning fires

The accumulation of dead lower branches, and the resins of many of the other plants in a spruce forest, make it particularly vulnerable to fire. Perhaps surprisingly, fires caused by lightning are of major importance in these forests, opening the way for succeeding plant communities and maintaining the diversity of species in the ecosystem.

Black spruce is well adapted to fire. Its cones can remain on the trees for five years or more without opening; when fire strikes, the heat triggers the release of large quantities of seed, which enables the species to reestablish itself. Pines produce similar cones, and they too may release abundant seeds after a fire. Aspens seldom reproduce by seed; instead they sprout freely from their roots. After fires, dense stands of aspen saplings spring up, but they decline as the growing conifers cut out the light and the soil becomes depleted of nutrients.

Labrador tea (*Ledum groenlandicum*), a lowgrowing shrub 30–80 cm (12–30 in) tall, which is characteristic of northern forests, is also adapted to survive fire. It sprouts from charred stem bases, and the young shoots grow rapidly with the flush of nutrients that are released from burnt vegetation.

Mosses, coral-roots and lichens

Much of the ground in northern forests is densely covered with the feather mosses *Hylocomium splendens* and *Pleurozium schreberi*. These mosses slow down the evaporation of moisture from the soil. Unlike higher plants, they are able to absorb mineral nutrients directly from rain. The nutrients are later released at the base of the slowly decomposing moss layer, where the fine roots of black spruce absorb them.

Branched lichens (*above*) Cladonia, like all lichens, is a partnership between a fungus and an alga. The fungus surrounds and protects a layer of green alga, which manufactures sugars by photosynthesis. Water is absorbed through the surface of the organisms.

Vegetation pattern of a bog (*below*) Peatlands and *Sphagnum* bogs cover large areas of the north. Trees and lowgrowing shrubs colonize the raised areas of peat, while in the surrounding wet fens sedge (*Carex*) and cattail (*Typha*) dominate.

Tamarack (*Larix lariciana*), labrador tea and dwarf juniper (*Juniperus communis* var. *depressa*) form forests on raised peat

On gently sloping ground, birch (*Betula pumila*) and a variety of peat-forming plants occupy low ridges of peat known as "strings". Sedges (*Carex*) fill shallow pools between the ridges

Sedges and cattail (*Typha*) grow on the wet fen and marsh marigolds (*Calla palustris*) may also be found

Sedges, pitcher plants (*Sarracenia*) and bogmosses occupy the pools

Coral-root orchids (*Corallorhiza*) are also typical of northern forests. These plants are saprophytic – they live off dead matter. They consist only of an underground rhizome or stem – a yellowish, many branched coral-like structure. The rhizomes have no roots, but are heavily infected by a fungus that absorbs organic nutrients from the soil and supplies them to the orchids. When the plant has accumulated sufficient food, aerial stems develop measuring up to 40 cm (16 in) in height, each ending in an inflorescence of small cream to purplish flowers. There are no leaves on these stems, but to compensate, both the green stalk of the inflorescence and the plant's ovaries contain chlorophyll; their photosynthesis presumably supplements the food derived from the fungus.

Like coral-roots, lichens consist of an association between plants and fungi. The partners in this symbiotic relationship are algae and fungi. The algae, which contain chlorophyll and photosynthesize, supply the organic nutrients for both partners. Lichens have no roots to draw water from the soil, but the fungal hyphae are able to absorb both water and mineral nutrients from precipitation. They also form a protective sheath, contracting around the algal cells to reduce metabolic activity when sunlight, which dries the

White-flowered Labrador tea The tough leaves and rust-colored hairs on the undersides restrict water loss. Such precautions are necessary because the roots cannot function efficiently in the anerobic conditions of the boggy soils where the shrub grows.

lichen, penetrates the open woodland canopy, and expanding again when conditions become more moist and photosynthesis can be resumed.

Reindeer lichen (*Cladonia rangiferina*) and related species cover the ground in open woodland in the northern forests. These pale brown or whitish, branched structures, up to 15 cm (6 in) tall, resemble tiny shrubs. Above them, fine strands of old man's beard lichen (*Usnea*) festoon the tree branches.

Pale lichens grow in areas that receive heavy snow in winter, as a result of which they are inactive. In summer the lichens reflect the sun's rays, reducing water loss and extending their periods of metabolic activity. Black lichens reverse this pattern of seasonal activity. *Alectoria*, for example, grows in exposed places with only a thin snow cover. The black coloration increases their absorption of radiation from the sun, enabling them to melt the snow immediately surrounding their stems, and stimulating photosynthesis in spring and fall when meltwater is available. The black lichens are dry and inactive for long periods in summer.

TREES IN A COLD CLIMATE

Forests develop in areas where conditions are neither too cold, as in the tundra, nor too dry, as in the prairies. Even so, the conditions they have to withstand may be extreme. Some areas, such as southern Ontario, may have long, mild summers, but these alternate with winters cold enough to freeze the soil, which restricts the amount of water the trees can take up. These areas are characterized by broadleaf deciduous trees, which survive by shedding their leaves in winter. This minimizes the amount of water lost through transpiration.

In northern and upland areas, where winter temperatures are as low as −30°C (−22°F), evergreen conifers predominate. Here the growing season is very short, so deciduous trees, which can photosynthesize only when new leaves develop in spring, and have to invest considerable resources in leaves that function for only a few months, are at a severe disadvantage. In contrast, the needlelike leaves of evergreen trees, such as pine and spruce, remain active for several years whenever the weather is favorable. The trees are able to conserve water during the long, very cold winters because their leaves have a thick, protective outer layer and a reduced surface area.

PLANTS AND PEOPLE

Plants feature prominently in Canadian culture. The maple leaf on the national flag proclaims the distinctive nature of the Canadian landscape, particularly in the fall. Each of the twelve provinces and territories has adopted a characteristic plant species as an emblem. Newfoundland, for example, has chose the carnivorous pitcher plant (*Sarracenia purpurea*); the Northwest Territories selected the mountain avens.

The Canadian forests are famous for the berries they yield, such as blueberry (*Vaccinium myrtilloides*) and cranberry (*Oxycoccus macrocarpus*). These fruits are picked every summer for local domestic use, and are also harvested commercially on a small scale. The woods of Ontario are also well known for their maples. Following the ancient custom of the Iroquois Indians, the trunks of sugar maples are tapped in March, as the sap rises, to collect the sugary fluid that is refined and sold as maple syrup.

Native Canadian plants that are widely cultivated in gardens include the shrubby goldenrod (*Solidago canadensis*) and the dogwood tree (*Cornus alternifolia*) from the southeast, creeping wintergreen (*Gaultheria procumbens*) from the northern forests, the western temperate trout lilies (*Erythronium*) and Arctic alpines such as purple saxifrage. However, it is not always clear whether the cultivated stocks came from Canadian populations or from elsewhere within the range of the species.

Commerce and conservation

The exploitation of forest resources, both in natural stands and increasingly in plantations, is a major industry. Important timber species include hemlock, douglas fir, ponderosa pine and red cedar in the west, and white pine, sugar maple and white oak (*Quercus alba*) in the east. Across the country various species of spruce are logged, and are particularly important in the pulp and paper industry.

The western coastal rainforests, the

Maples in the fall (*right*) The brilliant reds and yellows of the maples now attract tourists. Sugar maples were once the only source of sweetness in North America; a large tree can produce up to 115 litres (25 US gallons) of sap in a single spring.

Blueberries (*below*) Growing on boggy soil, these fruits were an important part of the diet of the Indian people, who dried any surplus for the winter. Blueberries are also eaten in vast quantities by birds and other animals, especially bears.

central deciduous forest, and the mixed forests in much of the east have mostly been felled, either for timber or to make way for agriculture and urban development. Regrowth forests develop rapidly, whether by succession in abandoned fields or following replanting. However, it will take a long time for them to match the grandeur of the few remaining primeval stands; those of western hemlock reach 40–50 m (130–165 ft) in height and have taken up to 500 years to develop.

The best way to conserve the forests is to increase the extent of protected reserves, harvest timber on a sustainable yield basis, and practice selective rather than clear-felling (in which all the trees in an area are felled). The last strategy has the added advantage of retaining some forest cover, which benefits orchids and other plants of the forest floor.

Pinus strobus
white pine

Picea pungens

Thuja occidentalis
American or white cedar

Tsuga heterophylla
western hemlock

Conifers of Canada These are primarily timber trees, but they and their decorative varieties are planted for their beauty. The foliage and cones vary considerably from genus to genus.

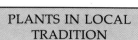
PLANTS IN LOCAL TRADITION

In a land of limited natural resources, the indigenous people demonstrated great ingenuity in their use of local plants. Pacific Coast Indians fashioned western red cedar into massive square houses, totem poles and dugout canoes, as well as boxes and bowls. They also used strips of cedar bark and spruce roots in weaving and as twine. Red cedar and other softwoods are easily carved, and were fashioned into elaborate ceremonial masks.

Indian women capitalized on the absorbent, antibiotic properties of sphagnum moss to diaper their babies, and to stem menstrual blood. In the east and north the men built canoes from strips of white birchbark stretched over a cedar frame, sewing them in place with the fine, pliable roots of white spruce. They could later be repaired with pine resin. Birchbark was also used to make barkcloth, which served as a fabric for clothing.

Many of the indigenous people have always relied on plants to nourish the animals that are their principal source of food. In the past the prairie grasses supported bison, the mainstay of the Plains Indians, while in the Arctic many Inuit relied on the annual migrations of caribou, one of the few animals able to digest the lichens of the northern woodlands.

It is not only the forests that have suffered from economic pressure. Most of the natural grasslands have been replaced by fields of Eurasian cereal grasses. Many of the native prairie species are now restricted to a few scattered reserves and to roadside verges, where they are increasingly threatened by herbicides and other agricultural chemicals. No native plants are used significantly in agriculture. This is not a new trend; even the traditional crops of the Iroquois Indians (maize, pumpkins, beans and tobacco) were introduced from farther south.

The state of the far north
In contrast to those of the south, the plants of the northern and Arctic areas, including Greenland, have so far not been much disrupted by agriculture. The plants here are, however, particularly susceptible to pollution. The emission of sulfur dioxide and heavy metals by nickel smelting activities at Sudbury, Ontario, has had a devastating effect on nearby forest. Local disruption of tundra vegetation has also been caused by the oil industry, both through oil spillage and because the heavy vehicles used in oil exploration erode the soil so the permafrost begins to melt.

The northern territories are so vast, inhospitable and remote that there is little prospect of largescale human settlement, and little imminent danger of the native vegetation being seriously disturbed. More significant is the potential threat of acid rain and other pollutants spreading to the north from existing centers of population and industry. Global warming and the depletion of ozone in the upper atmosphere could also have a major impact. Any significant change in climate is likely to disrupt existing vegetation patterns, particularly in the Arctic, and plants are damaged by increases in ultraviolet radiation. These are international problems. The causes are largely not of Canada's making, while the effects could seriously damage ecosystems throughout the world.

Survival in the Arctic

The Arctic is one of the most rigorous environments on Earth. The summers are short and cool, with average temperatures above freezing (0°C–6°C/32°F–43°F) for less than three months during the year. Summer days are long, with continuous daylight in midsummer, but the intensity of the sunlight is low. In winter there is a corresponding period of continuous darkness, and prolonged severe frost. Only a thin surface layer of the soil thaws in summer – beneath this the soil is permanently frozen. The soil is usually poor in available nutrients, particularly nitrogen and phosphorous. There is little moisture in inland areas, and although snow protects the plants from the severe cold and drying winds, late-lying snow can restrict plant growth in the spring.

Many plants have adapted to survive the severe conditions. Several of the plants are evergreen, which enables them to make maximum use of the summer period for photosynthesis. Most are low-growing, as wind speed is usually lower, and temperature and relative humidity higher, near the ground, and most have a compact form. Their surfaces absorb solar radiation, increasing plant temperature considerably above air temperature during sunlight hours, while the dense canopy of shoots reduces the movement of the air and therefore lessens the loss of heat and moisture.

Reproduction strategies

Many Arctic species flower within a few days of the spring thaw or, like the purple saxifrage, push their flowers through the last remaining snow. The seeds are released in late summer; they require relatively high daytime temperatures to promote germination, which is thus delayed until the following spring.

Reproduction by seed is unreliable in the Arctic, where both flower and fruit development is very slow, there is a shortage of insect pollinators, and the cold climate means that seeds do not always succeed in germinating. There are consequently very few annuals in this region, and many of the perennials reproduce vegetatively as well as by seed. Arctic communities of alpine sorrel are particularly well adapted, developing both flowers and rhizomes (the underground plant stems used for food storage). In contrast, communities that live in the less severe alpine habitats farther south do not produce rhizomes.

Apart from rhizomes, plants such as creeping willows and cushion plants reproduce by putting out roots where the stems come into contact with the ground. New shoots arise as the roots become established; eventually the stem rots and breaks, and the new plant becomes independent. This process is known as layering. Some plants even replace a few or all of their flowers with vegetative bulbils (small bulbs). These include nodding saxifrage (*Saxifraga cernua*) and grasses such as *Poa alpina*, where the bulbils develop into young plants with leaves and partly developed roots before they

are shed – an effective means of ensuring successful reproduction.

Many members of the daisy family (Compositae), rose family (Rosaceae) and other groups overcome the unreliability of seed production by producing flowers and seed asexually. By one method, a cell in the ovule repeatedly divides to form an embryo without fertilization having taken place. There is an unusually high proportion of such apomictic plants in the Arctic; they include many species thought to have evolved recently in order to occupy new habitats formed since the last ice age ended some 10,000 years ago.

Arctic bells (*above*) *Cassiope tetragona* is a dwarf shrub with tiny leaves pressed close to the stem. These are produced very slowly, but are capable of photosynthesizing for many seasons. It has been known for them to function for as long as 15 years.

Kidney-shaped leaves (*left*) The growth of the mountain sorrel (*Oxyria digyna*) is governed by daylength. As the days get longer growth begins; as the daylength decreases to 15 hours, buds begin to develop. These will not open until the days lengthen and the next growing season begins.

Spider plant (*right*) The extraordinary appearance of *Saxifraga flagellaris* is due to the numerous runners, creeping stems capable of producing tiny bulbils that will grow into daughter plants. This additional method of reproduction is particularly useful in the Arctic tundra, where pollinating flies are infrequent visitors.

AGRICULTURE

WESTWARD HO! · FAMILY FARMS, WORLD MARKETS · SUPPORTING AGRICULTURAL GROWTH

Although Canada is the second largest country in the world, its agricultural lands are limited. Farming occupies just 8 percent of the total land area of nearly 1 billion ha (2.5 billion acres), and only a tiny proportion of this farmland has high agricultural capability. Almost half the land is under forest; the rest is covered by lakes, swamps and high mountains, or is in areas with Arctic or subarctic climates that are unsuitable for agriculture. The best agricultural land is in the Great Lakes/St Lawrence lowlands, close to the border with the United States. To the west, the wheat-growing prairies – the northern part of the Great Plains of America – have been Canada's "bread basket" since the 1880s. Forestry predominates on the Pacific coastlands, with intensive agricultural production occupying the fertile valleys.

COUNTRIES IN THE REGION

Canada

Land (million hectares)

Total	Agricultural	Arable	Forest/woodland
956 (100%)	78 (8%)	46 (5%)	354 (37%)

Farmers

472,000 employed in agriculture (4% of work force)
97 hectares of arable land per person employed in agriculture

Major crops
Numbers in brackets are percentages of world average yield and total world production

	Area mill ha	Yield 100kg/ha	Production mill tonnes	Change since 1963
Wheat	13.5	19.3 (83)	26.0 (5)	+69%
Barley	5.0	27.9 (120)	14.0 (8)	+262%
Rapeseed	2.7	14.4 (101)	3.8 (17)	+1,284%
Oats	1.3	23.7 (129)	3.0 (7)	−51%
Maize	1.0	70.2 (193)	7.0 (2)	+554%
Linseed	0.6	12.3 (216)	0.7 (29)	+42%

Major livestock

	Number mill	Production mill tonnes	Change since 1963
Cattle	11.7 (1)	—	+4%
Pigs	10.5 (1)	—	+101%
Milk	—	8.0 (2)	−4%
Fish catch	—	1.6 (2)	–

Food security (cereal exports minus imports)

mill tonnes	% domestic production	% world trade
+23.5	45	11

WESTWARD HO!

French settlers first introduced European-style agriculture to eastern Canada in the early 17th century, and further waves of immigrants from France, Britain and other European countries then progressed westward across the country during the course of the 18th and 19th centuries. The prairies were not really opened up to cereal farming until the passing of the Homestead Act (1870), which offered free land to prospective settlers. Many different ethnic groups took part in the surge of pioneer settlement during the last quarter of the 19th century, giving rise to distinctive local communities: Ukrainian, German and Scandinavian settlers were among those who benefited from the emerging export trade in grain. Settlement continued into the 20th century, with mining and forestry opening up new areas north of the established agricultural frontier. Even parts of the extreme north

Fish drying (*above*) The Inuit, the indigenous Indian people of the north, remain largely unchanged by colonial influences. Isolated by the harsh climate, they follow a traditional way of life based on hunting and fishing. Fish is an important source of protein and is preserved by air drying.

Opening up the wheatlands (*right*) The vast expanses of the prairies began to be exploited after 1870, when pioneer settlers were offered free land. The introduction of a drought-resistant variety of wheat and of dry farming techniques caused a massive increase in the area of land under wheat cultivation over the next few decades.

developed a limited amount of agriculture to provide food for mining settlements.

The influence of climate

From colonial times, Canadian agriculture has mainly been determined by the widely different physical conditions across the country. The cold, harsh climate of the north generally discouraged European settlers, so that is one area where the indigenous Inuit people's traditional way of life, based on hunting and fishing, has been preserved. Elsewhere in the country indigenous Indian peoples, mostly hunter–gatherers, were displaced by the European colonists and were eventually confined to designated reserves.

The early settlers in the Great Lakes/St Lawrence lowlands found extremely favorable conditions for agriculture. The fertile soils, the ample rainfall evenly distributed throughout the year, and the hot summers that compensated for cold winters were all factors that encouraged

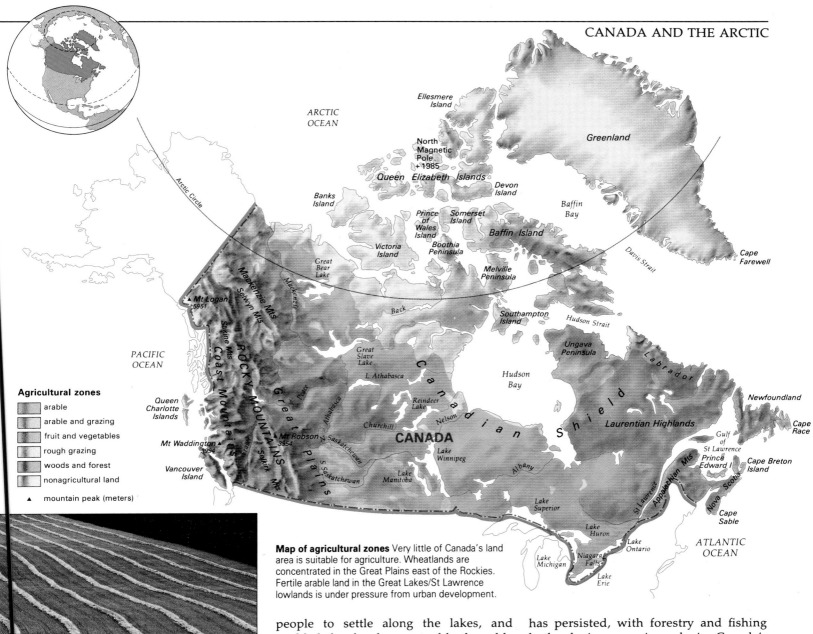

Map of agricultural zones Very little of Canada's land area is suitable for agriculture. Wheatlands are concentrated in the Great Plains east of the Rockies. Fertile arable land in the Great Lakes/St Lawrence lowlands is under pressure from urban development.

Agricultural zones

- arable
- arable and grazing
- fruit and vegetables
- rough grazing
- woods and forest
- nonagricultural land

▲ mountain peak (meters)

people to settle along the lakes, and enabled the development of both arable and livestock farming to take place. Fruit growing was introduced on the Niagara peninsula, which is free of frost for 190 days of the year.

Farther west, the harsher winters of the prairies reduce the length of the growing season, and rainfall in the south of the region is less than 400 mm (15 in) per year. Nevertheless, settlers were able to produce good cereal crops thanks to the timely summer rains and humus-rich chernozem soils. To the west of the Rocky Mountains, the mild, damp climate gives a frost-free period of over 250 days, supporting mixed farming and fruit growing in the valley lowlands. By contrast, the Maritime Provinces of eastern Canada have severe conditions, with harsh winters and cool springs that restrict agricultural activity.

Natural riches

From the earliest European settlement of eastern Canada, farming was only a part of a diverse rural economy. This diversity

has persisted, with forestry and fishing both playing a major role in Canada's economic development. The physical and climatic restrictions on agricultural activity have been offset by favorable conditions for forestry, particularly on the Pacific coast in British Columbia and in northern parts of Ontario and Quebec. Forest products are now the single most important component of Canada's international trade, accounting for nearly a third of the country's exports.

Fishing played an important part in the European colonization of the Atlantic seaboard, and continues to be an important industry in the region. About 1,000 communities along the coast are wholly or mostly dependent on income derived from fishing; it is particularly important to the local economy of Newfoundland, in the east of the region, where the waters of the Grand Banks to the southeast of the island provide rich catches of cod, haddock, flat-fish, mackerel and herring. The fishing industry in British Columbia yields valuable exports of processed salmon and tuna.

FAMILY FARMS, WORLD MARKETS

Grains, notably wheat, provide nearly half of Canada's agricultural revenue. Cultivation is concentrated in the three prairie provinces of Alberta, Manitoba and Saskatchewan, which were settled in the years after Canada's Confederation in 1867. A special variety of wheat – Marquis – was developed to withstand the dry climate and short growing season, and the wheat economy boomed with the coming of the railroads, particularly the Canadian Pacific Railroad in 1886. Rapid transportation to eastern ports provided access to world markets, and large grain elevators were built to store grain beside the railroads.

A system of "dryland farming" was first introduced into the prairies in the 1880s, thereby facilitating the spread of large-scale cereal farming. It involves the systematic use of summer fallow to limit the effects of low annual rainfall. Once a crop has been harvested, the land is allowed to remain fallow throughout the following year, enabling it to store moisture and yield a good crop the next year.

The adoption of dry farming methods, as well as the introduction of fast maturing grain varieties, helped Canadian farmers to bring about an increase of 15 million ha (37 million acres) in the area of land under cultivation in the first three decades of the century. Although dryland farming gradually reduces soil fertility over a long period of time, this can be restored by the use of fertilizers, and the system is still widely used as a means of conserving moisture.

Wheat still dominates farming in the prairies, except in the driest areas where it has been replaced with cattle ranching. Between 1900 and 1930 the area under wheat rose from 610,000 ha (150,700 acres) to 10 million ha (almost 25 million acres). This phenomenal expansion was halted during the 1930s by drought and world economic depression, and subsequently by the disruption of World War II. But by the 1950s output and exports were again increasing. Longterm contracts to supply wheat to China and the Soviet Union opened up new markets, in addition to

Ontario cereals Wheat gives way to maize and rye in eastern Canada, where the ample rainfall reduces reliance on dry farming. The barn reflects the north European influence in the province.

Specialist fruit production Canada supports a wide range of fruit growing in areas where the climate permits. Most of the fruit comes from specialist farms in the southeast, but there is also an important fruit area in British Columbia. Apples are a major crop, and are sold either as fresh produce or for processing.

the traditional ones in Britain and Japan. The 1960s saw an expansion of beef production in the region at the expense of some wheat production, but since then higher grain prices have led to a new resurgence in wheat growing, and grains have now overtaken livestock as the largest single source of revenue in the Canadian agricultural economy.

Unlike the grain monoculture of the prairies that stretch across central Canada, the agriculture of the eastern provinces has tended to be more diverse. Commercial dairy farming became locally significant, supplying the growing cities of Ontario and Quebec; horticultural farming developed in the Niagara peninsula and southwestern Ontario; and greater reliance was placed on livestock production in mixed farming systems.

The tendency toward specialist dairy and livestock farming grew stronger after World War II as demand for most meat and livestock products increased. By 1981 the number of cattle had risen by 60 percent, pigs by 50 percent, and poultry by 53 percent. On the other hand, the size and number of sheep flocks fell in the face of cheaper competition from Australia and New Zealand.

While a number of long-established crop specializations, such as potatoes on Prince Edward Island, have been overtaken by a greater reliance on livestock, in general the high prices available during the 1980s for crops such as maize, soybeans, tobacco and vegetables have stimulated greater production. There has been a particularly rapid expansion of the cultivation of oilseed rape (canola) in the east of the country, as well as on the prairies, where the area devoted to it rose from 100,000 ha (247,150 acres) in 1960 to 2 million ha (almost 5 million acres) in the mid-1980s. Higher cereal prices, and the practice of using grains with rapemeal and silage for livestock feed, also brought about a significant increase in grain production in Ontario.

The price of efficiency

The move away from mixed farming in favor of specialist production of a single crop or livestock animal demands high capital investment. Very often this brings greater financial returns, but it also makes producers more vulnerable to fluctuations in market prices and has led to a high rate of farm business failure.

The need to use costly inputs of fertilizers and machinery to sustain high productivity has meant that many farms have had to amalgamate to achieve economies of scale. The postwar period has consequently witnessed a sharp fall in the number of farm holdings: from 623,000 individual farms in 1951 to 293,100 in 1986. In the eastern Maritime Provinces the drop has been enormous – as much as 80 percent – and fishing and forestry here are now much more important in the rural economy.

Despite the highly commercial nature of Canadian agriculture, the vast majority of farms are still family run. Nearly two-thirds of farms are entirely family owned, and many others constitute a mix of owned and rented land. This high level of owner occupation has its roots in the early pioneer days, when colonists were able to buy land outright from the colonial, federal or provincial authorities.

THE NORTHERN LIMITS FOR FRUIT

Harsh climates, particularly the length and severity of winter frosts, limit the areas where fruit and vegetable production is possible in Canada. However, there are significant pockets where the climatic conditions of the region are modified by the natural features of the landscape to allow earlier spring warming and a longer maturing season. One of the most important of these is the Okanagan valley of British Columbia in the extreme west of the region.

The valley lies in the central plateau to the west of the Rocky Mountains and in the rainshadow of the Pacific coastal range. Fruit growing here is therefore dependent on irrigation, and this means that a wide range of fruit can be grown. Apples are the major crop, however, accounting for two-thirds of the area of production.

Most of the orchards are situated on terraces on the top and sides of the slopes above Okanagan Lake. The terraces are divided by deep gullies running from the high slopes down to the lake. These enable cold air to "drain" down the hills to the valley bottom, thereby preventing damage from frost. Nevertheless, this can be a hazard if there is a severe frost in late spring. Very low winter temperatures can also damage the apple trees; sometimes as much as a fifth of the orchard stock has been destroyed.

Most of the apples grown are sold as fresh produce, but there is also a large local fruit processing industry that makes juice concentrates, apple sauce, pie fillings and frozen apple slices.

SUPPORTING AGRICULTURAL GROWTH

The importance of agriculture to Canada's national economy is recognized in the government's record of supporting water and land conservation measures and of exercising price controls to help maintain farm incomes. After Confederation, the government's agricultural policy was designed to encourage farming on the prairies, and freight rates and the grain handling system were both regulated. The Prairie Farm Rehabilitation Act (1935) was passed to counter the effects of drought and economic depression, which had led to the abandonment of farmland. It introduced better management of water resources, improved farming methods, and some resettlement schemes. Irrigation has been substantially extended as a result of government policy, especially in Alberta and dry southern Saskatchewan. Nevertheless, no more than 1.5 percent of Canadian land is irrigated, indicating the continued reliance on dryland farming on the prairies, and the plentiful rainfall in other agricultural regions.

An agricultural revolution

More recent government measures have helped to stabilize the farming industry by raising commodity prices, making agricultural credit easier to obtain, and encouraging mechanization and the development of more efficient farms.

To meet the demands of the expanding Canadian and world markets, farmers have turned more and more to the use of expensive inputs to generate higher yields. There was a fivefold increase in the use of chemicals in the 1960s and 1970s, a doubling in the area of land sprayed with pesticides, and a near doubling in the real value of investment in farm machinery. The rising costs of these inputs in the 1970s prompted an extension of both federal and provincial income maintenance programs for farmers. Intervention in the marketing of eggs, poultry and dairy produce meant that the producers were able to have more control over the price of commodities.

In effect, what has taken place has been a rapid process of agricultural industrialization, with high capital investment and more sophisticated methods of business management. The average size of farms has more than doubled since 1951, and

despite government measures to protect them, many smaller, less efficient farmers have been driven out of business. In order to remain in farming many have resorted to off-farm work to supplement their incomes; about 40 percent of Canadian farmers are now engaged in paid employment off their own farms for an average of 171 days a year.

Urban sprawl

The loss of agricultural land to urban development is a serious concern in a

Reaching the world market The construction of railroads to connect the prairies with eastern ports was vital for the wheat economy. Grain destined for Europe was stored in vast grain elevators beside the tracks. Many are no longer in use following the reorganization of the railroads.

country where prime agricultural lands are limited. In many cases this conflict is inevitable, since urban centers in the past were established to serve good agricultural areas, and they have expanded as farming and its related industries have grown. A highly efficient monitoring

When the prairies were opened up to agriculture in the 19th century, the surveys used by the pioneers to allocate land divided the territory into 259 ha (640 acre) farm "sections". Usually the land given out to individual farmers measured one-quarter of the size of these original sections, or 65 ha (160 acres). Rationalization of farming in recent years has seen the disappearance of many of these small, family-owned farms as land is amalgamated into larger, more efficient units that can be farmed using huge machines rather than human and animal labor. At the same time, the reorganization of the railroad network led to the closure of more than 2,500 grain elevators between 1953 and 1983. These huge structures, left empty and abandoned in the flat, bare prairie landscape, symbolize what many regard as the death of oldstyle farming in the prairies.

Many people have had to abandon farming to find employment in the towns and cities, and in some cases whole farming communities have been broken up. Those that remain have been forced to change their traditional way of life: scores of small local schools have been closed down, along with other rural services. This movement away from the country is typical of a dramatic decline in rural populations throughout Canada. Between 1951 and 1990 – a period when the total population rose from 14 million to 25 million – the number of people employed in agriculture fell from just under 3 million (21 percent of the population) to slightly less than 1 million – a mere 4 percent.

system was established in 1966 to chart the transfer of farmland to nonagricultural uses; in some provinces there has been legislation to protect farmland. British Columbia, for example, has created Agricultural Land Reserves that strictly control the extent of urban expansion in order to protect its valuable fruit growing areas, and similar controls in the Niagara fruit belt in Ontario have helped to maintain production there.

Since monitoring began, losses have been greatest in Ontario. More than a third of the total amount of agricultural land lost to other uses is in this province – more than 17,000 ha (nearly 50,000 acres) of prime land was surrendered to urban use in the early 1980s. A triangular area that extends northward from Toronto and contains most of the province's best farmland is now threatened by the rapidly encroaching city. By contrast, in the northern prairies the agricultural frontier has expanded in recent years.

In response to the continually expanding world market for cattle fodder, the federal government has supported long-term research on plant breeding to adapt certain crops – most notably wheat and oilseed rape – to withstand Canadian climatic conditions. It was the development of the Marquis variety of wheat in the 19th century and early in the 20th that helped push the frontier of cultivation on the prairies northward. More recently new varieties have been bred that are able to reach maturity even more rapidly, and this has resulted in the expansion of grain production in areas like the Peace river area of Alberta. In particular, a completely new cereal crop, triticale, has been developed by crossbreeding wheat and rye. Triticale is very high in protein, and is grown as a food grain for humans as well as for livestock feed.

Forestry and the logging industry

Forests cover well over a third of Canada's land area; they account for 7 percent of the world's forests. The exploitation of this vast natural resource has played a critical part in the country's development, and today forestry generates jobs for over three-quarters of a million workers. A substantial export earner, it makes a greater contribution to the balance of trade than any other commodity group.

Three-quarters of Canada's forests form part of the cold climate boreal forest that extends across the high latitudes of the northern hemisphere into Alaska, Siberia and Scandinavia. The main species of trees are white and black spruce, but other conifers such as balsam fir, jack pine and tamarack are also widely distributed. Both inaccessibility and the unfavorable climatic conditions of large parts of the forest, especially in the far north, means they are not economically productive; it is in the eastern part, in a belt stretching from Manitoba east to Newfoundland, that Canada's principal area of pulpwood production lies. In parts of Ontario and Nova Scotia the conifers give way to deciduous forest. These were once much more extensive; they are all that survive of the forests cleared by the original European settlers. West of the Rocky Mountains along the Pacific coast there is temperate, mainly coniferous, forest. It is more productive than the boreal forest.

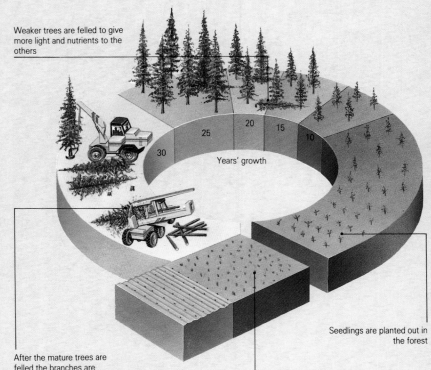

Weaker trees are felled to give more light and nutrients to the others

30 25 20 15 10

Years' growth

After the mature trees are felled the branches are stripped and the trunks sawn into logs for transportation to the processing plant

Seeds are planted in a nursery where they grow to seedlings

Seedlings are planted out in the forest

A plentiful resource

The forests yield a wide range of products. From the logging industry come logs, plywood, pulp chips and poles; from sawmills, a variety of boards and milled wood; from the paper industry, newsprint, pulp, paper and tissue. In addition

Forests for the future (*above*) Forests – unlike fossil fuels – are a renewable part of the Earth's resources. Responsible forestry can fulfill both commercial and environmental aims.

A valuable cargo (*below*) Timber forms a significant part of Canada's export trade. Logs are transported from the forest to mills that convert them into a range of products from lumber to plywood and paper.

there are specialist ventures such as the supply of Christmas trees and the manufacture of maple syrup.

From the earliest days of the colonial period, the forests of eastern Canada became the major supplier of timber to Britain. They still provide a range of forest products for export, but since 1917 British Columbia has been the leading export producer in the country. The favorable climate, with cool winters and warm, moist summers, contributes to the forests' high productivity, especially of western hemlock, western red cedar, sitka spruce and Douglas fir. In the first half of this century too much forest was felled for any natural regeneration to take place, but efforts are now being made to manage the forests as a renewable resource.

Rivers were the only way of moving the logs out of the forests in pioneer days, and water transportation is still used in British Columbia to carry logs from isolated islands or coastal inlets. Logs are taken by truck to the rivers and then formed into rafts of log bundles for transportation to the mills. Bundling the logs reduces losses from sinkage and prevents logs from breaking away.

British Columbia's forest industry supplies two-thirds of Canada's softwood lumber and nearly half its woodpulp, which it exports in great quantity to the United States. The unrestricted market that was created by the Free Trade Agreement concluded between Canada and the United States in 1988 was consequently greeted with enthusiasm by British Columbia's timber exporters, though other interest groups are concerned about the industry's encroachments in one of the world's last remaining areas of temperate rainforest.

Commercial forestry operations are dominated by private companies, 40 percent of which are foreign owned. In recent years the trend has been for smallscale saw mills or pulp and paper mills to be replaced by large complexes that produce a range of products under single corporate control. Although the number of individual processing plants has fallen, both output and the influence of foreign investment have increased.

River of wood The transportation of logs by water was the standard method in pioneer days, and is still widely used in some areas. Water transportation is cheap, and allows huge quantities of wood to be moved at one time. It is still the only way of moving timber from inaccessible areas.

INDUSTRY

A WORLD SUPPLIER OF RESOURCES · A CENTURY OF GROWTH AND DECLINE · SUPPORT STRATEGIES

Canada's huge expanses of territory of-fer a rich diversity of natural resources far beyond the needs of its small popula-tion. It has therefore had to look outside its boundaries for markets, and its leading role as supplier of raw materials to the rest of the world has shaped the pattern of its industrial development. The difficulties and heavy financial costs of extracting and shipping huge volumes of ore or timber across remote terrain have favored the involvement of giant corporations. Only in the most heavily populated areas of Quebec and Ontario is there significant manufacturing diversity. However, recent decline in the world demand for raw materials, and intensified competition from other suppliers, means that Canada today is having to redefine its industrial role and seek new challenges.

A WORLD SUPPLIER OF RESOURCES

To the first European settlers, Canada's vast spaces offered seemingly inexhaust-ible biological resources for exploitation – fur-bearing animals, plentiful fish in rivers and coastal waters, endless forests of fir and pine. At first fur was the most attractive of these resources, and fur traders, both French and British, pene-trated the country's interior, setting up trading posts along the rivers from the Great Lakes to Hudson Bay. Extensive exploitation of Canada's forest reserves began when Britain's involvement in the American War of Independence (1775–83) and the Napoleonic Wars (1803–15) cre-ated an urgent demand for large quan-tities of timber for shipbuilding.

Throughout the 19th century the de-velopment of Canada's resources con-tinued apace. From the 1880s the prairies were opened up for agriculture, and the production of lumber in British Columbia enjoyed rapid growth. Settlers also began to discover Canada's rich mineral re-sources. Deposits of nickel, silver, zinc

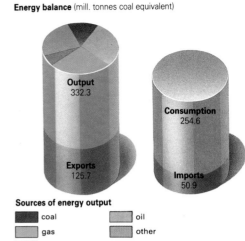

Energy balance (mill. tonnes coal equivalent)

Output 332.3
Exports 125.7
Consumption 254.6
Imports 50.9

Sources of energy output
- coal
- gas
- nuclear
- oil
- other

Energy production and consumption (*above*)
Domestic gas, oil and hydroelectric power are the mainstays, though nuclear power is becoming increasingly important.

Map of principal resources and industrial zones (*right*) Canada's scattered natural resources include metals, coal, gas and oil. Manufacturing is concentrated in the Montreal–Toronto corridor.

A paper mill (*below*) on British Columbia's Gold river is ideally located. The river provides hydroelectric power and free transportation of logs.

COUNTRIES IN THE REGION

Canada

INDUSTRIAL OUTPUT (US $ billion)

Total	Mining	Manufacturing	Average annual change since 1960
171.3	19.7	94.3	+3.5%

INDUSTRIAL WORKERS (millions)
(figures in brackets are percentages of total labor force)

Total	Mining	Manufacturing	Construction
3.3	0.2 (1.5%)	2.3 (17.1%)	0.8 (6.3%)

MAJOR PRODUCTS (figures in brackets are percentages of world production)

Energy and minerals	Output	Change since 1960
Coal (mill tonnes)	70.6 (1.5%)	+713%
Oil (mill barrels)	615.7 (2.8%)	+327%
Natural gas (billion cu. meters)	90.8 (4.9%)	+625%
Iron Ore (mill tonnes)	40.8 (7.2%)	+13.5%
Copper (mill tonnes)	0.8 (8.8%)	-8.5%
Lead (mill tonnes)	0.4 (11.5%)	+29%
Zinc (mill tonnes)	1.5 (20.9%)	+14%
Nickel (mill tonnes)	0.2 (24.6%)	-18%
Uranium (1,000 tonnes: U content)	12.4 (33.7%)	No data

Manufactures		
Aluminum (mill tonnes)	1.6 (7.2%)	+72%
Steel (mill tonnes)	15.1 (2.1%)	+286%
Woodpulp (mill tonnes)	21.0 (16.5%)	+16%
Newsprint (mill tonnes)	10.0 (31.5%)	+15%
Sulfuric acid (mill tonnes)	3.8 (1.4%)	+45%
Automobiles (mill)	2.0 (4.3%)	+509%

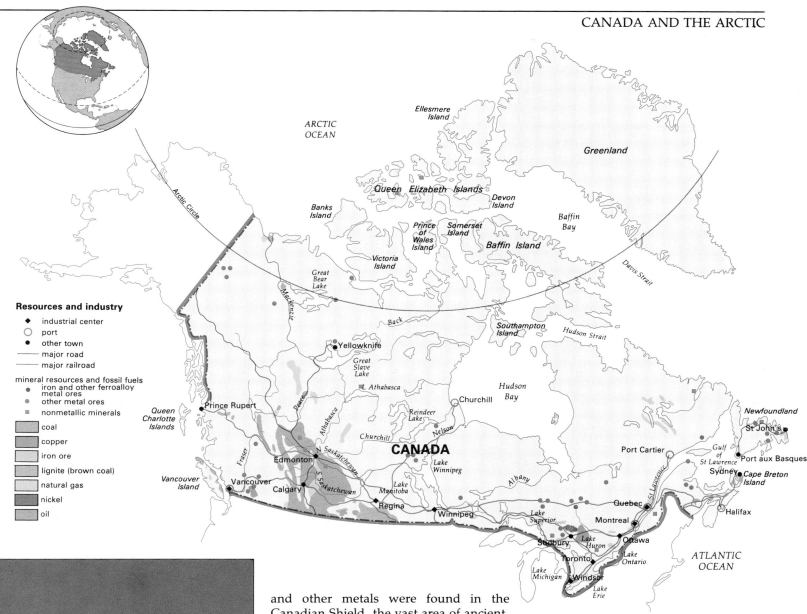

Resources and industry
- ◆ industrial center
- ○ port
- ● other town
- —— major road
- —— major railroad

mineral resources and fossil fuels
- ● iron and other ferroalloy metal ores
- ● other metal ores
- ■ nonmetallic minerals

- coal
- copper
- iron ore
- lignite (brown coal)
- natural gas
- nickel
- oil

and other metals were found in the Canadian Shield, the vast area of ancient, eroded rock that encompasses Hudson Bay. In the late 1890s the discovery of gold nuggets in the Klondike, a tributary of the Yukon river in north British Columbia, sparked off the greatest outbreak of prospector fever ever recorded.

Many mineral deposits lie in the far north under permafrost, soil that is frozen for much of the year. This makes them difficult to extract, and before 1945 exploitation was sporadic. Since then resource development has continued to grow, especially in the west and north. Today Canada is a leading world producer of nickel, uranium, asbestos, zinc, iron ore and molybdenum.

It is richest of all in energy reserves. Coal (which it increasingly exports to Japan), petroleum and natural gas lie beneath the prairies, and there are petroleum fields in the Arctic Ocean and off the Atlantic coast. Rivers are used to generate hydroelectricity, though this is not so significant a source of energy as in the past. By contrast, nuclear power is on the increase. During the fuel crisis of the early 1970s Canada's energy exports became increasingly important, exceeding nonfuel mineral exports for the first time in 1975, though they have declined somewhat since then.

Neighborly concerns

Proximity to the economically powerful United States, always a major market for Canadian commodities, has often had a direct influence on resource development. For example, the northern forests of the Canadian Shield were first exploited at the end of the 19th century to supply newspaper publishers in the United States with woodpulp. After 1945, Canadian exports of raw materials to the United States grew and diversified as large American corporations, concerned about shortages of indigenous resources, sought new sources of supply.

One such corporation was the United States-owned Iron Ore Company of Canada. It began to mine the massive iron-ore

deposits of northeast Quebec in the 1950s to supply its mills in the United States. The town of Schefferville was built, as well as power stations, crushing plants, a 573km (355mi) railroad and port facilities at Sept Isle on the St Lawrence Seaway. Subsequent industrial decline in the United States led to measures to protect American industries by restricting imports of raw materials, and the Schefferville mines closed in 1983.

A prime reason for Canada's signing the Free Trade Agreement (FTA) with the United States in 1989 was to free Canadian exports from these protectionist restrictions. One likely effect of the FTA was to spell out for Canada a future role as the leading supplier of resources to the North American continent, rather than the world.

A CENTURY OF GROWTH AND DECLINE

By the end of the 19th century Canada's growing tide of exports had created an economic boom. Specialized machinery was needed to process minerals, lumber and agricultural products at their source. Railroads, ports and shipping facilities were built to transport these commodities to their markets in the United States and Western Europe. Canada's rapidly growing population created a demand for housing, domestic goods and food products. All this acted as a spur to the urgent development of largescale manufacturing industry.

Before Confederation in 1867, a few small manufacturing industries, supplying the local population with farming implements and equipment, had existed in southern Ontario and Quebec. It was here that a much more diversified range of industries now began to develop. Several factors encouraged the area's industrial preeminence – its relatively large population, its central location within Canada and its proximity to the industrial belt of the United States. The tendency for its industries to attract related industries, and a tariff policy designed to protect manufacturing, were also important.

The Quebec–Ontario corridor
Today an industrialized, urban belt runs from Quebec in the northeast to Windsor, Ontario in the southwest. Although manufacturing is highly diversified in the two large centers of Montreal and

Toronto, it is much more specialized within the numerous smaller towns of the area. Those in Quebec have a greater emphasis on textiles and clothing, while Ontario concentrates on automobiles, iron and steel, and electronics. This more favorable mix of industries helps explain Ontario's faster growth. Food processing and brewing are also important industries throughout the area.

A distinctive and significant element in Canada's industrial structure was created in 1965 by the Canada–United States Autopact. Under this agreement, tariffs on automobile export–imports between the two countries were lifted, allowing Canadian assembly plants – at that time entirely American-owned – to specialize more and produce a greater volume of vehicles for the United States. A required level of parts had to be purchased from Canadian sources. As a result, Canada now exports significant numbers of automobiles to the United States. Sales outside North America are rare, however, and imports are high. Research and development has been concentrated in the United States. Recent investment by Japanese automobile companies in plants in southern Ontario and Quebec seem likely to repeat this pattern.

During the 1980s unprecedented manufacturing job losses occurred in southern Ontario and Quebec as a result of three factors: technological change, overseas competition from both Japan and the developing countries and increasing economic integration with the United States. Canadian sales taxes and the FTA encouraged people to shop for retail goods in the United States, at the expense of local manufacturing. Hopes for the future prosperity of Canada's traditional manufacturing heartland rested on the attraction of more service industries and research-intensive activities.

The rest of Canada

Outside of the Quebec–Ontario corridor, industry has traditionally been based on local resources. Despite prolonged attempts to diversify the manufacturing base of eastern Canada, industry here is mainly restricted to fish processing and pulp and paper manufacture. Offshore oil reserves, however, encourage optimism for future development.

Western Canada has even richer resources than the east. In addition, both the petroleum processing industry in Alberta and the forestry industry in British Columbia have spawned a number of manufacturing industries making heavy equipment and machinery.

In the early 1980s, however, many of Canada's traditional resource-based industries began to experience decline. There were various reasons for this. The increased strength of the Canadian dollar lessened the competitiveness of exports to the United States. Technological changes and the development of new products and alternative sources of supply reduced the demand for certain minerals. A number of resources were becoming exhausted, and the exploitation of others was inhibited by widespread concern about environmental damage. As a result, attention turned from the bulk export of raw materials to finding ways of processing them at source that would add value to exports, and to establishing new markets for these products.

Attempts have also been made to diversify into new areas of enterprise and industry by expanding tourism, as well as developing sporting, educational, and arts and crafts activities. The construction industry concentrated on developing the new market potential of retirement housing. In addition, to meet the demands of British Columbia's rapidly increasing, affluent population, a number of industries oriented to this consumer market sprang up along the Pacific seaboard, including an electronics sector.

Oil extraction in Alberta (*left*) This huge paddle dredge dwarfs the people working at its base but is scaled to the vast open spaces of the prairies, which conceal rich deposits of natural gas and petroleum. United States' companies have played a considerable role in developing the petroleum industry, which requires high capital investment. The Canadian government sponsors research and regulates the privately controlled industries that exploit these resources.

Cutting coats in Winnipeg (*right*) The distinctive white coats with multicolored stripes, called Hudson's Bay coats, are products of Canada's crafts industry. The original Hudson's Bay Company was founded in 1670 by French fur traders and London merchants. Today, the fur trade is still flourishing, and Hudson's Bay coats are popular local souvenirs.

THE PETROLEUM BOOM IN THE PRAIRIES

Alberta, the most westerly prairie province, contains most of Canada's petroleum and natural gas. As recently as 1947 oilfields were discovered at Leduc, Redwater and Pembina, all within a radius of 120 km (75 mi) of the provincial capital of Edmonton. An extensive network of pipelines was quickly laid down, and these now deliver crude oil and natural gas from Alberta to eastern Canada and California in the United States.

During the 1950s a relatively small petrochemical industry was built up in Edmonton, producing fertilizers and industrial chemicals, but Canada's largest petrochemical complexes grew up closer to the major markets in central Canada, fed through the pipeline.

As crude oil prices escalated during the energy crisis of the early 1970s, Alberta's abundance of relatively cheap natural gas attracted much attention. As a result, a number of world-class, gas-based petroleum complexes were established in the area. Two giant ethylene plants at Joffre, near Red Deer, began production in 1979 and 1984, providing the raw material for a wide range of plastics and chemicals manufacturing processes.

The decline in international oil prices in the early 1980s removed Alberta's advantage, making further development of the petrochemical industry unlikely, but not before the boom had brought new prosperity to Canada's prairie capital.

SUPPORT STRATEGIES

Canada's rich resources are scattered across vast, often inaccessible territory. Operations to extract and process minerals, carry petroleum and natural gas long distances through pipelines, and fell and transport trees to processing plants on rivers and the coast are expensive. In the past, Canada lacked the manpower, the communications network and the financial capital to exploit its reserves of minerals and timber.

Foreign-owned companies were consequently pursuaded to speed up the rate of resource development and industrial growth by being offered cheap supplies of raw materials in return for capital, expertise and access to export markets. This open-door policy provided a means of generating export income, creating employment and encouraging regional development. Inevitably, however, it favored largescale industrialization in the hands of giant corporations.

Building the railroad
The interrelation between government policy, private investment and industrial development is well illustrated in the story of the Canadian Pacific Railway (CPR). The decision to build a transcontinental railroad was taken in 1872, just after the acquisition of British Columbia on the Pacific coast. This would link Canada's widely scattered territories, allow manufactured goods from Montreal and Toronto to reach new markets in the recently settled prairies, and carry wheat and lumber back to ports on the Great Lakes for shipment overseas.

However, economic depression called a halt to further construction soon after work had started. It was not until 1878, when the government granted land, money, the sections of the line already built and other concessions to the Canadian Pacific Railway Company of Montreal, that work pushed ahead rapidly. At the same time a new National Policy of tariff protection revived the manufacturing industry in Montreal and Toronto and encouraged investment in the enterprise.

The CPR quickly became the means of opening up mining areas in the Canadian Shield and western Canada, giving the company considerable influence over settlement patterns and resource develop-

ment. It has benefited from this advantage to become, over the years, one of Canada's largest transportation and resource conglomerates. The building of the railroad also reinforced Montreal and Toronto's leading role in Canada's expanding industrial economy, placing them at the center of the country's banking system and other support industries.

The labor force that built the railroad was made up to a very large extent of Chinese immigrants. Until comparatively recently, Canadian governments consistently encouraged immigration to build up a work force to develop the country's natural riches. Particular ethnic groups tended to specialize in particular industries. For example, Eastern Europeans (Ukrainians, Czechs, Slovaks, Poles and Hungarians) were instrumental in opening up the agriculture of the prairies, the Germans established the shipbuilding industry in Nova Scotia, and the Japanese worked in the expanding fishing industry of British Columbia.

The growing role of the provinces
In the early years of industrialization, policy-making for resource development was regarded as the preserve of the federal government, located in Ottawa in southeastern Ontario. This emphasized

Cement for construction (*left*)
Lime, sand and clay are found in several Canadian provinces, and cement is one of the main industrial products of Manitoba. Although materials tend to be produced close to sites, Manitoba is well positioned to deliver cement to a wide area, by rail or by the Trans–Canadian highway, or by water in summer and by sled and tractor in winter.

Maintaining the power lines (*right*)
Workers at the James Bay station, Quebec. Quebec province has more than 50 hydroelectric power plants, and Hydro-Quebec is Canada's largest producer of electricity. Federal control of resources is especially sensitive in the province, where separatist feeling frequently runs very high.

General Motors in Ontario (*below*)
Ontario has Canada's highest manufacturing output and employs half of the national workforce. With United States' firms in control, Canadian factories have been vulnerable to fluctuations in the American economy, and have also suffered from the decline of the steel and automotive industries from the mid 1970s onward.

the dominant position held by Ontario and Quebec (representing the English and French-speaking cultures of Canada respectively) within the country's administrative and commercial structure. Until the early 20th century the federal government retained direct responsibility for developing resources in the Canadian Shield around Hudson Bay, and in the western parts of the country. The Shield areas were incorporated within Quebec and Ontario only in 1920, and it was not

The forestry industry of British Columbia produces two-thirds of Canada's lumber, half of its woodpulp, and important quantities of other forest products such as newsprint, paperboard and particleboard. Large, highly-efficient, integrated processing plants operate along the coast. In these complexes, logs supply either the wood processing or pulping operation. The residue of chips, sawdust or bark are used as fuel, as inputs for pulping, or in the manufacture of composite woods.

The biggest and most innovative of British Columbia's forestry companies is MacMillan Bloedel. In 1919 H.R. MacMillan (1885–1976), who had previously worked in a variety of jobs in the forestry and timber industries, founded a lumber trading company. It quickly became the province's largest lumber exporter, acquired plywood and sawmills, and in the 1940s built the province's first kraft (paperboard) pulp mill. It then merged with two other companies to create MacMillan Bloedel, Canada's largest forestry corporation.

In 1957 MacMillan Bloedel located its headquarters in Vancouver, building what was then the tallest skyscraper in the city – a decision that reflected Vancouver's growing importance as a regional center and also marked its rise as a city of metropolitan status to match Toronto and Montreal. In the recession of the 1980s, a controlling interest in the company was acquired by conglomerates based in Toronto, leading to considerable restructuring, but MacMillan Bloedel remains the giant of British Columbia's forestry industry.

until 1930 that the federal government transferred resource management rights to the prairie provinces.

After 1945 the governments of Canada's ten constituent provinces assumed increasing responsibility for the resources within their jurisdictions. In the main, priority was given to funding the building of pipelines, communications networks and roads to support large, export-oriented resource projects. Most provincial governments also tried to attract secondary manufacturing activities and to encourage new and rapidly expanding industries such as tourism. These provincial initiatives, usually supported by the federal government, were of great importance in promoting regional development throughout Canada.

Yet by the 1970s and 1980s many commentators had begun to argue that the decentralized and independent policy-making of the individual provinces with regard to the use of their resources had helped to create a national economy that served North American rather than Canadian interests. Barriers had been raised against trade between the different provinces, and too great a reliance placed on the United States as a market.

All this had occurred in a situation of growing tension between the provincial and federal governments. Control over resources played a crucial role in the debates over Canada's federal structure and the decentralization of power that divided opinion in the country during these years. The eventual outcome of the discussion will doubtless have profound implications for the development of Canadian industry, and for Canada's future as a nation.

Speaking to the world

Industrial competitiveness increasingly depends on the ability to diversify into new activities and the willingness to invest in new technologies. By comparison with other countries, industrial research and development in general in Canada has been underfunded. Typically, foreign-owned plants manufacture goods for the Canadian market that have been researched and developed by parent companies elsewhere. However, within the electronics and communications industry, Northern Telecom's longterm commitment to research and development is a prominent exception, showing that such commercial strategies for survival and growth are possible in Canada.

Canada's involvement in telecommunications is of long standing. Alexander Graham Bell (1847–1922) migrated to Ontario from Scotland before moving to the United States. In 1876 he made the first one-way, long-distance telephone call over a 13km (8 mi) line that he had set up in southern Ontario.

Thereafter, progress was rapid. Telephones were installed in Victoria on the west coast in 1878, the first telephone exchange was built in Vancouver in 1888 and the first transcontinental telephone exchange took place between Vancouver and Montreal in 1916.

However, from the very beginning the telephone companies in Canada (both those supplying services and also those manufacturing equipment) were subsidiaries of American-owned companies. It was not until the 1950s that Bell Canada became a wholly owned Canadian corporation. In 1956 it bought out the equipment-manufacturing company of Northern Telecom (then called Northern Electric) and channeled considerable investment capital to its research and development laboratories in Ottawa, in southeastern Ontario.

Today Northern Telecom is easily Canada's largest telecommunications firm with an impressive record of innovation. Its chief activity is in the manufacture of sophisticated telephone and telephone-switching technology, and in 1989 it had sales of over US$6 billion and a payroll in excess of 47,000 employees. It spends over 11 percent of its revenue on research and development. As a result, Northern Telecom has widely expanded its original market by becoming a leading global supplier of fully digital telecommunication systems. Northern Telecom products are used in over 90 countries and it has established many manufacturing operations in Canada, the United States, Europe and Asia.

Satellite Earth station, Alberta (*above*) spread out against the sky like a giant fan. The Telesat system in Canada links isolated areas such as the Northwest Territories to the rest of the country; innovations have included broadcasts in the Inuit languages. In 1958 the first ever satellite operated for 13 days on batteries; now they last for years and are retired due to obsolescence, not failure.

Computerized telephone chips (*left*) The Novatel factory in Calgary is an example of Canada's new high-tech industry. Its location in Canada's western corridor is a counterbalance to the domination of the older southeastern industrial sector. Computer chips play an important role in satellite communications. For example, largescale integrated chips help to cancel echoes on long-distance telephone calls.

Communication over longer distances

This success is not altogether typical. Canada's electronics industry is small by international standards and of the 100 largest firms, almost 75 percent are foreign owned. However, in recent years Canada has developed a wide range of internationally recognized competitive strengths, especially in the field of long-distance communications. Most significant have been the contributions it has made to the development and manufacture of communications satellites. These make possible the exchange of live television programs, and of telephone and radio communications, between countries and across continents and oceans. Signals from an Earth station are sent to an orbiting satellite, which amplifies them and then transmits them to a station in another region of the Earth.

The federal government has played a significant role in developing expertise in satellite technology by initiating a series of research projects over the years. The Alouette satellites launched in 1962, the Anik satellites launched a decade later (developed in conjunction with private industry and built in the United States) and the Hermes satellite launched in 1976 all significantly extended long-distance broadcasting capability.

In the private sector, Spar Aerospace of Toronto is Canada's leading developer and manufacturer of satellite communication systems. It was responsible for developing Canadarm, the remote manipulator system used on the United States' space shuttle.

Treasure Island

The spectacular and intricate scenery of Canada's Maritime Provinces was created by glacial action during the last ice age. These same glaciers invested a wealth of mineral and metal resources in the islands and mainland of the area. One of the most abundant natural metal resources in Canada is copper.

Found in quantity mainly in Nova Scotia around the Cap d'Or, but also scattered throughout the country, Canada's reserves of copper make it one of the world's leading producers. Because copper is so important in manufacturing, the mining industry in Canada is very large and profitable.

Copper may have been the first metal used by humans. Today its use in manufacturing ranks second, exceeded only by iron. Copper has several special properties that contribute to its extensive use throughout the world. Apart from silver, which is much more expensive, copper is the best conductor of thermal and electrical energy. This makes it an ideal lining for furnaces, pans and other utensils that need to be heated and cooled rapidly, as well as being essential in the electronics industries. Copper is also the base for several alloy metals, including bronze (copper and tin) and brass (copper and zinc).

Although it is an essential biological element, concentrations of the metal can be toxic, one of the hazards of working with copper. Waste from mining and refining damages the mine's surrounding environment. This is particularly true of the fragile ecosystems off some of Canada's island mines.

A copper mine off Canada's northeast coast. Most of the copper mined in Canada is used by the country's growing high-tech and electronics industries.

ECONOMY

The Canadian economy has grown and diversified considerably over the last hundred years, and Canadians now have one of the highest standards of living in the world. This has been achieved despite the potential handicaps of a limited population, regional political pressures and a harsh northern climate. Much of Canada's success springs from the profitable exploitation of natural resources. In the past, an insatiable world appetite for raw materials and primary products allowed Canada to compete effectively in the global marketplace and develop robust manufacturing and service sectors. However, in recent years it has become clear that controlling unprocessed resources can no longer guarantee prosperity. Canada must diversify its economy and seek new markets to maintain its enviable record of growth.

COUNTRIES IN THE REGION	
Canada	

ECONOMIC INDICATORS: 1990

	HIE* Canada
GDP (US$ billions)	570.15
GNP per capita (US$)	20,470
Annual rate of growth of GDP, 1980–1990 (%)	3.4
Manufacturing as % of GDP	13
Central government spending as % of GNP	23
Merchandise exports (US$ billions)	133.5
Merchandise imports (US$ billions)	126.5
% of GNP donated as development aid	0.44

WELFARE INDICATORS

Infant mortality rate (per 1,000 live births)	
1965	24
1990	7
Daily food supply available (calories per capita, 1989)	3,482
Population per physician (1984)	510
Teacher–pupil ratio (primary school, 1989)	1 : 16

Note: The Gross Domestic Product (GDP) is the total value of all goods and services domestically produced. The Gross National Product (GNP) is the GDP plus net income from abroad.

* HIE (High Income Economy) – GNP per capita above $7,620 in 1990.

CREATING AN INDEPENDENT ECONOMY

During the 18th and early 19th centuries Canada, then a British colony, supplied raw materials (fur, fish, wheat, and timber) to Britain and the United States. In turn Canadians bought manufactured goods from their trading partners, but had little or no domestic industry. After Confederation in 1867 the government attempted to strengthen the country's economic base and develop a manufacturing sector. A national railroad was created, encouraging settlement and development to spread westward, and protective trade restrictions were introduced to promote local manufacturing.

The industrial base
By 1900, with improved transport and communications and rising domestic production, the Canadian economy was ripe for expansion. Important mineral finds in areas such as the Klondike fueled growth, followed by a massive boom in wheat production as Britain's demand for grain grew and the prairies were opened to cultivation by immigrant farmers. The manufacturing sectors of Ontario and Quebec in the southeast also expanded in order to supply the increasingly prosperous population to the west with both consumer goods and heavy engineering. On the eve of World War I, Canada was on the verge of becoming a mature industrial economy.

Economic slump followed the war years and the demand for many key Canadian products declined. Exports did not return to their wartime levels until 1926. As wheat prices fell and the nation's foreign policy became increasingly independent of Britain, the Canadian economy became more closely linked to the United States. By the mid 1920s many large United States' firms had established branch plants over the border in Canada and their level of investment continued to rise even during the Great Depression of the 1930s. By the 1940s Canada was incorporated into a global trading economy very much dominated by the United States.

Rich neighbors
Following World War II, the Canadian economy experienced another period of sustained economic growth. This was stimulated by increased demand from major trading partners and the investment of almost $1 billion in industry by the federal government. The United States made unprecedented direct investment in the Canadian economy as its manufacturing companies sought a stable supply of raw materials and entry into Commonwealth markets. Production increased dramatically, unemployment fell and workers' wages in Canada rose faster than in the United States. Nevertheless, some Canadians were already expressing fears about the extent of control exercised

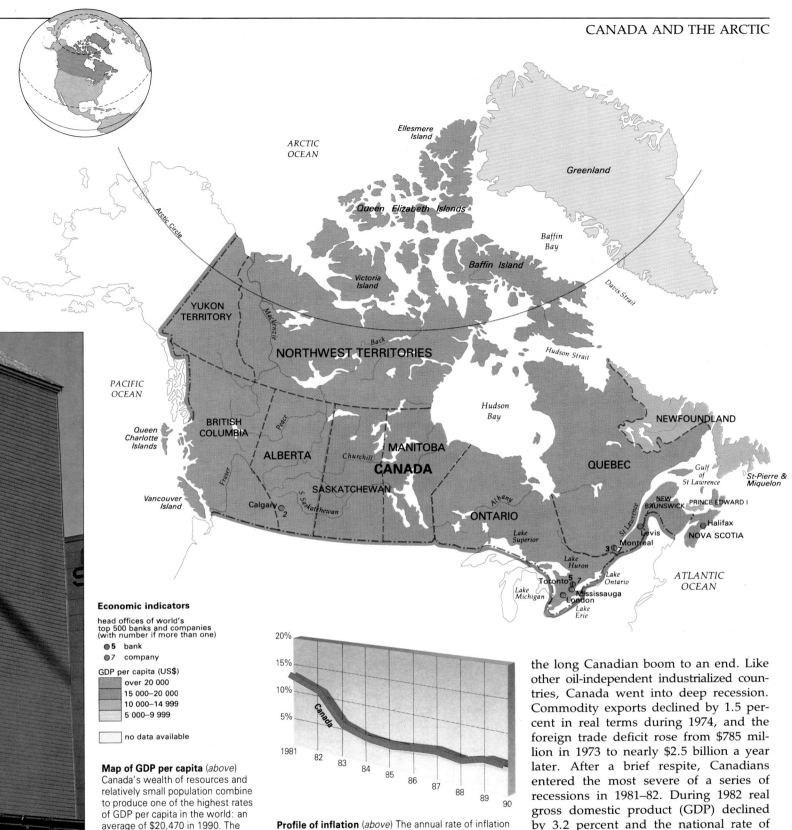

ARCTIC OCEAN

Ellesmere Island

Greenland

Queen Elizabeth Islands

Baffin Bay

Baffin Island

Davis Strait

Arctic Circle

Victoria Island

YUKON TERRITORY

Mackenzie

NORTHWEST TERRITORIES

Back

Hudson Strait

PACIFIC OCEAN

Hudson Bay

NEWFOUNDLAND

Queen Charlotte Islands

BRITISH COLUMBIA

Peace

Fraser

ALBERTA

Churchill

MANITOBA

CANADA

QUEBEC

Gulf of St Lawrence

St-Pierre & Miquelon

Vancouver Island

Calgary ○ 2

S Saskatchewan

SASKATCHEWAN

Albany

ONTARIO

St Lawrence

NEW BRUNSWICK

PRINCE EDWARD I

Lake Superior

Levis

Montreal

3 ○ 7

Halifax

NOVA SCOTIA

ATLANTIC OCEAN

Lake Huron

Lake Ontario

Toronto 5 7

Lake Michigan

Mississauga

London

Lake Erie

Economic indicators

head offices of world's top 500 banks and companies (with number if more than one)

● **5** bank
● **7** company

GDP per capita (US$)

- over 20 000
- 15 000–20 000
- 10 000–14 999
- 5 000–9 999

☐ no data available

Map of GDP per capita (*above*) Canada's wealth of resources and relatively small population combine to produce one of the highest rates of GDP per capita in the world: an average of $20,470 in 1990. The average annual growth rate of GDP of 3.4 percent (1980–90) was bettered only by Japan among the world's top seven economic powers.

A vast grain elevator (*left*) stores Canadian wheat before shipping to countries all over the world. Wheat is one of the country's principal agricultural exports. In the late 19th and early 20th centuries, revenues from wheat and other farming and forestry industries helped to fund the rapid growth of Canada's manufacturing sector.

Profile of inflation (*above*) The annual rate of inflation in Canada hit a high of nearly 13 percent in 1981. In response, the government's tight monetary policies brought inflation down to a fairly steady 5 percent from 1983 onward.

by the United States. By the 1970s, almost 60 percent of all financial assets in mining and smelting were owned by United States firms, and the same proportions in the oil and gas industry. In all, United States' companies controlled over half the value of Canadian manufacturing output.

The oil price shock of 1973–74 brought the long Canadian boom to an end. Like other oil-independent industrialized countries, Canada went into deep recession. Commodity exports declined by 1.5 percent in real terms during 1974, and the foreign trade deficit rose from $785 million in 1973 to nearly $2.5 billion a year later. After a brief respite, Canadians entered the most severe of a series of recessions in 1981–82. During 1982 real gross domestic product (GDP) declined by 3.2 percent and the national rate of unemployment peaked at 12.7 percent.

The rapid shifts in Canada's economic fortunes throughout its history displayed the classic "boom-bust" pattern of a resource-based economy. Although the Canadian economy was far more diversified in 1980 than a century earlier, it was still at the mercy of rapid fluctuations in commodity prices. In addition, recessionary pressures in the United States' market still had a major impact on the Canadian economy.

BREAKING THE BOOM–BUST CYCLE

Following the 1981–82 recession, Canada experienced nearly a decade of sustained growth. While the impetus for much of this growth came from traditional sectors such as forestry, mining, agriculture and heavy industry, the economy continued to diversify. High-technology sectors such as telecommunications grew rapidly as did many areas of the service sector. By the end of the decade over 70 percent of Canadian workers were employed in service occupations.

The 1980s also witnessed shifts in trading patterns. Over 30 percent of Canada's income derives from trade, with export businesses providing over three million jobs. The United States' market dominates, accounting for about 75 percent of Canadian exports and 65 percent of imports. While the role of the United States has been strengthened by the 1989 Free Trade Agreement, Canada has also expanded trading relations with Pacific

Loading timber (*above*) on a Canadian quayside. Products from Canada's vast forests (including pulp and paper) make up the country's most valuable commodity group. New legislation is forcing forestry companies to invest in more sustainable forestry techniques.

Rim nations such as Japan and South Korea and aims to gain a stronger foothold in Europe.

Gearing up for competition
Canada faces a number of economic challenges in the 1990s. It is competing in an increasingly global marketplace and recent political events have changed the shape and nature of many of its major markets. The liberalization of Eastern Europe, European economic integration through the European Community (EC) and the inclusion of Mexico in a North American Free Trade Agreement (NAFTA) create potential obstacles for Canadian industries. Manufacturers will have to produce high-quality goods efficiently and cheaply as well as investing heavily in new technologies and in research and development if they are to remain competitive. The resource-based sectors must

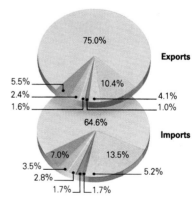

Trading partners

- United States
- Japan
- Britain
- Germany
- South Korea
- Taiwan
- other EC countries
- other countries

Canada's balance of merchandise trade (*above and right*) The United States is by far Canada's most important trading partner, receiving a massive 75 percent of Canadian exports and supplying almost 65 percent of the country's imports. Exploitation of natural resources contributes a substantial amount to export earnings, especially energy (oil, natural gas, coal and hydroelectricity) processed metals and forest products including paper. Imports are dominated by machinery and industrial equipment.

THE COST OF ENVIRONMENTAL PROTECTION

In recent years the environment has emerged as an important public policy issue throughout the developed world. Canada is committed to spending $6 billion on its ambitious Green Plan, which will result in more stringent environmental regulations. Pressure from consumer concern is forcing many Canadian companies to produce environmentally friendly products and to invest heavily in pollution-control technologies. Such protective measures are extremely costly and companies fear a decrease in profits as they are obliged to make investments in expensive environmental protection programs.

The Canadian pulp and paper industry, for example, employs over 120,000 Canadians and accounts for 9 percent of the nation's manufacturing shipments. It is estimated that Canadian companies will have to spend $5 billion by the mid 1990s to comply with new environmental legislation. The public is increasingly aware of the depletion of

Canada's vast woodlands, and forestry companies are being forced to develop improved logging techniques as well as investing more heavily in replanting schemes. But the cost of failing to protect the environment is equally high: Canadian farmers experience annual production losses of $500–900 million due to erosion through environmentally unfriendly farming methods. Several power generating authorities in the United States have begun to reevaluate contracts to buy electricity from Quebec in view of the environmental damage caused by the construction of hydroelectric dams. The state of Maine canceled its $9 billion contract in 1992, and the future of other important contracts is under review. In another market sector, Canadian newsprint producers fear that stringent United States' recycling legislation providing for greater use of recycled paper will restrict their access to a traditionally lucrative market.

---

add greater value to their raw materials by processing them or using them in manufacturing before trading. Most will have to improve productivity if they are to escape the worst effects of further boom–bust cycles.

To prepare for the challenges ahead, the federal government has adopted a series of free-market policies designed to make the economy more competitive. In particular, direct government participation in the economy has been minimized through the reduction of tariffs, the deregulation of a series of sectors including energy and financial services, and the privatization of a range of publicly owned operations.

Quebec as an economic issue
Meanwhile, economic growth is threatened by political instability and cultural clashes between various ethnic groups.

One of the most damaging conflicts is the issue of Quebec's separation from the rest of Canada. French Canadians supporting independence for Quebec want political sovereignty while retaining an economic association with Canada (including a customs and monetary union).

Many commentators feel that such a separation would have dire economic consequences, not only for Quebec, but also for Canada as a whole. The political reorganization of Canada into two sovereign states might tempt the United States to reopen, or reinterpret, existing trade agreements. Also, while a sovereign Quebec would be rich by international standards, it would be distinctly poorer than its neighbors. It would have to shoulder its share of the national deficit, but would no longer receive the federal aid that has, so far, contributed to many of Quebec's social programs. With its existing high taxation, it is not clear how Quebec would raise extra tax revenues and at the same time maintain the competitiveness of its economy.

Debt and taxes
Increasing levels of debt also threaten Canada's economic future. In March 1990 the net federal debt (the money borrowed by the government to cover successive budget deficits) stood at $379,565 million or nearly $15,000 per person. The debt shows little sign of diminishing. Consumer debt, or the money owed by individuals to banks and other institutions, more than doubled during the 1980s to reach $101,500 million in 1990. This is equivalent to 21.5 percent of the average Canadian's after-tax personal income. Such high levels of debt pose serious questions for the future since Canadians will be paying interest on the national debt, much of it to foreign institutions, for many years to come. This in turn prevents reinvestment in the Canadian economy and raises levels of international dependence.

In response, the federal government has cut domestic expenditure, reduced levels of overseas aid and increased tax revenue through a goods and services tax levied on most consumer purchases. While these policies may eventually improve the economy's competitive stance and reduce budget problems, many fear that a shift away from a welfare economy may lead to growing social and economic inequalities within the nation.

Agricultural produce and food 6%
Consumer goods 11%
Industrial supplies 18%
Automobiles and other transport equipment 21%
Industrial plant and machinery 29%

Energy products 5%
Others 10%

Imports $126.5 bn

Exports $133.5 bn

Automobiles and other transport equipment 22%
Industrial supplies 20%
Industrial plant and machinery 18%
Forest products 14%
Energy products 9%

Others 9%
Agricultural produce and food 8%

A NATION OF CONTRASTS

The average standard of living in Canada ranks among the highest in the world, but members of some ethnic groups and the inhabitants of certain regions fare much worse than others. Unemployment rates and the potential for improving conditions for the inhabitants vary greatly between the provinces. Earlier in the nation's history the Atlantic provinces (Prince Edward Island, New Brunswick, Nova Scotia and Newfoundland) and prairie provinces (Saskatchewan and Manitoba) grew rapidly as a result of resource-based booms. In recent decades, however, they have had to fight hard against low levels of economic growth. Newfoundland in particular has suffered from a decline in its fisheries and some small towns in the region register unemployment rates above 30 percent.

Since World War II the provinces with the most vibrant economies have been British Columbia, Alberta and Ontario. While the average unemployment rate for Newfoundland during the 1980s ranged between 15 and 20 percent, these three regions were characterized by rates of only half this level. Quebec remains something of a special case. While it has a great deal of industrial potential and remains, after Ontario, the second largest producer of manufactured goods, political uncertainty and a dependence on declining sectors such as clothing and textiles have affected its performance in recent years. Montreal now has the highest urban unemployment rate in the nation. Canada has attempted to overcome these inequalities through a system of transfer or equalization payments. These redirect federal tax money from the wealthier to the poorer provinces.

Evening the odds

Canada has long prided itself on its relatively fair system of welfare support. As in the United States, the way government-funded education is organized varies from province to province. In particular, the federal government takes responsibility for education in the Yukon

Vive la difference! (*below*) French Canadians campaigning for separatism. Quebec's declining economy has been assisted by federal resource transfer schemes recently, and experts doubt that an independent Quebec could survive economically.

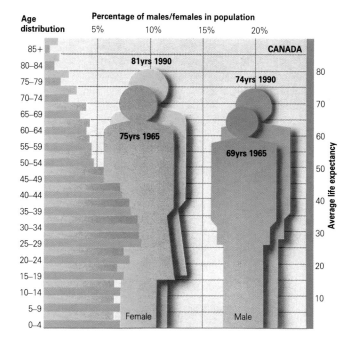

A day at the lake (*left*) City-dwellers taking a relaxing break on the shores of Lake Ontario. The highly urbanized Canadian population enjoys one of the highest standards of living in the world, including ample time and money to spend on leisure pursuits. Affluent city-dwellers frequently own a second home in the countryside. By comparison, the standards of living of inhabitants of some isolated rural areas, particularly the indigenous peoples of the northwest, are low.

Life expectancy and age distribution (*right*) In common with other developed countries, life expectancy in Canada is high – the average female life expectancy (81 years) is second only to Japan's. Among the indigenous Inuit population, however, the average life span is shorter, even though access to healthcare and other social services is relatively equitably distributed. Since the 1960s' baby boom, birthrates have dropped steadily.

Age distribution

Percentage of males/females in population

CANADA

81yrs 1990

74yrs 1990

75yrs 1965

69yrs 1965

Average life expectancy

Female   Male

and Northwest territories where the majority of schools cater specifically for Canada's indigenous peoples including the Inuit and native Indians. The Federal Government also contributes to the higher education budget of each province. Most Canadian children go to elementary school at the age of six, and spend eight years there. Virtually all students go on to secondary school at 14, and spend five or six years there (depending on the province). Bilingual or French-language instruction is increasingly common in English-speaking areas.

The government also provides health and welfare services, through universally funded taxation programs. Nevertheless, inequalities appear to be growing as the economy enters the 1990s and the international political trend moves away from the welfare state. Canada has begun to cut transfer payments and there has been some discussion about the possibility of partly privatizing the healthcare system. It is estimated that 3.5 million Canadians (over 10 percent of the population) live below the poverty line.

THE INUIT: MAKING A LIVING

Approximately 35,000 Canadian Inuit live in small, isolated villages spread throughout the Northwest Territories and the Yukon. In these government-built communities, incomes are well below the national average and unemployment rates are generally high. Social welfare assistance is a fact of everyday life. This state of affairs is mostly the result of long-standing problems: the disadvantage of the remote location coupled with high transportation costs; low levels of education leading to poorly skilled workers; the sheer lack of people to sustain large-scale ventures; and a limited range of occupations and business activities.

Hunting, fishing and trapping remain important occupations among the Inuit, providing food that would otherwise have to be imported and raw material for clothing. While these traditional forms of economic activity also provide some cash income, the market for seal and other furs has been cut drastically as a result of international bans on fur trading and changing consumer demand. In consequence, traditional economic activities are no longer sufficiently profitable in the modern economy. Inuit communities have to rely heavily on handicrafts, especially carving, as a source of income. The main chance for future economic development is seen to lie with tourism, bringing with it the risk of cultural and environmental damage.

Conditions for the disadvantaged

Some ethnic and cultural groups can be identified as being more impoverished than others. In the 1960s restrictions that had effectively encouraged only European immigration were relaxed and more immigrants began to arrive from developing countries, particularly from Asia. As this flow of new workers and their families has continued, they have tended to settle in the inner cities and a number of related problems have arisen.

A lack of training has restricted migrants to jobs in the nonskilled sector, which has become substantially reduced as industries have modernized and relocated to hightech offices in outer city areas. While the federal and provincial governments have introduced a variety of assimilation and training schemes, several ethnic groups continue to experience unemployment rates that are well above the national average. Racial prejudice is becoming a growing problem in some parts of the country.

Perhaps the most pressing issue, however, is the relatively low standard of living of Canada's indigenous peoples. In the north and on native Indian reservations across the country, unemployment rates often exceed 40 percent and average life expectancy is much lower than for the nation as a whole. In most of these areas, harsh climatic conditions and limited resource bases reduce the potential for future economic development and create a cycle of poverty that is difficult to break.

The free-trade debate

The Free-Trade Agreement (FTA) between Canada and the United States is the most significant economic treaty ever signed by Canada. It took effect in January 1989 and, according to the original terms, virtually all goods produced in the two countries will be traded without restriction by 1998. Predictably, the FTA has fueled a great deal of political and economic debate on both sides on the potential benefits and damaging side effects of freer trade.

Opponents of the agreement believe that Canada still requires some form of protection for its economy if it is not to be overwhelmed by its larger neighbor. They argue that by 1991 over 200,000 jobs had already been lost as a result of the FTA. This has happened mostly because Canadian firms moved south of the border into the United States to preserve their competitiveness by taking advantage of lower labor costs there. Political opponents of the agreement also argue that the United States is already in economic decline and that Canada has tied itself to the wrong economic partner if it wishes to improve its competitive position in the global economy.

Supporters of the agreement argue that any firms that have closed would have been forced to rationalize their operations regardless of the agreement. They point out that 75 percent of all trade between the two countries was already free of barriers before 1989. Proponents believe that while free trade will increase competition at home, it will also provide secure access to a market of some 275 million consumers. They are confident that the market will be large enough to offer Canadian industry the possibility to obtain economies of scale and improve productivity. In this way the FTA will actually assist Canada in becoming more competitive in the global marketplace.

North America, Inc.

Supporters of the FTA believe that only by extending the nation's trading links can Canadians continue to enjoy the standard of living achieved by the end of the 1980s. It is this thinking that led the country into negotiations with both the United States and Mexico for the establishment of a North American Free-Trade Agreement (known as NAFTA).

New trade links between Canada and

Mexico amounted to C$2.3 billion in 1989, of which imports from Mexico accounted for C$1.7 billion. When compared with the Canada–United States' trading figure of C$185.8 billion for the same year, the partnership with Mexico does not appear to be significant. However, Mexico is Canada's leading trading partner in Latin America. Canada's imports from Mexico are mainly manufactured products (principally transportation equipment and parts for machinery) while its exports to Mexico are largely agricultural products and some transportation equipment.

The NAFTA treaty was signed in Texas in 1992, but it was not ratified by the Canadian government. There are still important issues to be discussed before

Left out in the cold (*right*) Trade union members protest against the Free Trade Agreement. Representatives of selected industries voiced widespread opposition to the agreement in 1988 on the grounds that free trade with the United States would cause substantial job losses and damage the economy.

Steeled for change (*below*) Workers in steel manufacturing and the related automobile industry are likely to be hit hard by redundancies as a result of factory relocation to the United States or Mexico where wages are lower.

Canada can agree to abide by its stipulations. Mexico is at a far lower level of development than Canada. The large differences in wage levels and productivity that exist between Canadian and Mexican manufacturing plants mean that free trade with Mexico will have to be introduced gradually. An agreement that quickly removed tariffs on most trade with Mexico could make it difficult for Canadian producers to compete with cheaper Mexican goods. Many unions are already strongly opposed to the NAFTA treaty, believing that it may encourage manufacturers of certain goods to shift their operations to Mexico in order to take advantage of cheap labor and lax environmental regulations.

Supporters of NAFTA think that consideration must be given to Mexico's potential for growth. They argue that labor costs are only one of the elements to take into account, and that factors such as the overall efficiency of the economy, the skills of the workforce, the quality of management and the cost of capital will provide Canada with a competitive advantage. For example, as Mexico modernizes, it will have to invest heavily in transportation and communications. With its expertise in these areas, Canada would be well positioned to take advantage of free trade. Proponents also believe that only by participating in NAFTA can Canada influence the flow of future trade and investment in the region.

PEOPLES AND CULTURES

TWO CULTURAL TRADITIONS · A DISTINCT NATION · TOWARD A MULTICULTURAL SOCIETY

Canadians are not easily defined. The population of 26 million, living in scattered pockets stretched out in a narrow belt along a vast east–west territory that covers almost 90 degrees of latitude, is made up of a collection of diverse ethnocultural groups, the result of Canada's history of welcoming immigrants from Europe, and more recently from Asia and Latin America. Yet these groups are accommodated within a fundamental cultural dualism that divides the country into an English-speaking and a French-speaking community. The question of national identity has inevitably been an abiding concern: are national icons English, French, neither or both? Are dominant loyalties regional or national? How are the indigenous populations of Native Indians and Inuit (Eskimos) to be integrated into a modern state?

COUNTRIES IN THE REGION
Canada, Greenland (dependency of Denmark)

POPULATION
Canada	26.6 million
Greenland	56,000

LANGUAGE
Countries with two official languages (English, French) Canada; (Danish, Greenlandic) Greenland

Percentage of population by first language (Canada) English (61%), French (24%), other (11%), bi- or multilingual (4%), indigenous languages (0.3%)

RELIGION
Canada Roman Catholic (46.5%), Protestant (41%), nonreligious (7.4%), Eastern Orthodox (1.5%), Jewish (1.2%), Muslim (0.4%), Hindu (0.3%), Sikh (0.3%)

Greenland Protestant (97.8%); other (2.2%)

TWO CULTURAL TRADITIONS

The original inhabitants of Canada made their way over a land bridge across the Bering Strait from northern Asia about 30,000 years ago; to the far north were Inuits belonging to the group of hunter–gatherers that lived along the edge of the Arctic ice from Siberia to Alaska. The first contact with Europe came about 1000 AD when Norse explorers established a brief settlement at L'Anse aux Meadows in Newfoundland – an event that is recorded in the Icelandic sagas. Nothing more occurred for more than 500 years until, following the discovery by English and French sailors of the Newfoundland coast and the St Lawrence river, fishing fleets from European ports started to exploit the rich North Atlantic fisheries and established seasonal settlements along the coast. Gradually, as some people decided to spend the winter there, these became permanent settlements.

The making of French Canada
At this time, the region was inhabited by between 220,000 and 250,000 indigenous peoples belonging to one of 12 major language groups. Apart from the Iroquois, who were settled as farmers in the area around Lake Ontario, most survived by hunting and fishing, moving around with the seasons through much of the continental interior. Trading contacts were established, first by the French and then by the English, with these migratory groups, who exchanged furs, highly valued in Europe, for a variety of goods. Competition for trade between European rivals was fierce. The introduction of firearms brought substantial changes to the traditional Native Indian patterns of hunting and warfare. Gradually they were displaced by European settlement, and were compelled to abandon their seasonal migratory way of life.

The French were the first Europeans to open up the interior to settlement. Progress, following the course of the St Lawrence river, was slow, limited by the climate and the volatility of relations with indigenous groups. Quebec, founded in 1608, was by 1800 the largest settlement away from the coast, and the center of French-speaking Canada, yet its population was only about 8,000 – roughly the same size as Halifax, the capital of Nova Scotia, which was the largest coastal

town. After 300 years of European contact, the total European population of the seven colonies of British North America, which would come together in the course of the 19th century to form the Canadian confederation, was no more than 340,000 – and 60 percent of these inhabitants were French-speaking.

The British influence
The French-speaking people, however, were living within a territory that since 1763 had been British-owned. The British element in Canada (at this time predominantly Scots and Irish) was strengthened by the addition of thousands of loyalist emigrants from the newly independent United States of America to the south, and the division of the colony into English-speaking Upper Canada and French-speaking Lower Canada (corresponding to Ontario and Quebec today) confirmed the existence of two parallel cultures. The English-speaking community looked to Britain for its laws, its models of government and its Protestant Christian culture; French-Canadians retained the use of their own language, their distinctive system of land-holding, and their Roman Catholic religion.

Expansion westward across the continent did not fundamentally alter this cultural division. In 1901 only 10 percent of the population fell outside the Anglo-Canadian or the French-Canadian communities, or were not members of the indigenous peoples. These included the *Métis*, people of mixed Indian and French or British ancestry, who had developed a distinctive way of life and thought of themselves as a nation with rights in the area that was to become Manitoba, west of Hudson Bay.

Control of political and economic resources made the British influence culturally dominant in most of Canada. Although there were some local concentrations of minorities – for example, Asian settlers, predominantely Chinese and Japanese, accounted for 11 percent of the population of British Columbia in 1901, and there were communities of European immigrants (particularly Scandinavian, Dutch, Italian, German, Polish and Ukrainian) across the continent – they were islands in a much broader ocean of Anglo-Canadian culture.

Even in Montreal, the commercial center of the province of Quebec, the English-speaking minority successfully

dominated local business and politics – a change that had started to come about when the French fur trade was taken over by British interests. They came to form a ruling elite that was segregated by language, religion, class and residence from a largely rural, Roman Catholic French-Canadian majority.

British influence in Canada attained its highwater mark between 1914 and 1918. Many Canadians fought on the British side in World War I – the Molsons, one of Montreal's leading industrialist families, sent 30 members to the war in Europe, more than half of whom were killed or wounded in action. However, by the

A Quebec street scene (*above right*) highlights some of the influences at work in Canadian society. French shops and chateau-style architecture reveal European links; the rise in popularity of American sports shows the impact of the United States.

Urban convenience (*above*) Huge American-style shopping malls, where shoppers can park and purchase all their needs under one roof, are well suited to Canada's often rigorous climate.

A sign of belonging (*left*) Canada's national symbol of a red maple leaf helps to unite its diverse population. It is, however, relatively recent: the Canadian flag bearing the maple leaf only became official in 1965.

1920s United States' investment in Canada had outstripped British investment and in the period since then its popular culture – spread through newspapers and journals, television, movies, and the increased movement of population – has become a pervasive element in Canadian culture. Even to the people of Quebec the United States' border has become increasingly permeable. Over a quarter of a million older Quebecois are today permanently resident in Florida.

A DISTINCT NATION

The establishment of a coherent cultural identity has been an elusive goal in Canada. This is common to most former colonial nations, but in Canada the problem is compounded by the distances that divide its centers of population, the bicultural nature of its society, and the fact of its living next to an economically more powerful neighbor. Canada has, in many respects, substituted one dominant presence for another. Sharing an immense land boundary and with an economy and population some ten times smaller than the United States, it has a major task in defining its distinctiveness.

One example of how this distinctiveness expresses itself at the popular level is found in the area of sport. Hockey (which in Canada means ice hockey) is a major national interest, and a powerful symbol of national unity. For decades one of the most popular television programs has been the Canadian Broadcasting Corporation's *Hockey night in Canada*. Yet even in the context of sport, competition from the United States is evident. Baseball is growing in popularity, and Canadian baseball teams compete in the United States' leagues.

The threat from the south

Canada's cultural tug between its own identity and that of the United States makes itself felt in a number of ways. For example, there is confusion over the style of spellings used in written English – although the government and large business corporations (including United States-owned multinationals) will usually follow the British spellings of words ("neighbour" rather than "neighbor", for example). At the popular level, including newspapers, an inconsistent mixture of British and American spellings is used.

During the 1970s and early 1980s, concerns over Canada's cultural and economic independence led to the then Liberal administration's program of "Canadianization": attempts were made to nationalize the economy, and the constitution was freed from British parliamentary control by the passing of the Canada Act. These moves stimulated a wide-ranging debate on national identity, which came to a head with the vehement discussion over the signing of the Free Trade Agreement (FTA) with the

National passion (*above*) Ice hockey, developed in its present form in Canada during the 19th century, is the country's most popular sport. Children are encouraged to compete for the big teams from an early age. Thousands of amateurs play in leagues across the country, and top professional players have the status of national heroes. Team loyalties are affected by ethno-religious boundaries.

Canada's changing face (*left*) The image that many Canadians have of themselves is colored by the country's recent pioneer past, but belies the fact that theirs is now a highly urbanized society. Highrise commercial buildings dominate the center of Edmonton, capital of the western prairies, dwarfing its earlier, more modest architecture.

United States in 1988, opponents (who failed in their political attempt to prevent the agreement) arguing that it would erode Canadian identity by threatening its cultural and social traditions.

Among the people who spoke most vociferously against the FTA were artists and other members of the cultural media. The arts, broadcasting, publishing and film industries have always enjoyed a privileged position in Canada, provided with subsidies and tax incentives to advance the cause of Canadian distinctiveness. There are, for example, specific guidelines to regulate the degree of Canadian content in broadcasting: the 1968 Broadcasting Act identifies the need "to safeguard, enrich and strengthen the cultural, political, social and economic fabric of Canada" through the Canadian

ownership of broadcasting.

Canadian artists and intellectuals consequently possess significant material grounds for resisting Americanization, in addition to their own individual emotional response to the issue. They have played an important role in contributing to Canada's images of nationhood. In the 1920s and 1930s, the Toronto-based Group of Seven established the first major school of Canadian art. Their paintings, which represented "the true north, strong and free", portrayed natural landscapes; typically, though not always, they showed primitive yet colorful wilderness scenes devoid of settlement.

Rural pioneers to urban dwellers
These images of northern austerity and purity were offered as icons of Canadian

THE HUTTERITES – A RURAL COMMUNITY

While most of the European immigrant groups to Canada have sought to preserve some elements of their old-world culture, they have been assimilated to a greater or lesser degree into Canadian society. A few, however, have sought complete seclusion in rural settlements to maintain their distinct ways of life free from contamination from mainstream cultures.

One of the most interesting of these groups is the Hutterites. Originally from Moravia (today part of Czecho-slovakia), they take their name from Jacob Hutter (d. 1536), a religious leader who was burned as a heretic. Taking their authority from a strict interpretation of the Bible, they hold all goods in common, and are the oldest and the largest communal group in the Western world. On emigrating from Europe in the 19th century, they first settled in the United States and only moved into the prairie provinces of Canada in 1940, during World War II, to avoid persecution for their pacifism.

Living on collective farms, Hutterites pursue a modern commercial agriculture, and have a reputation as innovative and successful farmers. Their farming colonies increased rapidly from 52 communities in 1940 to nearly 247 a little more than 25 years later, reflecting their high birthrate: colonies divide once the population reaches about 150. This is done to safeguard the financial wellbeing of the parent colony, and it is the Hutterites' successful pursuit of a modern commercial economy that enables them to preserve their culture.

Ethnic diversity in Canada The map shows clearly the dominant areas of French-Canadian and British-Canadian culture in the eastern half of the country, and Inuit in the north. The picture is more varied elsewhere in the region.

distinctiveness, and continue to draw a lively following. It was perhaps no accident that Canadian artists looked to the wilderness for their inspiration: the choice of a maple leaf to symbolize Canada's nationhood on the country's flag points to a deep-rooted identification with the natural environment. But such an image today overlooks the fact that Canada is now one of the most urbanized of nations. Canadians may seek to recreate their pioneer past by weekending at lakeside cabins and taking part in log-rolling competitions, and the northern wilderness may offer a useful symbol of national cohesiveness, but it is far removed from the everyday life of most Canadians working in office blocks in large urban centers.

For these people, the rural conservatism and traditional religious values of the past (whether the strict Protestant Christianity of those of Scottish, German and Scandinavian descent, or the devotional piety of French Roman Catholics) have mostly been replaced by urban, secular values. This transformation has been most marked in Quebec, where the role of the church as the dominant institution in the province was successfully

challenged and displaced in the 1960s by the "Quiet Revolution" of the Liberal administration, led by Jean Lesage. In this period of rapid secularization and modernization, Quebec's birthrate plummeted from being one of the highest to one of the very lowest to be found among Western societies.

The division between urban and rural values has been at the root of two bitter ideological struggles that have divided Canadian society in recent years. The base of support for the "pro-choice" lobby in the debate over abortion, enunciating the right of women to control their own fertility, has been in the major urban centers, while "pro-life" advocates have drawn their strength from the suburbs and small towns. Similarly urban opinion has been unequivocally expressed on a range of environmental questions, in particular the culling of seals on the Atlantic coast, while small town residents balance these arguments against their own economic livelihood.

TOWARD A MULTICULTURAL SOCIETY

From the earliest days of British power in Canada, the interests of the distinct French cultural community in Quebec were legally safeguarded within the constitution. This has not been the case with Canada's other cultural groups. For example, would-be Chinese immigrants to British Columbia at the turn of the century had to pay a head tax. In 1895 this was rated at $50 per immigrant, but it increased dramatically to $500 in 1905 – a figure that reflected contemporary anti-Oriental sentiment.

British Canada's prevailing rhetoric of race and Empire established a clear ethnic pecking order among immigrants, and many groups faced a marginal existence, whether in Irish Catholic slums in Montreal, deprived Eastern European districts in Winnipeg's North End, or in the barely tolerated ghetto of Vancouver's China-

Kensington market, Toronto, is a lively meeting place for people of many different cultural traditions and from many parts of the world. One-third of recent immigrants to Canada, particularly from Hong Kong, Southeast Asia and India, have settled in the city.

town. However, as the numbers of various groups increased, their social status slowly improved. Canada's Jewish population – principally made up of immigrants from Eastern Europe – had grown from 16,000 in 1901 to 126,000 in 1921. Most were initially employed within the garment industries of Toronto and Montreal, and as they grew they prospered to form a significant merchant class. Progress among the Asian communities, however, was delayed by a lingering anti-Orientalism. During World War II this found political expression in the decision to intern Japanese-Canadians and confiscate their property.

More liberal policies in the postwar years have seen the flow of immigrants increase in national diversity. In 1957, 95 percent of immigrants were from Europe or the United States, by far the greater number of them from Britain. Ten years later this figure had fallen to 80 percent, declining still farther to 47 percent in 1977 and 24 percent in 1987. The leading countries of origin in 1989 were Hong Kong, Poland, the Philippines, India and Vietnam. Before the war most immigrants were unskilled laborers; but since then greater numbers of middle-class immigrants have been admitted, a trend that the Canadian government's policy of welcoming political refugees encouraged.

Pressure from ethnic groups
By far the greater number of new arrivals seek a life in the cities. In 1988, more than a third of all immigrants settled in the Toronto metropolitan area. This has had a significant influence on the nature of small businesses setting up in commercial streets, and has led to changes in domestic styles of architecture.

There has been among these groups a growing sense of exclusion from Canada's bicultural society, particularly in the light of the debate about national identity that the Quebec separatist movement has stimulated. Under pressure from ethnic groups, positive attitudes to multiculturalism have been encouraged by providing funds for the promotion of ethnic festivals and community centers. A growing consciousness of ethnic rights is reshaping public policy in other ways, too. Japanese-Canadians have launched a campaign to gain redress for wartime losses, and the issue of multiculturalism looms large in debating current immigration policy.

French voices
In Quebec, the ideals and policies of multiculturalism collide uncomfortably with regional goals. The province's falling birthrate means that immigrants are needed to sustain its economy and labor force. But few are native French-speakers, and since 1977 French has been the language in which all work and education are legally conducted: immigrants are required to send their children to French-language schools.

The increasingly protective nature of legislation to preserve the French language in Quebec has led to some unusual situations. In 1983 the Language Commission had to pass a ruling on a case that involved the daughter of a woman who had died in hospital. She complained that her mother "didn't die in French", and the Commission – which heard evidence from a doctor and three nurses — concluded that the woman had died only 66 percent in French, since she had been treated by English speakers for 34 percent of her last months in hospital.

As a result of the campaign for French language rights, there is today a fuller and more confident consensus in Quebec society than ever before. That Quebec

separatism continues to pose a most serious challenge to national unity was made clear in the constitutional crisis that erupted in 1990 following opposition to the government's plan, set out in the Meech Lake Accord, to secure Quebec's standing as a "distinct society" within Canada and its further rejection in a referendum in 1992. Opposition arose from the demand of some other provinces for an equal recognition of distinctiveness, in effect suppressing Quebec's claim of a unique cultural status.

Northern frontier, northern homeland

When the French established their trading post at Quebec in 1608, the surrounding area was home to the Huron-Petun group of the Iroquois family of Native Indians, settled agriculturalists who then numbered between 20,000 and 30,000. Outbreaks of measles, influenza and smallpox, all introduced by the Europeans, had immediate and devastating effect upon them: by 1639 only some 12,000 survived. This pattern of events was repeated many times across the continent in the next 300 years.

The combined effects of disease, enforced relocation to accommodate European settlement, and wars aided by the use of European arms brought widespread destruction to Canada's indigenous peoples. Their numbers reached their lowest point in about 1920. Since then greater immunity from disease and the provision of improved health care have contributed to a rapid growth in numbers, and by 1981 the populations of Native Indians, *Métis* and Inuit had climbed to threequarters of a million. Most of these groups today are found in the Yukon and Northwest Territories.

Even in Canada's most remote areas, their way of life is under threat. The Inuit people of the Arctic inhabit one of the most inhospitable environments on Earth. Survival in these severe conditions was dependent on a seminomadic hunting–gathering culture – winter settlements of between 500 and 1,000 people

ing conditions bring new threats and pressures from outside. The campaigns of animal rights' activists around the world have limited demand for furs and skins, the trapping of which provided a means of support for many Inuit communities. Rapid cultural change leads to demoralization and displacement – Inuit suicides are four times the national average, and violent crimes, almost invariably associated with dependency on alcohol, are also high.

Campaigning for lost rights (*above*) Mohawks and other Indian nations have become increasingly politicized in their pursuit of cultural independence and restoration of their territory.

Under pressure (*left*) Inuit communities have been severely disrupted by the commercial exploitation of their land. The breakdown of their traditional way of life has led to serious social problems and alcohol abuse.

Artistic heritage (*below*) Inuit craftsmen continue the skill of their ancestors in soapstone and bone carving. Craftwork is now an important source of income.

broke up into small hunting bands in summer, and social life was communal, with strong family bonding.

Today, the far north is Canada's last frontier. Exploitation of its mineral resources has exposed the Inuit to modern pressures, and their traditional way of life has been almost entirely abandoned. Survival, materially and culturally, is pursued in other ways. Inuit art, particularly carving and printmaking, has become a significant economic activity, and cultural integrity is protected by the Inuit Tapirisat, an umbrella organization that safeguards Inuit interests, including the Inuktitut language. But chang-

A culture in transition

A study of a remote village in the Yukon, carried out by Robert McSkimming over a long period of time, shows how a traditional indigenous economy and culture has been affected by European contact. The Kutchin people who live today in Old Crow were originally fishermen and caribou hunters – the village became a permanent settlement only when a trading post was established there in 1912. The villagers quickly turned to trapping for their main means of support. The acquisition of firearms meant that hunting could be carried out quickly, leaving more time for trapping. Their communal hunts were abandoned, and by the 1940s perhaps three-quarters of the adult population were trappers; their trap lines reached 240 km (150 mi) south of Old Crow.

By 1973 all this had changed. With a declining market for furs, only 10 percent of Old Crow adults remained trappers, and few young people knew how to set trap lines. There was widespread unemployment. Nevertheless, a quarter of the village's income, and over half of its food needs, were still derived from the land.

"Without land, Indian people have no soul, no life, no identity, no purpose. Control of our own land is necessary for our cultural and economic survival." These words of the Yukon Native Brotherhood lie at the heart of the land claims movement. For Canada's indigenous peoples, possession of their land not only has symbolic meaning, but fundamental material importance. Substantial land claims offer an opportunity for economic and cultural survival. The first agreement, made with the Council for Yukon Indians in 1990, included a cash settlement of $232 million and ownership of an area of land covering 41,000 sq km (15,830 sq mi). Such land claims are likely to increase in the future.

The Mounties

The Royal Canadian Mounted Police – commonly called the Mounties – are an important symbol of Canadian nationhood. Founded in 1873, they began as a small mounted force charged with keeping the peace between the indigenous peoples and European settlers in the vast territories acquired from the Hudson Bay Company. From a series of posts and forts they maintained order first in western Canada and then later in the northwestern gold fields and inside the Arctic Circle. Canadian folklore contrasts the peace and stability brought by the Mounties to these frontier lands with the violence and disorder that ruled south of the border.

In their scarlet tunics and blue pants – the uniform they still wear – Mounties were used on immigration pamphlets and tourist advertisements as early as the 1880s. Through novels, paintings and movies, they acquired an almost mythical status that was, in some ways, reminiscent of the European tradition of the romantic knight. The image of the calm, dutiful, honest and courageous individual provided an archetypal hero for a society undergoing rapid change. The heroes were, however, strictly English, men from yeoman and aristocratic backgrounds bound together by ties of mutual loyalty and respect, engaged in tackling the threat from outsiders, usually American or Chinese. The Mounties were never so popular among either French–Canadians or Native Indians.

The legendary character of the Mounties was such that they were able to withstand a series of scandals in the 1970s over their involvement in illegal surveillance and bomb-planting activities, much of which was directed against Quebec separatists. They are now a force of 20,000 men, and training on horseback is no longer essential, although their Musical Ride remains a popular show and an important source of publicity.

Mounted cavalcade Mounties are no longer required to be skilled horseback riders – except those that take part in the famous Musical Ride.

CITIES

The popular image of Canada as a land of wide open spaces, vast forests and ice-capped mountains takes little account of the country's towns and cities. Yet Canada is highly urbanized – just over three-quarters of the population are urban-dwellers. Moreover, urban settlement is highly concentrated. The vast majority of people live within 320 km (200 mi) of the border with the United States, nearly one-third of them within the three dominant metropolitan areas of Toronto, Montreal and Vancouver. The transformation from a rural to an urban society is a relatively recent one. The mechanization and rationalization of farming methods in the course of the 20th century have led to massive rural-urban migration, while urban growth has been boosted by high levels of immigration from many parts of the world.

COUNTRIES IN THE REGION

Canada

POPULATION

Total population of region (millions)	26.6
Population density (persons per sq km)	2.9
Population change (average annual percent 1960–1990)	
Urban	+1.7
Rural	+0.4

URBAN POPULATION

As percentage of total population	
1960	68.9
1990	75.6
Percentage in cities of more than 1 million	29.7

TEN LARGEST CITIES

	Population
Toronto	3,427,000
Montreal	2,921,000
Vancouver	1,381,000
Ottawa †	819,000
Edmonton	785,000
Calgary	671,000
Winnipeg	623,000
Quebec	603,000
Hamilton	557,000
St Catharines-Niagara	343,000

† *denotes capital city*

SETTLING A HARSH LAND

Canada's indigenous peoples were mainly migratory hunter–gatherers until they were displaced by European colonists after the 15th century and forced into a more settled way of life. The earliest Canadian towns were founded during the early colonial period when control of land and trade along the course of the St Lawrence river was contested between Britain and France. Quebec City, for example, was founded by the French in 1608; Halifax in Nova Scotia was established in 1749 as a British stronghold.

Following the American War of Independence (1775–83), the influx of British Loyalists from the new republic of the United States and fear of a Yankee takeover stimulated urban settlement along the border. Places such as Kingston (Ontario) and St John (New Brunswick) grew as Loyalist centers, and new defense-oriented towns such as London in southwestern Ontario were founded.

Lingering distrust of its larger neighbor, as well the need to balance Anglo-Canadian and French-Canadian interests, was a factor in the decision in 1852 to locate Canada's new federal capital in Ottawa, on the border between Ontario and Quebec.

Resource-based settlement

Of even greater significance to the nature and location of urban settlement in the region has been the drive to exploit its rich natural resources. In Newfoundland, the town of St John's developed around a magnificent ice-free harbor to serve both inshore and deepsea fishing. The fur trade provided the original stimulus to Montreal's growth; later in the 19th century it developed as the hub of the country's transportation network.

As the export of lumber and timber products from Canada's forests grew into

Historic landmark (*below*) The walled Citadel of Quebec City dominates the busy harbor below. The capital of French-speaking Canada, the city was one of the first European settlements on the mainland.

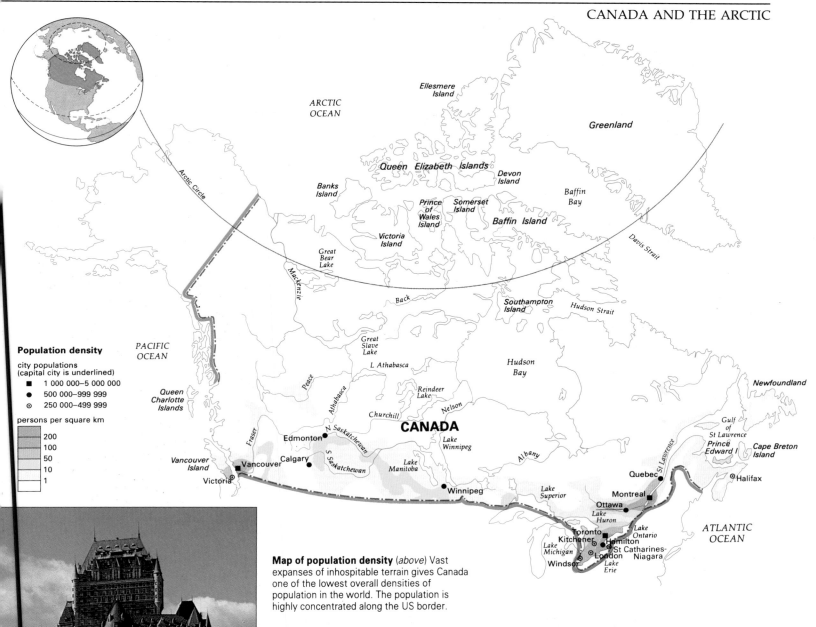

Population density

city populations
(capital city is underlined)
- ■ 1 000 000–5 000 000
- ● 500 000–999 999
- ◎ 250 000–499 999

persons per square km
- 200
- 100
- 50
- 10
- 1

Map of population density (*above*) Vast expanses of inhospitable terrain gives Canada one of the lowest overall densities of population in the world. The population is highly concentrated along the US border.

a major international trade, mill towns developed right across the country. Some of these – such as Trois-Rivières in Quebec and Prince George in British Columbia – have grown into significant provincial centers. However, management of the huge national complex of forest industries has mainly benefited the larger metropolitan areas, notably Vancouver on the west coast.

The extraction, and sometimes processing, of mineral resources also gave rise to a scattering of small towns in the interior of the country. A few, such as Sudbury in northern Ontario, have become important regional centers. Others were reduced to ghost towns as the mineral that brought them into life became exhausted or ceased to be mined because of falling world prices. More recently, the exploitation of oil and natural gas reserves in western Canada has boosted the growth of centers such as Edmonton, Calgary, Vancouver and Saskatoon.

Finally, a large number of small towns developed to serve the needs of dispersed rural farmers and their families. The expansion of the railroads, especially in the Prairies of western Canada, was a key factor in their growth: a school, a church, a few stores and houses would grow up beside the grain elevator and railroad siding from which wheat and other agricultural produce was dispatched to the larger cities and distribution centers.

Some of these places – such as Regina, Calgary or Winnipeg – have become important centers by virtue of location, entrepreneurialism and sheer good luck. But drastic changes in farming have led to the stagnation and decline of many others, as more and more people have left the rural areas of Canada to find work in the cities. As recently as the 1920s there were more rural-dwellers in Canada than urban, no metropolitan area exceeded 1 million, and only six cities had populations of more than 100,000. The transformation from a rural to an urban society has taken place within a single lifetime.

ISLAND CLUSTERS OF POPULATION

By the early 1990s more than three-quarters of Canada's population inhabited a comparatively small number of cities dispersed across a vast territory: it is 8,000 km (4,970 mi) from St John's (Newfoundland) in the east to Victoria (British Columbia) in the west, and 4,000 km (2,485 mi) from Windsor (Ontario) in the south to Whitehorse (Yukon) in the north. Most cities, however, lie in a narrow corridor running parallel to the border with the United States. The area of metropolitan Vancouver, located at the

Glittering metropolis The city skyline of Toronto is dwarfed by the CN tower, the tallest freestanding structure in the world. Toronto is the largest of Canada's three major metropolitan areas, and the country's leading commercial center.

international boundary, is exceeded in size only by Toronto and Montreal. Other cities along the border pair off with American cities on the other side. For example, a bridge and tunnel connect Windsor in southeast Ontario with Detroit, Michigan, and Fort Erie, also in Ontario, is linked by a bridge with Buffalo in New York state.

The exceptions to the borderland concentration of population are the few towns of Canada's far north (Whitehorse,

Yellowknife) and the resource-oriented towns of the mid-northern areas (Edmonton, Prince George, and Thunder Bay, on the northwest shore of Lake Superior). Although the towns of the eastern Maritime Provinces also lie geographically distant from the border, in the past communication links brought them within the sphere of influence of Boston in the northeastern United States, rather than that of any of the major cities of Quebec or Ontario province.

Main Street, Canada
At the heart of Canada's urban system is a densely populated urban area stretching almost 1,200 km (745 mi) from Windsor to

ARCTIC TOWNS

Towns in Canada's vast Arctic regions are few, far between and very small. Apart from a handful of government and mining centers, there are between 50 and 60 settlements where the predominantly indigenous population is about 1,000. Even Whitehorse, the largest Arctic settlement, has a population of less than 20,000.

The character of these Arctic towns reflects a mixture of influences. A "modern" economy – which provides seasonal work for many indigenous people – has been grafted on to an age-old way of life based on hunting and fishing for survival and fur-trapping for trade. Mining is particularly important in the Yukon, while oil and gas exploration and extraction are carried out throughout the northern Canada. The presence of government is increasingly evident in the larger towns. Yellowknife in the Northwest Territories has been transformed in two decades from a small mining town to an important regional center, with high-rise office buildings and hotels to house public officials and visitors.

Although government of the northern territories has moved significantly toward self-government, with greater inclusion of the Dene and Inuit peoples, economic dependency on external corporate and public sector interests is likely to increase. The struggle of the Dene and Inuit to preserve their land, traditional resources and way of life against modernizing and urbanizing pressures will continue.

Dawson City lies on the Yukon river about 80 km (50 mi) east of the Alaskan border, and serves as the receiving and distribution center for the Klondike mining region.

Quebec, referred to as Main Street – a label that ironically reflects American influences. This urban corridor, which accounts for only 14 percent of the country's occupied land area, contains half of the national population and most of its manufacturing and service industry.

Urban development is not continuous throughout this corridor, but is broken up by areas of farmland, forests and scrub. The agriculture of the area is very profitable – it accounts for 30 percent of national farming receipts. But its rich farmlands are under constant threat from urban expansion.

The two great cities that dominate this urban corridor, Toronto and Montreal, have a long history of rivalry that mirrors the tense relationship between Canada's English-speaking and French-speaking populations. In some respects, the competition seems to have been decided in favor of Toronto, which increasingly dominates the national economy. It is a major focus for immigration – in the early 1980s its growth rate was four times that of Montreal. Unemployment rates are twice as high in Montreal than Toronto, and though living costs – especially housing – are high in Toronto, its citizens earn almost 25 percent more per head than those of Montreal.

Leaving aside economic considerations, if criteria such as cultural vitality and quality of life are considered, then the rivalry is far from over. In the past, it was traditionally expressed through fervent support for the cities' sports teams. However, in the national game of ice hockey the once-proud Toronto Maple Leafs have long ceded superiority to the Montreal Canadiens.

Government and growth
A recent development has been the increasing challenge to Toronto and Montreal's dominance of Main Street by the growing metropolis formed by the two cities of Ottawa and Hull (across the border in Quebec), which now contains nearly 1 million people. Expansion of this

metropolitan area has been fueled by the increasing scope of federal government, with its related employment, since World War II. An increase in the activities of the provincial government of Ontario, the most populous and affluent of the Canadian provinces, also accounts for some of the growth of Toronto, its capital.

Montreal has benefited less directly from public sector growth in Quebec province, since Quebec City is the capital as well as being the seat of the bilingual National Assembly. The latter's metropolitan area has grown rapidly in recent years as the provincial government has become an increasingly critical instrument in the expression of the national identity of the Quebecois. However, Montreal – accounting for almost half of the province's politically important population – has been the beneficiary of considerable federal investment. In response, the provincial government has asserted its physical presence in Montreal's urban landscape by funding the construction of office buildings and public works.

INSIDE THE CITIES

There is a great deal of variety in the architectural forms and styles of Canada's cities, reflecting the different historic, ethnic and cultural influences that have shaped them. The walled center and Citadel of Quebec City is almost medieval in character, as is the old city of Montreal, currently being preserved. In the fishing community of St John's, Newfoundland, brightly colored wooden houses cling to the rocky hillside above the harbor, dominated by a towering basilica. The solid limestone mansions of Kingston, Ontario, are a legacy of the commercial prosperity and political success of the Loyalists, and of later British and German immigrants.

In many Canadian cities, Victorian housing styles predominate in the wide residential streets that were laid out to accommodate the streetcar. However, the bungalow style that became popular in 19th-century Vancouver, influenced by

Colorful mansard roofs (*above*), reflecting strong French influences, in the St Denis area of Montreal are an example of the rich variety of architectural styles and motifs that enliven the older residential districts of Canada's major cities.

Chinatown (*below*) A street of narrow redbrick houses in downtown Toronto has become the center of a thriving Asian community, one of many that are found in cities across the country.

Many of this latter group work in the central business district (CBD) where recent new development has been funded by public and private investment.

These new residential and commercial developments posed a direct threat to the older residential areas of the core city. The middle-class professionals who typically resided in these areas mounted articulate campaigns to preserve their neighborhoods by blocking further expansionary schemes. In some cases they were even able to stop the construction of new expressway systems designed to deliver suburban workers to downtown office complexes. Although modern development continues in the CBD, in the inner areas immediately surrounding it much greater emphasis is now being given to restoring and upgrading existing building stock.

ETHNICITY IN THE CITY

The long-prevailing vision of Canada as a bicultural, bilingual society has been effectively challenged in recent years by the changing pattern of immigration, which has brought people from virtually every continent of the world to swell the numbers of Canada's urban populations. Canada's large cities today are multicultural, multiethnic societies in which a new, less polarized national identity is being asserted.

Residential districts and shopping neighborhoods with distinctive ethnic characters have developed in several of the larger cities, including the suburbs. For example, there is a Chinatown in Vancouver and in many other cities across Canada, Portuguese areas in Toronto, Italian areas in Montreal, Sikh areas in Vancouver and Polish and Ukrainian areas in Winnipeg.

Although there are few ghettos of the kind that house African-American populations in the United States, many of Canada's indigenous peoples live in adverse conditions in inner-city districts in Winnipeg, Edmonton, Regina and other western cities. Effectively excluded from the earlier bicultural vision of Canadian society, they are now actively campaigning for inclusion within the larger multicultural perspective that is emerging.

the western United States, differs sharply from the more densely-built redbrick Victorian houses of Toronto.

The coming of suburbia

The age of the automobile has had major impact on Canadian cities. Since the 1940s urban development has mainly taken the form of low-density, detached homes in the suburbs. These sprawl ever farther from the city center to accommodate an increasingly mobile population. Many suburban housing densities are as low as 30 per hectare (12 per acre).

Industrial enterprises have also moved out to larger, more efficient plants in suburban locations, together with shopping malls and a legion of other private and public services. Thus the out-of-town urban areas of Canada's major cities have come to resemble, on the surface at any rate, the auto-oriented, extensive single-family suburbs that characterize contemporary American cities.

In contrast to the more complex, racially divided inner cities of the United States, those in Canada have not experienced such dramatic declines and have been less adversely affected by suburbanization. There has been an infusion of new investment through the building of highrise apartment complexes to house the elderly, young people and childless couples.

Vitality in the city

The continuation of residential and mixed land-use districts within inner city areas contributes to their vitality. The population in a majority of Canadian cities, buoyed in key instances by worldwide immigration, has more often increased than declined. This distinguishes Canada from the United States. Until the 1970s most new arrivals to the cities came from Europe, including Britain, but then the pattern changed. Growing numbers of immigrants from Asia, the Caribbean and Central and South America have resulted in a more multiracial urban society, and this too helps to make the inner cities lively, vital places.

Canadian cities generally have higher residential densities than their counterparts in the United States. They provide more efficient public transportation, rather than relying on extensive freeway systems, and are safer and better served with public facilities provided by less fragmented municipal government and administration. Nevertheless, with their sprawling suburbs, enormous shopping malls and entertainment complexes, and with the spectacular highrise development of their CBDs, Canadian cities belong to a common North American urban experience that sets them apart from the rest of the world.

Montreal
– city on the St Lawrence

No other city encapsulates the volatile politics of Canada's language issues in quite the same way as Montreal, the largest city of Quebec province. Founded by French settlers in 1642 on a strategic site on the St Lawrence river as a center for the fur trade, Montreal acquired the bicultural and bilingual character it partly retains today when the British displaced the French as the ruling power in Canadian North America in 1763: the settlement's military and ruling elite was British, while the majority of the population were French-speaking "canadiens".

Power remains closely related to language in Montreal. Although English-speakers are numerically smaller – today accounting for about 20 percent of the population – they traditionally filled elite positions in commerce, trade and industry. A French-speaking elite also existed, but was concentrated in the professions, the church and the regional administration. The French-speaking majority was therefore commonly perceived as being economically ruled by a privileged English-speaking minority.

This long-felt inequity provoked a political response during the 1960s and 1970s when the French-speaking majority sought change under the slogan "Masters in our own house", and Quebec's provincial government introduced a number of measures to support it. These included the encouragement of a French-speaking business community, which is now well represented in the skyscrapers of downtown Montreal. The city has been the principal battleground in the struggle to make French the everyday working language in Quebec. During the early 1990s this found expression in a complex, drawn-out legal and political wrangle over commercial signs.

Bicultural city (*right*) From the towering offices of Montreal's CBD, traditionally dominated by English-speaking economic interests, the view sweeps down toward the French-speaking working-class area of the city, with the modern port beyond.

Montreal's strategic site (*below*) on an island in the St Lawrence river has made it Canada's largest port. Joined to the coast by the St Lawrence Seaway, it serves both ocean-going and inland shipping, though it lies 1,600 km (1,000 mi) from the Atlantic.

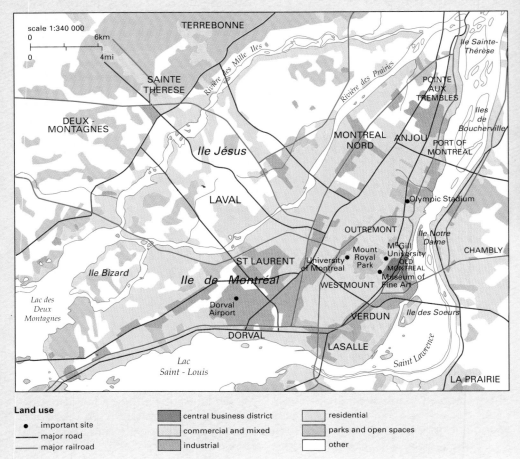

scale 1:340 000

Land use
- important site
- major road
- major railroad

- central business district
- commercial and mixed
- industrial
- residential
- parks and open spaces
- other

Linguistic complexities

Over 1 million of the population speaks only French. A further 1.4 million is bilingual, and the majority of these have French as their first language. It is often claimed that Montreal is the second largest French-speaking city in the world after Paris, and it has acquired a significant place within the global French-speaking community that makes it attractive to a large number of international organizations.

Almost 300,000 speak only English, and they are the most privileged sector of the

population, for a complex institutional structure has developed to meet their needs. English-speaking schools, hospitals, newspapers, radio and television stations, colleges and universities parallel their French-speaking counterparts. Outside the confines of the old city boundaries there are residential enclaves of English-speakers. The district of Westmount, for example, is an affluent community of about 20,000 people.

Within the inner city there is a longstanding division between the English-speaking West End and the larger, poorer working-class French-speaking East End. Between them lies a "buffer" area where recent immigrants to the city live: at present accounting for about 10 percent of the population, the rising numbers of people whose first language is neither English nor French is adding a new layer to the city's linguistic complexity. The social geography of the city and its suburbs gives tangible expression to the interweavings of class, language and power within the city. The tension that underlies these inter-relationships makes Montreal appear an exciting – sometimes even disturbing – city to outsiders.

Montreal faces an uncertain future. It has relatively high level of unemployment, serious pollution and a creaking governmental structure. Economic power has been lost to Toronto, and many Montrealers fear that it has irrevocably slipped to second place in Canada's urban system. Growing numbers believe that the longterm solution is for Montreal to become the leading center of an autonomous Quebec within a restructured political system encompassing the whole of North America.

Living by the sea

In 1497 the Italian-born sailor John Cabot (c. 1450–c. 1499), in the service of the English crown, made landfall on the coast of Newfoundland or southern Labrador. Like Christopher Columbus only five years before, he had sailed west in search of a route to the Far East. The wealth he discovered was more prosaic than gold and exotic spices: fish. He told of schools of cod so large they stopped his ships from passing. Once news of his discovery spread, fishing fleets sailed regularly to the rich fishing grounds of the North Atlantic from England, France and Portugal, but stayed only long enough to salt their catch before returning home.

Permanent settlement in Canada's Maritime Provinces dates from the French colony of Acadia, established in 1605. In 1629 the British set up a rival settlement nearby that they named Nova Scotia – New Scotland. Fishing villages, notable for their brightly colored wooden houses, grew up around the rocky coasts. It was a hard life, and the small coummunities – far from large centers of urbanization – remained self-sufficient and close-knit.

In recent decades the prosperity of the Maritime Provinces has fallen behind that of the central and western regions of Canada. Seasonal unemployment in fishing and logging is high, and regional income is one of the lowest in Canada. Throughout the 20th century there has been a steady flow of emigration from the provinces to the United States and, more recently, to the urban industrial centers of Canada.

In Newfoundland, where there were about 1,300 coastal villages, government programs have favored the creation of larger concentrations of population to make more economically viable communities. Over half the population is now classified as urban, with the greater number living in the metropolitan areas of St John's and Corner Brook.

Fishing memorial A whale's jawbone decorates the doorway of a traditional fisherman's house, now in the Fisheries Museum of Nova Scotia.

GOVERNMENT

Two European nations – Britain and France – were the earliest colonizers of Canada. Rivalry between them was great from the 17th century onward. Britain eventually acquired all France's possessions, and in 1791 the territory was divided into English-speaking Upper Canada and French-speaking Lower Canada. As the provinces of Ontario and Quebec they formed the federal Dominion of Canada in 1867, with Nova Scotia and New Brunswick. Westward expansion was rapid, reaching across the continent when British Columbia joined the Dominion in 1871. By 1905 four more provinces had been added; Newfoundland (a British colony since 1583) voted in 1949 to become the tenth. There are also two national territories, the Yukon Territory and the Northwest Territories, administered by the federal government.

COUNTRIES IN THE REGION

Canada

Dependencies of other states Greenland (Denmark); St Pierre and Miquelon (France)

STYLES OF GOVERNMENT

Monarchy Canada

Federal state Canada

Multi-party state Canada

Two-chamber assembly Canada

CONFLICTS (since 1945)

Nationalist movement Canada (Quebec)

MEMBERSHIP OF INTERNATIONAL ORGANIZATIONS

Colombo Plan Canada

North Atlantic Treaty Organization (NATO) Canada

Organization for Economic Cooperation and Development (OECD) Canada

Note: Greenland remains part of the Danish realm but acquired self-governing status in 1981.

WHAT IS A CANADIAN?

Canada's sheer size always presented something of an obstacle to national integration. Most Canadian citizens live within 320 km (200 mi) of the border with the United States, the world's longest undefended boundary. Regional interests have always tended to override wider national interests; the western provinces in particular have traditionally looked toward the United States not only for economic markets and investment but also for cultural ideas.

Rail links across the continent were built with the political aim of welding the western provinces more effectively into the young state structure, and to counter the northernward thrust of commercial interests from the United States. In the event, however, their construction had the effect of consolidating the political and economic dominance of the central provinces of Quebec and Ontario over the small, less developed maritime provinces in the east and the sparsely populated, though increasingly rich, western prairie provinces.

From the beginning, Canada's federal system of government (modeled on that of its giant neighbor, the United States) took account of the need to guarantee the rights of the French Canadian community within Quebec. Constitutional undertakings were given to protect the French language, the Roman Catholic church and the French tradition of civil law. This enabled a well-developed sense of ethnic community to survive within French Quebec, which expressed itself politically in periodic demands for either a renegotiated position within the confederation or secession from it.

A diverse population

The indigenous Inuit (once known as Eskimo) and Amerindian population probably numbered about 220,000 before the arrival of European settlers. It declined considerably afterward, until improved medical care and living conditions raised levels again in the present century. Growing protest led to increased opportunities for Amerindians – particularly those living on reserves (to whom the franchise was extended only in 1960) – to influence decisions affecting their own lives. The Nunavik district of northern Quebec has been designated as a homeland for the Inuit people.

During the initial period of settlement

Pierre Trudeau's colorful personality made him highly popular; he was elected to office four times between 1969 and 1984. His premiership saw a number of important political changes. Equal status was given to French and to English, and his vigorous defense of federalism defeated Quebec separatism.

in Canada until World War I, the population grew from 3 million to just over 7 million. Immigrants, who came mostly from Britain, northwestern Europe and the United States, settled first in eastern Canada, but efforts were later made to encourage settlement of the grasslands of the prairies to the west, particularly by farmers and others from central Europe. After World War II more than 4 million immigrants, many from Africa, Asia and Latin America, entered the country; they settled mainly in the urban centers of central Canada.

Most of the newcomers, who were assimilated rapidly into Canadian life, identified themselves by and large with the Anglo-Saxon, or British, cultural tradition. This heightened dissatisfaction among the French-speaking community, which came to feel that its interests were no longer central to Canadian national concerns and federal policy. As a result of increasing pressure for the separation of Quebec during the 1960s, Canada witnessed one of the most exhaustive debates on national identity ever carried out within a democratic society.

The Official Language Act

Under the premiership of Pierre Elliott Trudeau (Liberal prime minister 1968–79, 1980–84), who was a convinced federalist and opponent of separation though himself a Québécois, the Official Language Act, which made Canada a bilingual and bicultural state, was passed in 1969. The granting of equal status to English and French continued to be vigorously opposed by many people in western

The Canada Act, passed in 1982, established Canada's independence from the British parliament, which until then had the task of ratifying all constitutional changes made by the Canadian parliament. Like all legal and other official documents, it is written in both English and French.

A peaceful dominion The stability of Canada's territorial boundaries means that it has fought no major wars of its own making since the 18th century. Its great size posed problems of integration during the early years of westward expansion; the building of transcontinental railroads strengthened the dominance of Ontario and Quebec. In 1977 Canada extended its maritime limits to 370 km (200 nautical mi) to include resource-rich areas of the Arctic sea floor. These claims are disputed by the United States.

Canada, who argued that bilingualism was an eastern preoccupation, and that German or Ukrainian had a greater claim than French to be made the second official language of the prairie provinces.

Efforts were therefore made to place Canada's bilingual and bicultural policies within a multicultural framework that would recognize the permanent and positive contribution of other minority ethnic groups to Canada's national life. Nonetheless, regional and ethnic tensions made themselves felt in the opposition to the Meech Lake constitutional accord proposed by Prime Minister Brian Mulroney, which among other things asserted that Quebec is a distinct society within Canada. The failure of all ten provinces to ratify the clauses of the accord in June 1990 was prompted by the desire of some of them to wrest a number of further concessions for their own ethnic and indigenous minorities.

In 1992, new constitutional proposals put forward by the government to recognize Quebec's distinct status were rejected in a national referendum, amid strengthening demand in Quebec for separatism from the rest of Canada. The debate about national identity, regional competition and the division between federal and provincial authority – carried on in a more or less harmonious fashion – showed little sign of abating.

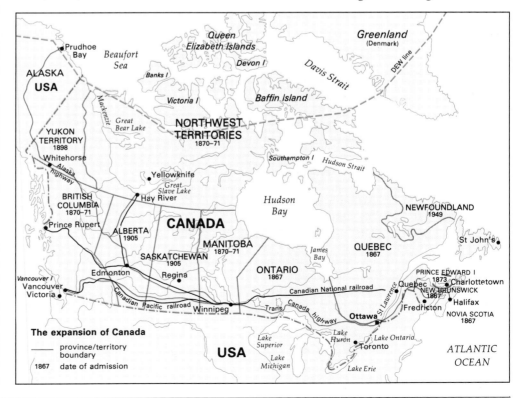

The expansion of Canada
— province/territory boundary
1867 date of admission

A PARLIAMENTARY FEDERAL SYSTEM

Canada's style of parliamentary democracy is based on the British model. The federal parliament in Ottawa, Ontario consists of a lower house (the house of commons), elected from single-member constituencies called ridings, and an appointed upper house (the senate). The head of state is the British monarch, represented by a governor-general who appoints the prime minister and cabinet from the party that has most support in the house of commons. The crown also has a representative in each province in the lieutenant governor. Each of the ten provinces has its own elected single-chamber legislature with a prime minister and cabinet. In the two territories there are locally elected councils that work with a commissioner appointed by the federal government.

Federal and provincial government

The federal government has exclusive or dominant power over external affairs, defense, commerce, finance and criminal justice. The provincial governments are responsible for education, health, social services and civil justice. Federal involvement in provincial matters has been seen to be increasing, especially with regard to the development and management of local resources.

Since World War II relations between federal and provincial government have been strained by a number of issues. These include the debate over Canadian identity and the question of Quebec separatism. A particular problem has been posed by the rapid development of the resource-rich western provinces; for example, Alberta has at times sought greater autonomy for itself, stretching the concept of federalism to its limit. By contrast, the poorer maritime provinces have attempted to secure more concessions and a greater share of federal tax revenues for themselves.

Underlying all these tensions were Canada's persistent efforts to disengage itself from political dependence on Britain. Not until 1982, with the passing of the Canada (or Constitution) Act, did Canada gain total control over its constitution (patriation). Before that date all constitutional changes agreed in the Canadian parliament had to be ratified by

the British parliament before becoming law. The new Act incorporated a charter of rights and freedoms.

Quebec – the key to electoral success

In the past the two main parties – the Liberals and the Conservatives (later the Progressive Conservatives) – received three-quarters of the votes cast in federal elections. The rest went to the third party, the New Democratic Party, and to minor parties. The party system at national level has been described as a "stable two and a half party system".

The Liberals have enjoyed long, unbroken periods in power this century, most notably from 1935 to 1957, and from

A powerful neighbor Canada's former premier, Brian Mulroney with George Bush, then vice president of the United States. Mulroney made the Free Trade Agreement with the United States an election issue in 1988 and won. In 1993 Canada's new liberal prime minister, Jean Chrétien, determined to renegotiate aspects of the Agreement arguing that free trade with Mexico had been obtained at the expense of protectionist measures against Canada.

1963 to 1979. For most of this time the Conservatives – identified as the party of the British interest – failed to win votes in Quebec. It gained fewer than ten seats here in nearly every general election from 1917 to 1958, and it was not unusual for the Liberals to have an absolute majority in Quebec while the rest of Canada favored the other parties.

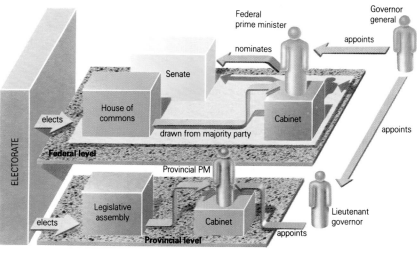

Canada's system of government has grafted the federalism of the neighboring United States onto a parliamentary system modeled on that of the British. The two-chamber federal parliament consists of the senate, whose 104 members are appointed for life, and the 282-member house of commons, elected for a maximum of five years. Legislation must be passed by both houses to become law.

The parliament building in Ottawa was built in Gothic style in homage to the British Houses of Parliament, from which its procedures were borrowed. It stands at the top of Parliament Hill dominating the city of Ottawa in southeastern Ontario, which was chosen as Canada's political and administrative capital by Queen Victoria in 1858.

The 1980s saw a reversal of this traditional arrangement. In 1980 the Progressive Conservatives held only one seat in Quebec, the Liberals 74. In the general election of 1988 the Progressive Conservatives, led by Prime Minister Brian Mulroney, won 63 seats – a truly remarkable turnabout.

The Liberal stranglehold on Quebec provided the national support base for Trudeau's two administrations, from 1968 to 1979 and from 1980 to 1984. These years saw the establishment of a strong federal government, in which the separatist demands of Quebec and regionalist pressure from the western provinces were recognized – and were met head on. Toward the end of his second period in office Trudeau's policies were more and more characterized by their vigorous defense of Canadian economic nationalism in the face of the increasing commercial pressure from the United States.

His successor, Brian Mulroney – like Trudeau, a lawyer from Quebec – turned these policies around. He became prime minister in 1984, when the Conservatives were elected with the largest parliamentary majority in Canadian history. The 1988 general election, fought on the issue of a comprehensive Free Trade Agreement (FTA) with the United States, gave the Progressive Conservatives a 45-seat majority in the house of commons (though only 43 percent of the votes cast).

However, continued economic and ethnic difficulties contributed to a drastic fall in Conservative popularity and in 1993 the Liberals presided over a crushing electoral defeat for the Conservatives who retained only two seats in the house of commons. Jean Chrétien headed the new Liberal government and immediately announced his intention to renegotiate aspects of the Free Trade Agreement in order to secure better terms for Canada, in particular to reduce the likelihood of punitive trade sanctions.

THE PROVINCIAL LEVEL OF GOVERNMENT

Canada's ten provincial governments mirror in structure its federal government. Each lieutenant governor is appointed by the federal cabinet on the advice of the prime minister; they represent the crown by summoning and dissolving the provincial assemblies, and by assenting to provincial legislation. It is an important and potentially powerful office, though in practice no lieutenant governor would act against the advice of the provincial premier or cabinet except in extraordinary circumstances.

The legislative assemblies and their various governmental departments are supported by a burgeoning civil service. This is responsible for providing services at provincial level, and for staffing provincial government enterprises, boards and agencies. With the employees of school boards, municipalities and hospitals they add up to some 75 percent of all Canada's public employees. Provincial government thus touches closely on the lives of very many Canadians. A large number of people, particularly regionalists and other disaffected citizens, have a greater sense of identity with it than

they do with federal government, which is frequently perceived as a distant, intrusive element in their lives. Several provincial governments have sought ways of directly involving their citizens in the formulation of policy.

Vast differences exist in the capacity of individual provinces to harmonize national standards of health care and the provision of education and social services. Prince Edward Island, for example, with a total population of only 128,000, can hardly be compared with the two largest provinces: Ontario (9 million) or Quebec (6.5 million).

The provincial government may be formed by a different party from the majority party representing the province in the federal parliament. Some sophisticated electoral behavior may be involved in this. For example, in the period after 1976 voters in Quebec chose the autonomist Parti Québécois at provincial level, but the Liberals at federal level. The third national party, the New Democractic Party, also performs well in provincial elections, and has formed governments in British Columbia (1972–75), Saskatchewan (1944–64) and Manitoba (1969–77, 1981).

THE CANADIAN PERSPECTIVE IN NORTH AMERICA

The single most important factor that affects Canada's external relations is the presence of the economic giant of the United States to the south. Wary of being drawn into its continental influence, Canadians have at the same time been irresistibly attracted by its cultural and material dynamism. Canada and the United States are each other's largest trading partners in goods, services, capital and manpower: three-quarters of Canada's trade is with the United States. But the exchange is clearly unequal, as the United States' economy is ten times larger than that of Canada. To capitalize on this degree of economic dependence the Free Trade Agreement (FTA) was signed with the United States in 1988 (and ratified by the Canadian parliament in 1989).

Defense strategies

Since the end of World War II Canada has been a partner in United States' military defense policies as well as in the economic sphere: it occupies a vital strategic position between the United States and the Soviet Union over the polar ice cap. Under the North American Defense Agreement (NORAD) of 1957, renamed the North American Aerospace Defense Command in 1981, the United States and Canada's air defense forces are integrated in a joint command system with head-

A radar station on the Distant Early Warning (DEW) line, which runs from Alaska across northern Canada was a major component of NORAD's defenses to protect the North American continent against Soviet long-range missile attack.

quarters at Colorado Springs, Colorado. A Canadian officer always serves as the deputy commander.

In 1949 the Canadian government supported the United States' proposal for an alliance of Western European and North American powers – the North Atlantic Treaty Organization (NATO) – that would

Working for peace between nations Since 1945 Canadian forces have served with the United Nations in many trouble spots in an effort to reconcile warring factions, and Canada has been a strong supporter of UN initiatives to aid the Third World.

provide for the collective defense of its member states from the perceived threat of Soviet domination in Eastern Europe. At Canada's insistence, Article 2 of the treaty (sometimes called the "Canadian article") gave a political and economic, as well as a military, dimension to the alliance. However, it has never been put to any significant use.

The discovery of potentially rich oil reserves in the Arctic Ocean reactivated Canada's claims to sovereignty over the icebound Arctic archipelago and all waters within 370 km (200 nautical mi) of the Canadian coastline, the counter interest of its southern neighbor and key defense partner notwithstanding. The United States recognizes Canada's coastal jurisdiction as extending over only a 20 km (12 mi) zone. The growing pollution of these Arctic waters is an enduring concern of the Canadian government.

In the past, Canada's historical links with Britain also helped to shape its external policies. Until World War II Britain and the United States frequently alternated as Canada's first and second most important trading partners. Canada now sends less than 5 percent of its exports to Britain, which accounts for just over 3 percent of its total imports. Japan has replaced Britain as Canada's second largest trading partner. Although most Canadians still regard Britain as an important part of their national heritage, the link has been given less and less political expression since the patriation of the Canadian constitution in 1982. In the same period closer ties have been nurtured with the worldwide association of French-speaking states.

An independent actor

Canada has attempted to distance itself from its image of being merely a northern outpost of the United States. Building on its connections with the Commonwealth and the community of French-speaking states it has sought a role as a middle-ranking power with global presence, prepared to take a responsible role in the resolution of worldwide conflicts. In the frequently uneasy period of decolonization after World War II troops and resources were committed to the joint security missions of the United Nations, and more recently Canada has been a powerful advocate of Third World needs.

Canada's strong commitment to the international community was initially

A base at Thule, on Baffin Bay in northern Greenland, is shared with the United States and forms part of the Arctic line of defense. Greenland is a self-governing province of Denmark, which is a member of NATO.

fostered by Lester Pearson (1897–1972), as foreign minister from 1948 to 1957 and as prime minister from 1963 to 1968. Pierre Trudeau subsequently developed these policies by establishing closer relations with many Third World states. In the early 1970s Canada supported the application of the People's Republic of China for a seat in the UN, and arranged wheat sales at preferential prices to ward off the worst ravages of the Chinese famine.

Successive governments since then have championed the cause of the developing nations of the South in the North–South dialogue by arguing for radical change in international terms of trade. Canada has continued to undertake humanitarian relief programs and to grant asylum to political refugees. It has promoted human rights campaigns to secure individual freedom as well as environmental programs aimed at ensuring global survival.

CANADA'S ARCTIC FRONTIER

In August 1985 the US Coastguard icebreaker *Polar Sea* sailed through the Northwest Passage. Its voyage through the strait, recognized by the United States as an international waterway, was in defiance of Canada's claims to sovereignty and produced a surge of Canadian national pride, leading to a series of measures aimed at strengthening Canada's hold in the Arctic.

The Arctic assumed significance as a bulwark against long-range missile attack across the polar ice cap at the onset of the Cold War period of East–West hostility in the late 1940s and 1950s. Awareness of the area's strategic importance was publicly expressed in the 1947 agreement with the United States to establish five joint weather stations in the Arctic islands, the construction of the Distant Early Warning (DEW) Line and Mid-Canada Line between 1955 and 1957, and in Canada's continuing commitment to its NATO and NORAD obligations.

However, Canadian public opinion was more consciously concerned with the activities of its southern neighbor in the area, and recent recognition of the Arctic's vast natural resource potential translated a rather passive defense policy into a fully fledged assertion of national sovereignty.

The *Polar Sea* incident showed that Canadian claims could not be enforced against challenge by the United States. Implementation of the planned measures to be taken to extend Canada's jurisdiction in the eastern Arctic included the acquisition of a force of between 10 and 12 nuclear-powered submarines to carry out sustained operations beneath the ice. In all, the package would require a growth in defense budgets of 2 percent in real terms for the next 15 years, and many questioned whether these targets could realistically be met.

With the ending of the Cold War the Canadian Arctic ceased to be a superpower buffer zone. This focused attention more sharply on the sovereignty issue, as the Canadian government finds ways to develop the area's resource potential while seeking to safeguard its environment.

Quebec: the French factor

The French colonization of Quebec took place in the first half of the 17th century, when some 10,000 French people came to settle on the shores of the St Lawrence river. After 1763, when the colony of New France was lost to the British, antagonism between the numerically dominant French-speaking and the economically dominant English-speaking populations was high. Quebec has fought hard to maintain itself as a distinct society.

Today about 80 percent of Quebec's population is French-speaking. In Montreal, Canada's leading banking city, where nearly half of Quebec's population lives, the figure drops to 68 percent. Historically most economic activities in Quebec were controlled by English speakers. It was the exclusion of French Canadians from economic and political life that kept alive the cause of Quebec nationalism.

In the early 1960s Quebec's Liberal prime minister, Jean Lesage (1912–80), conceived and directed the "quiet revolution", which successfully strengthened the powers of Quebec's provincial government by attacking the control of the Roman Catholic church hierarchy over education and the professions. Quebec was revolutionized and modernized. Social attitudes changed markedly, and a new generation of teachers, scientists, businessmen and accountants chose to use the French language, rather than English, in schools and universities, in the workplace and elsewhere.

Revived nationalist aspirations in Quebec, the cultural cradle of the French tradition in Canada, seemed to beckon in two directions. There were those like Lesage, who favored gradual social reform and language legislation – a policy summarized by the term *rattrapage*, to catch up – while remaining within the federal system. Others, led by René Lévesque, a former cabinet minister in Lesage's government, came to seek separate sovereign status for Quebec.

In 1967 Lévesque split with the Liberals to found the separatist Parti Québécois (PQ). As Lesage's revolution seemed to falter, the popularity of the PQ increased. It won power in 1976 with a program to give Quebec self-governing sovereign status while maintaining close economic ties with Canada (Sovereignty–Association). Although rejected by 60 percent of voters in a referendum in May 1980, the PQ was re-elected in 1981. Three bills

Stopping in two languages
Bilingualism did not receive an enthusiastic welcome everywhere – to many Canadians, particularly in the western provinces, it was an irrelevancy. Some English speakers in Quebec feel that legal measures to make French the sole language on public signs in the province erode their own language rights.

René Lévesque addresses a rally of the Parti Québécois, the party he helped to found in 1968 after he split with the Liberal Party led by Jean Lesage. Lévesque quickly built up a strong popular following for his democratic socialist policies and for his advocacy of Quebec separation, winning over a significant number of English speakers and supporters from other ethnic groups. Once in power, however, his measure to give Quebec sovereignty status was rejected. In 1985 the party voted to set aside the goal of separation for the foreseeable future, and Lévesque resigned.

passed by the Liberal government in the 1970s had strengthened French language rights. The PQ took these cultural policies even further, but alienation of the English-speaking minority and of many New Canadians, coupled with the threat of economic recession, led to their defeat by the Liberals in 1985.

In the late 1980s attention centered on the Meech Lake accord, which proposed assigning a special constitutional position to Quebec as a "distinct society" within Canada. Further extension of French language rights included a measure that all public signs on the outside of buildings should be in French only. This provoked a strong response from English-speakers, who argued that their right to their own language was being eroded within Quebec. Controversy over the accord brought the threat of Quebec's secession into sharp focus again. In 1992 a nationwide referendum to endorse Quebec's special status within Canada was rejected by a majority of Canadians. Those in Quebec voting against sought a greater degree of separation; many of those outside, particularly in the western and maritime provinces, wanted the same recognition for themselves.

Quebec's success

Quebec's language policies and its attempts to differentiate itself from other parts of Canada are often interpreted as cultural perversity and intransigence that

fly against current trends, but Quebec today is one of the most progressive and modern of Canadian provinces. It has an active energy and resource development program, based on its hydroelectricity, a fine record on social welfare, pension rights, medical provision and education, and a confidence in self-directed social change that others might envy.

Quebec has almost come to act as a sovereign state on the international stage. It has championed the rights of French speakers throughout the world, and has materially furthered both French culture and Canadian economic development. By challenging the Anglo-conformist basis of Canadian statehood, Quebec strengthened the bilingual and bicultural character of Canadian society, moving Canada farther away from its British past as well as from the assimilationist trends emanating from the United States.

Reevaluation of the cultural bases of Canadian identity also helped to redefine the role of its citizens of non-British and non-French ethnic origin, particularly Native Indians, Canada's policy of multiculturalism within a bicultural context offers a promising means to achieve state harmony without destroying group cultural identity. The majority of Canadians may not have realized it at the time, but Quebec's challenge in questioning the very foundation of Canadian statehood was the catalyst that produced this more open and honest approach.

ENVIRONMENTAL ISSUES

IMPRINTS ON THE LAND · THREATS TO LAND AND WATER · ADDRESSING THE PROBLEMS

Although Canada's natural resources have only been exploited on a significant scale for about 200 years, the region is not without serious environmental problems. Acid rain, originating from the highly industrialized, urbanized south, has blighted lakes, rivers and forests, while intensive agriculture in the prairie wheat belt has caused severe soil erosion. The vast northern wilderness is vulnerable to soil erosion from logging, and pollution from mining and oil drilling. Wildlife and the lifestyles of the indigenous peoples across the region have been threatened, for example, by huge hydroelectric schemes. However, there is strong local and national environmental awareness. In 1992, the Canadian government announced a 5-year, $3 billion program to clean up and protect the country's air, water and land.

IMPRINTS ON THE LAND

Long before Canada came under the re-shaping hands of the first European settlers in the early 17th century, the region was inhabited by indigenous peoples whose attitudes to the land and its riches were quite different. Native Indians and Inuit lived in harmony with their environment, utilizing its wealth, but not destroying it.

European settlement, located mainly in the south of Canada along what is now the border with the United States, profoundly changed the look of much of the country. It was the railroads that made this possible. In 1885 the 7,000 km (4,350 mi) long Canadian Pacific Railway (CPR) was completed, linking both sides of the continent and opening up the Canadian West to largescale exploitation. By the end of the century, immigrants from Europe were turning the flat prairies of Manitoba, Saskatchewan and Alberta – once home to Native Indians and great herds of buffalo – into vast seas of wheat.

The wheat fields of the prairie provinces have been a huge success in economic terms; in the late 1980s they produced 40 million tonnes of grain annually. But environmentally they have proved a disaster. Soil erosion, loss of soil fertility and the consequent over-reliance on chemical fertilizers and pesticides to maintain or improve productivity – often leading to river and groundwater pollution – are some of the major problems facing Canadian farmers and the environment today.

COUNTRIES IN THE REGION	
Canada	
POPULATION AND WEALTH	
Population (millions)	26.6
Population increase (annual population growth rate, % 1960–90)	1.3
Energy use (gigajoules/person)	291
Real purchasing power (US$/person)	17,680
ENVIRONMENTAL INDICATORS	
CO₂ emissions (million tonnes carbon/annum)	120
Municipal waste (kg/person/annum)	630
Nuclear waste (cumulative tonnes heavy metal)	11,000
Artificial fertilizer use (kg/ha/annum)	48
Automobiles (per 1,000 population)	432
Access to safe drinking water (% population)	100

MAJOR ENVIRONMENTAL PROBLEMS AND SOURCES

Air pollution: urban high; acid rain prevalent; high greenhouse gas emissions
River/lake pollution: medium; *sources*: agricultural, sewage, acid deposition
Land pollution: local; *sources*: industrial, urban/household
Waste disposal problems: domestic; industrial; nuclear
Major events: Mississauga (1979), chlorine gas leak during transportation; Saint Basile le Grand (1988), toxic cloud from waste dump fire

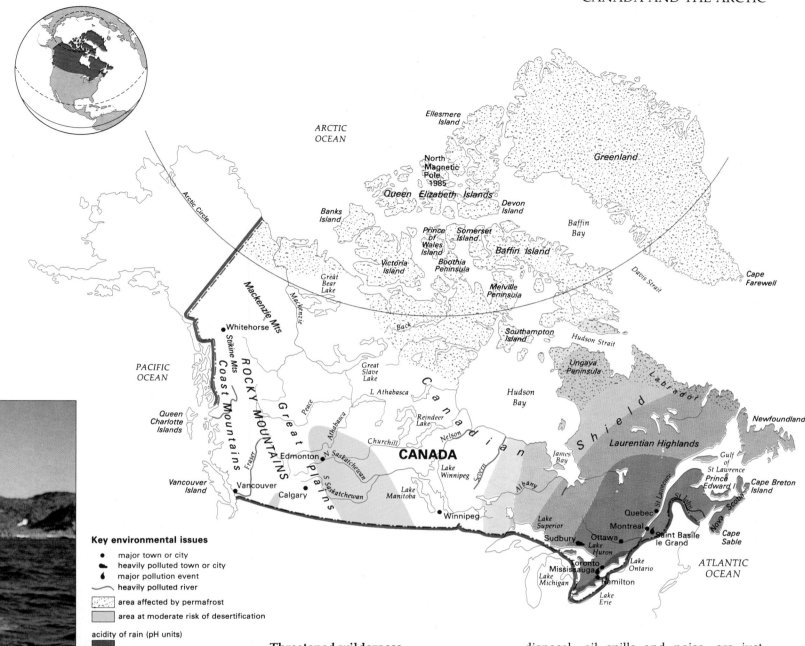

Key environmental issues

- ● major town or city
- heavily polluted town or city
- major pollution event
- ～ heavily polluted river
- ⦂⦂⦂ area affected by permafrost
- area at moderate risk of desertification

acidity of rain (pH units)

- 4.2 (most acidic)
- 4.4
- 4.6
- 4.8 (least acidic)

Map of environmental problems
(*above*) Global warming threatens the huge permafrost and Arctic areas of the far north, while farther south acid rain is having a major impact on eastern forests, and the western prairie provinces are increasingly at risk of desertification.

Politically or environmentally correct? (*left*) An Inuit fisherman brings in a ringed seal on Cumberland Sound, Northwest Territories. The fight to preserve the Inuits' traditional lifestyle has come into conflict with environmental issues: hunting seals is crucial to the Inuit diet and culture, but the sale of sealskin – a key source of revenue in their marginal economy – has been banned, and the skins must now all go to waste.

Threatened wilderness

Some 60 percent of Canada's 26 million people are concentrated in the corridor of urban development between Windsor, Ontario and Quebec City in the central southeast – only 5 percent of the total land area. This highly industrialized area is the source of considerable pollution of air and water. The country's vast subarctic and arctic areas, by contrast, are still relatively untouched; the isolation, the difficult terrain, mosquitoes and bitterly cold weather have acted as a deterrent to settlement and exploitation.

Nevertheless, though there are few settlements of significant size in the Yukon and Northwest Territories (the largest being Whitehorse in the Yukon, with a population of some 19,000), the area has been increasingly exploited for its mineral resources such as oil, copper, silver, lead, zinc and uranium. Largescale mineral extraction, together with waste disposal, oil spills and noise, are just some of the problems that now pose a serious environmental threat to the unique and fragile habitats of the Canadian Arctic. Global warming, a worldwide problem, is likely to affect the Arctic more seriously than elsewhere.

The original inhabitants of the Arctic, the Inuit, did not have to contend with such problems. As hunters who respected nature they had a strong empathy with their environment. Hunting and fishing provided a subsistence living. In recent decades, however, their traditional way of life has come under increasing pressure. The Inuit population density has always been low – roughly one person to every 1,000 sq km (400 sq mi). According to archaeologists, the number of Inuit living on the south coast of Baffin Island some 4,000 years ago was probably no more than about 100 to 150. By 1984 the figure had risen to just 290.

THREATS TO LAND AND WATER

Although Canada's industry is concentrated in a relatively small area, the country's vast wilderness regions are increasingly vulnerable to wind-blown air pollutants from the industrial south. In the Arctic zone these are increasingly noticeable as a thick haze over the land. In southeastern Canada acid rain or acid snow are common. They form when sulfur dioxide and nitrogen oxides – emitted by ore smelters, power stations and automobiles – react with water vapor in the atmosphere. Among the worst offenders within the region are the smelters of Sudbury, Ontario (the world's largest producer of nickel), which emit huge quantities of sulfur dioxide. Cross-border pollution from the United States exacerbates the situation. Canada now receives some 3.2 million tonnes of pollutants a year from the United States (almost twice as much as the United States receive from Canada).

As a result of this extensive aerial pollution, millions of trees in Canada's eastern forests (including sugar maples, vital to Canada's maple syrup industry) are sick or dying. The leaves or needles of affected trees turn yellow and drop off, while vital plant nutrients are leached from the soil. In addition, more than 14,000 Canadian lakes have now been pronounced "dead" as a result of acid rain; the acidity level of the water is too high to support most forms of aquatic life.

The Great Lakes on Canada's southeastern border have not only been affected by increased acidity; more than 300 toxic chemicals have been recorded in the water. Lake Erie, in particular, has undergone a catastrophic decline in water quality since the 1950s: urban, industrial and agricultural effluents turned parts of it into something approaching the state of an open sewer, and it is only now slowly beginning to recover.

Poisons in the food chain

The Canadian government recognized the grave dangers of waterborne pollution to human health in its "Green Plan", a comprehensive report on the state of the country's environment issued in April 1992: "Fish with tumors and diseases caused by toxins in water, birds with crossed bills and other deformities caused

A GIANT HYDROELECTRIC CONTROVERSY

Hydroelectric power is generally considered to be healthier for the environment than fossil fuel power generated from the burning of coal, oil or gas. However, although HEP produces none of the harmful sulfur emissions of fossil fuels, on a local scale it can be devastating to the environment. The world's largest hydroelectric project at James Bay, in northern Quebec, provides a striking example.

The first stage, completed in 1985, required the building of several dams along the La Grande river, which runs into James Bay. Its effect was to flood 30,000 sq km (11,600 sq mi) of Cree Indian hunting territory. This not only disrupted the Native Indians' tradi-

tional way of life, but also threatened their health: a dramatic rise in mercury levels in the reservoirs (caused by bacteria working on the inundated, mercury-rich vegetation) has poisoned the fish that form a major part of the Indians' diet.

The completed project – which will affect an area the size of France – could increase the salinity of James Bay and threaten its rich wildlife. However, the prospect of further flooding and diversion of rivers led to such strong protests from Native Indians and conservationists alike that in 1991 the second stage of the project was halted by the Canadian government pending an environmental review.

Hungry polar bears (*above*) raid a rubbish dump near an Arctic village. Waste disposal in the cold north is a problem since it cannot be buried and takes a long time to decompose. Dump sites, therefore, provide bears with opportunities to forage for food. The town of Churchill on Hudson Bay even draws tourists to observe the bears raiding the local dump. The bears are often captured and moved away to prevent them from being shot by frightened residents.

Disfiguring the landscape (*left*), a modern village in arctic Quebec surrounded by unsightly tracks in the permafrost. Recovery time from environmental damage in this fragile landscape is painfully slow: vehicle tracks can remain carved into the frozen land for a decade or more after just one vehicle has crossed the winter snow. Arctic tundra plants are extremely sensitive and very slow growing.

by eating contaminated fish, and reproductive failures in mammals feeding on the top predators of the aquatic food web all suggest that human health may be in jeopardy".

Studies of mercury levels in the food chain have highlighted the dangers. Under acidic conditions, bacteria living in the mud at the bottom of lakes can convert naturally occurring mercury into methyl mercury, which is highly toxic. Its noxious effect is magnified as it passes up the food chain. Plankton, for example, may take up only 0.05 parts per million (ppm) in their bodies, but this is concentrated to 0.25 ppm in small fishes and 2.0 ppm in the large fish that feed on them. The uptake of mercury in fish-eating birds and mammals can reach 15.0 ppm.

In humans, high levels can cause liver, kidney or brain damage, and can produce birth defects. In the St Lawrence river, Beluga whales are so contaminated with pollutants that their bodies are regarded as toxic waste.

In the Arctic, pollution in the food chain has reached alarming proportions. High levels of toxic chemicals have been found in all life forms – from zooplankton, through to fish, seals, polar bears and the Inuit themselves, who absorb the chemicals from the animals they eat. The worst contaminants are PCBs (polychlorinated biphenyls) – compounds that are used especially in the manufacture of electrical transformers. Some PCBs are carried by air currents to the polar region from industrialized areas farther south,

while others from marine paint on the hulls of ships pollute the water. In the early 1990s, the breast-milk of Inuit mothers was found to contain five times the level of PCBs found in mothers in southern Canada. The effects include damage to the immune systems of new-born babies, making them vulnerable to disease and infections.

Across northern Canada the land is strewn with hazardous waste from mines and military bases: rusting fuel and chemical drums, dumped into rivers and lakes, stand empty, their contents long since leaked into the water. Rivers downstream of settlements such as Whitehorse are also polluted by untreated sewage.

Perils of development

Massive logging of the great Canadian forests is having a devastating effect on the land. According to the government's Green Plan, the old growth forests of British Columbia in the far west may disappear by 2008. The results will include widespread soil erosion, landslides, the loss of unique animal and plant species, and perhaps a deleterious effect on climate stability.

In the wheatfields of the western prairies, intensive agriculture – including the application of over 1 million tonnes of phosphates and nitrogenous fertilizers on the land annually – has seriously reduced the binding power of the soil. As a result, the prairie soil has lost up to half of its original organic matter, making it vulnerable to erosion by wind and rain. Soil loss costs Canadian farmers between $500 million and $900 million (Canadian) in lost production every year.

ADDRESSING THE PROBLEMS

Since the 1980s Canadian environmental groups have been increasingly vocal in expressing their concern about the country's forests, soil, air and water. The Canadian government's Green Plan took a significant step forward in terms of confronting the issues of environmental deterioration. The government agreed to provide some $3 billion over 5 years in a program to reduce solid waste and eliminate pollutants from the air, land and water; cut back on greenhouse gases and ozone-depleting chemicals; encourage ecologically sound logging, fishing and farming; purchase lands for national parks; and provide for environmental education and research, as well as "outreach" programs to Native Indians and nongovernmental organizations. In addition, in June 1991 the government recognized the importance of preserving Canada's natural heritage when it voted unanimously to protect 12 percent of the country in its pristine state.

Heightened national awareness
A new attitude to the environment can be seen in various areas of development. Typical of the new environmentally sensitive approach to major engineering projects has been the Canadian Pacific Railway route across Rogers Pass in the Rocky Mountains of British Columbia. Completed in 1989, this project was undertaken within the ecologically sensitive Glacier National Park. Before any work was done, there were exhaustive evaluations of the vegetation, fish and other wildlife of the area, the impact of the route on rivers, the possibility of increased erosion and the potential impact of noise and visual disturbance. The effects of construction were monitored throughout, and more than 1 million trees and shrubs were planted after the project was completed.

Replanting is a priority, too, for the British Columbia logging industry. Although the province contains only 2 percent of Canada's forests, it accounts for 25 percent of the country's timber production – much of this from the old growth forests. However, the early period of exploitative clear-cutting without replanting ended over half a century ago. Today British Columbia replants 50 percent of felled sites.

In some areas, progress in environmental protection has only been made very recently and in response to specific threats. In Prince Edward Island, Canada's smallest province, situated in the Gulf of St Lawrence, there is serious concern about chemical contamination of the groundwater, which provides the islanders with their only source of natural drinking water. Most of these chemicals are agricultural pesticides and nitrates, some of them severely toxic, but other contaminants include fuel spilled from underground storage tanks.

To deal with this problem, the island's provincial and local authorities have developed an overall strategy to manage water resources. Future sewage facilities and petroleum storage tanks, for example, may be diverted from groundwater areas likely to be easily contaminated; the storage of hazardous wastes, including materials such as dry-cleaning solvents, is prohibited on the province's territory; and the use of certain agricultural chemicals is restricted. The highly toxic insecticide Aldicarb, widely used on potatoes (Prince Edward Island's main crop), was banned in 1989.

The risks involved in storing toxic waste were belatedly brought home to Canada in August 1988, when a warehouse at Saint Basile le Grand, east of Montreal, in Quebec, caught fire. The warehouse contained 90,900 liters (19,800 gallons) of liquid PCB wastes, as well as other contaminants. The dangerous smoke plume drifted far to the west, and residents living in the area had to be immediately evacuated. Since then, a nationwide inventory of all PCB waste storage sites has been made; stringent and legally enforceable requirements regarding PCB waste storage have been created under the Canadian Environmental Protection Act; and a federal PCB Destruction Program has been established, offering to provide mobile PCB destruction facilities in those areas with large quantities of PCB wastes.

Garbage disposal at source (*left*) An enormous municipal incinerator in Quebec provides an alternative to hauling the city's waste to rural landfill sites for dumping. Correct sorting makes incineration less polluting and more efficient.

Insulated pipes (*right*) in the village of Inuvik, Northwest Territories, ensure that water supplies and sewage disposal pipes do not freeze. The pipes, warmed by radiators, are elevated above the frozen ground to prevent the permafrost from melting.

Protecting the Inuit

Conservation issues are never clear cut, as the debate over the Canadian fur trade has shown. Conservationists from the south regard the sale of sealskins or beaver pelts as an affront to civilized standards, and the slaughter of wildlife as pandering to the luxury market. For Native Indian and Inuit hunters, however, the sale of skins has long been a major source of income. Now, following an international ban on sealskin products, the seals are still being killed for their meat but the skins go to waste. High rates of unemployment exacerbate many of the social problems affecting the Inuit. Such problems are often the result of cultural disruption and displacement.

Critical issues facing Canadian, Greenland and other Arctic Inuit – such as degradation of their land and culture – are the concern of the Inuit Circumpolar Conference, a nongovernmental organization representing the interests of the Inuit peoples. They are also being addressed by the Inuit Regional Conservation Strategy, a project fostering international cooperation on Arctic issues.

KEEPING THE ARCTIC COLD

Major accords such as the Arctic Environmental Protection Strategy cover the development of broad conservation policies for northern Canada, but the day-to-day priorities of those working in the Arctic are more practical. One of the main problems facing construction workers, for example, is not the Arctic cold, as many may think, but the opposite – heat.

The permanently frozen ground (a condition called permafrost) has great strength and resilience when frozen, but becomes weak if it thaws out. Arctic engineers, therefore, concentrate on insulating the ground from any heat generated by the things they build. Roads and runways carry thick gravel pads to prevent their frozen foundations from thawing out and collapsing. Buildings, too, are constructed on gravel foundations or piles. In some cases, heat extractors (giant versions of the domestic refrigerator) are buried on site to keep the permafrost frozen.

Oil pipelines, water supply pipes and sewage disposal pipes, however, have to be kept warm to prevent the contents from freezing solid. They consequently run above the permafrost on stilts, and are fitted with heat radiators and insulated trenching.

Turning on the heat

Scientists working at the tiny settlement of Resolute Bay on Cornwallis Island in the Arctic have found that the ice sheet became thinner by 30 percent between 1976 and 1989. Although local ice-thinning does not reflect global conditions, and computer climate models are imprecise, for more than a decade governments and individuals have been coming to terms with the prospect of "global warming" – a serious rise in the Earth's atmospheric temperature – caused by the build-up of "greenhouse" gases. Methane, CFCs, carbon dioxide (largely emitted as a result of burning fossil fuels for power), and nitrous oxides (from vehicle emissions) warm the atmosphere by trapping the heat that radiates from the Earth's surface.

Forecasts about what will happen as a result of global warming are many and varied, and have been viewed from both scientific and economic perspectives. Some scientists believe that the temperature will rise significantly over the next century, and that this will be greatest in higher latitudes where the increase may be by as much as 6°C or 9°C. This could be accompanied by a rise in sea level over the next century of 50 to 100 cm (20 to 40 in) – though some scientists have forecast a rise of up to 1.8 m (6 ft) – largely due to the melting of glaciers and polar ice.

A rise in the sea level would devastate many low-lying islands and heavily populated delta areas around the world, such as in Bangladesh. The long coast of Canada could also suffer significantly. At the international Earth Summit conference in Rio de Janeiro, Brazil, in 1992, the participating countries agreed to try to reduce greenhouse gas emissions by the year 2000, with the understanding that 1990 levels would be a desirable target.

For better or worse?

Higher temperatures could have some benefits for farmers in the region, enabling them to grow frost-sensitive crops much farther north than at present. However, high daytime temperatures and widespread drought could cancel out many of the gains in cereal-growing provinces, such as Ontario.

In the Arctic itself, scenarios of the future are varied. One view suggests that plants in the treeless tundra may grow quicker and their productivity increase, and that this could even slow down global warming if the mosses, lichens and other tundra plants absorb some of the surplus carbon dioxide. If, however, a lack of nutrients in the soil prevents this growth, then progressive melting of the permafrost might release large amounts of methane – one of the greenhouse gases – which would then reinforce the process of global warming.

The thawing of the frozen ground would have serious consequences for people living in the Arctic. If surface soils become saturated with water and weaken, roads and runways would collapse and many building foundations – previously anchored firmly into the permafrost – would founder. In this scenario, global warming seems set to challenge the ingenuity of polar engineers more than ever before.

SUMMER TEMPERATURES
1965   2020
1990   2050

-3 -2 -1 0 1 2 3 4 5
ΔT (°C)

Red marks the spot (*left*) of the greatest projected temperature increases due to global warming and the "greenhouse effect" as mapped by the Global Climate Model of NASA's Goddard Institute for Space Studies. Based on current global environmental patterns, a powerful NASA computer program is used to predict likely changes in the Earth's climate up to the year 2050.

Flood in waiting? (*right*) The Greenland ice sheet is the largest area of freshwater ice in the northern hemisphere, up to 3,000 m (10,000 ft) deep in places. Widespread melting in this area due to global warming could have catastrophic effects all over the world. However, some scientists argue that greater snowfall will be associated with the warming and will redress the balance.

GLOSSARY

Acid rain Rain or any other form of PRECIPITATION that has become more acid by absorbing waste gases (for example, sulfur dioxide and nitrogen oxides) discharged into the ATMOSPHERE.

Acid soil Soil that has a pH of less than 7; it is often PEATY.

Added value A higher price fetched by an article or RESOURCE after it has been processed. For example, crude oil has added value when it has been refined.

Agricultural economy An economy where most people work as cultivators or PASTORALISTS.

AIDS, Acquired Immune Deficiency Syndrome, a disease that damages the body's natural immune system and therefore makes people more susceptible to disease. The Human Immunodeficiency Virus (HIV) is the name given to one of the viruses that can lead to AIDS.

Air pollution The presence of gases and suspended particles in the air in high enough concentrations to harm humans, other animals, vegetation or materials. Such pollutants are introduced into the atmosphere principally as a result of human activity.

Alkaline soil Soil that has a pH of more than 7; chalk or limestone soils.

Alpine (1) A treeless ENVIRONMENT found on a mountain above the tree line but beneath the limit of permanent snow. (2) A plant that is adapted to grow in the TUNDRA-like environment of mountain areas.

Amphibian An animal that lives on land but whose life cycle requires some time to be spent in water, eg the frog.

Apartheid A way of organizing society to keep different racial groups apart. Introduced in South Africa by the National Party after 1948 as a means of ensuring continued white political dominance, it is now being dismantled.

Aquifer An underground layer of permeable rock, sand or gravel that absorbs and holds GROUNDWATER.

Arctic The northern POLAR region. In biological terms it also refers to the northern region of the globe where the mean temperature of the warmest month does not exceed 10°C (50°F). Its southern boundary roughly follows the northern tree line.

Arid (of the climate) Dry and usually hot. Arid areas generally have less than 250 mm (10 inches) of rain a year. Rainfall is intermittent and quickly evaporates or sinks into the ground. Little moisture remains in the soil, so plant life is sparse.

Atmosphere The gaseous layer surrounding the Earth. It consists of nitrogen (78 percent), oxygen (21 percent), argon (1 percent), tiny amounts of carbon dioxide, neon, ozone, hydrogen and krypton, and varying amounts of water vapor.

Atoll A circular chain of CORAL reefs enclosing a lagoon. Atolls form as coral reefs fringing a volcanic island; as sea levels rise or the island sinks a lagoon is formed.

Autonomy The condition of being self-governing, usually granted to a subdivision of a larger STATE or to a territory belonging to it.

Balance of payments A statement of a country's transactions with all other countries over a given period.

Balance of power A theory of political stability that is based upon an even distribution of power among the leading STATES.

Basalt A fine-grained IGNEOUS ROCK. It has a dark color and contains little silica. Ninety percent of lavas are basaltic.

Bible The book of scriptures of CHRISTIANITY and JUDAISM. The Jewish Bible contains many books in common with the Christian version describing historical events and prophetic teachings, but the latter also includes accounts of the life and teachings of Jesus Christ.

Biodegradable (of a substance) easily broken down into simpler substances by bacteria or other decomposers. Products made of organic materials such as paper, woolens, leather and wood are biodegradable; many plastics are not.

Biodiversity The number of different species of plants and animals found in a given area. In general, the greater the number of species, the more stable and robust the ECOSYSTEM is.

Biomass The total mass of all the living organisms in a defined area or ECOSYSTEM.

Biosphere The thin layer of the Earth that contains all living organisms and the ENVIRONMENT that supports them.

Biotechnology Technology applied to biological processes, including genetic engineering, the manipulation of the genetic makeup of living organisms.

Birthrate The number of births expressed as a proportion of a population. Usually given as the annual number of live births per 1,000 population (also known as the crude birthrate).

Black economy The sector of the economy that avoids paying tax.

Bloc A group of countries closely bound by economic and/or political ties.

Boreal Typical of the northern climates lying between the ARCTIC and latitude 50°N, characterized by long cold winters and short summers. Vegetation in these regions is dominated by BOREAL FOREST.

Boreal forest The name given to the CONIFEROUS FORESTS or TAIGA of the northern hemisphere.

Brown coal A peat-like material, also known as lignite, which is an immature form of coal. It has a lower energy value than more mature forms of coal.

Buddhism A religion founded in the 6th and 5th centuries BC and based on the teachings of Siddhartha Gautama; it is widely observed in southern and Southeast Asia.

Bureaucracy The body of STATE officials that carry out the day-to-day running of government. It may also refer to a system of administration marked by the inflexible application of rules.

Capital Variously refers to machinery, investment funds or a particular employment relationship involving waged labor.

Capitalism A political and economic system based on the production of goods and services for profitable exchange in which labor itself is bought and sold for wages. Capitalist economies can be more or less regulated by governments. In a capitalist mixed economy the government will own some of the country's utilities and industries as nationalized companies. It will also act as a major employer of labor.

Cash crop A crop grown for sale rather than for SUBSISTENCE.

Caste (1) (among people) A system of rigid hereditary social divisions, normally associated with the Hindu caste system in India, where an individual is born into the caste of his or her parents, must marry within it, and cannot leave it. (2) (among insects) A system within a single colony where there are different types of functional individual, usually distinguished by morphology, age and/or sex. For example, queens, workers and drones are distinct castes within a beehive.

Caucasian (1) A racial classification based on white or light skin color. (2) An inhabitant of the Caucasus region or the Indo-European language of this people.

Cereal A cultivated grass that has been selectively bred to produce high yields of edible grain for consumption by humans and livestock. The most important are wheat (*Triticum*), rice (*Oryza saliva*) and maize (*Zea mays*).

CFCs (chlorofluorocarbons) Organic compounds made up of atoms of carbon, chlorine and fluorine. Gaseous CFCs used as aerosol propellants, refrigerant gases and solvent cleaners are known to cause depletion of the OZONE LAYER.

Christianity A religion based on the teachings of Jesus Christ and originating in the 1st century AD from JUDAISM. Its main beliefs are found in the BIBLE and it is now the world's most widespread religion, divided into a number of churches and sects, including Roman Catholicism, Protestantism and Orthodox churches.

CITES (Convention on International Trade in Endangered Species) An international agreement signed by over 90 countries since 1973. SPECIES (FAUNA and FLORA) placed in Appendix I of CITES are considered to be in danger of EXTINCTION, and trade is prohibited without an export permit. Signatory countries have to supply data to the World Conservation Union, which monitors IMPORTS and EXPORTS. Appendix II species could be threatened with extinction if trade is not regulated.

City-state An independent STATE consisting of a single city and the surrounding countryside needed to support it. Singapore is an example of a modern city-state.

Class (1) A group of people sharing a common economic position, for example large landowners, waged-laborers or owners of small businesses. (2) (in zoology and botany) A rank in the taxonomic hierarchy coming between phylum and order. See CLASSIFICATION.

Classification A system of arranging the different types of living organisms according to the degree of similarity of their inherited characteristics. The classification system enables organisms to be identified and may also reveal the relationships between different groups. The internationally accepted classification hierarchy groups organisms first into divisions, then phyla, CLASSES, orders, FAMILIES, GENERA, SPECIES and SUBSPECIES.

Cocoa One of the ingredients of chocolate, cocoa is derived from cocoa beans, which are the seeds of the cacao tree (*Theobroma cacao*). They are found in yellowish pods that grow directly from the trunk. The tree is native to tropical America, but is cultivated mainly in west Africa.

Collectivization The organization of an economy (typically communist) by collective control through agencies of the state. See COMMUNISM.

Colonialism The political practice whereby a foreign country is occupied for settlement and economic exploitation.

Colony (1) A territory under the sovereignty of a foreign power. (2) (in zoology) A group of individual animals or plants that are physiologically connected to each other. (3) A distinct localized population of animals, for example termites, seabirds etc.

COMECON The Council for Mutual Economic Assistance, formed in 1947 as an organization to further trade and economic cooperation between communist countries. It had 10 members before its collapse in 1989 – the Soviet Union, Bulgaria, Czechoslovakia, Hungary, Poland, Romania, East Germany, Mongolia, Cuba, and Vietnam.

Commonwealth A loose association of STATES that are former members of the British EMPIRE with the British monarch at its head.

Communism A social and economic system based on the communal ownership of property. It usually refers to the state-controlled social and economic systems in the former Soviet Union and Soviet-bloc countries and in the People's Republic of China. See SOCIALISM.

Coniferous forest A forest of mainly coniferous, or cone-bearing trees, frequently with evergreen needle-shaped leaves and found principally in the TEMPERATE ZONES and BOREAL regions. The timber they produce is known as SOFTWOOD.

Conservation The use, management and protection of NATURAL RESOURCES so that they are not degraded, depleted or wasted and in order to maintain their sustainable use and ecological diversity. See SUSTAINABILITY.

Constitution The fundamental statement of laws that defines the way in which a country is governed.

Consumer goods Goods that are acquired for immediate use, such as foodstuffs, radios, televisions and washing machines.

Continental climate The type of climate associated with the interior of continents. It is characterized by wide daily and seasonal ranges of temperature, especially outside the TROPICS, and by low rainfall.

Continental drift The theory that today's continents, formed by the breakup of prehistoric supercontinents, have slowly drifted to their present positions. The theory was first proposed by Alfred Wegener in 1912.

Continental shelf An extension of a continent, forming a shallow, sloping shelf covered by sea.

Convention on International Trade in Endangered Species. See CITES.

Coral A group of animals related to sea anemones and living in warm seas. Individuals, called polyps, combine to form a COLONY.

Council for Mutual Economic Assistance See COMECON.

Culture (1) The beliefs, customs and social relations of a people. (2) The assumptions that a people makes in interpreting the world around them.

Cyclone A center of low atmospheric pressure. Tropical cyclones are known as HURRICANES or typhoons.

Dead lake (or **Dead river**) An area of water in which dissolved oxygen levels have fallen as a result of acidification, overgrowth of plants, or high levels of pollution to the extent that few or no living things are able to survive.

Debt The financial obligations owed by a country to the rest of the world, usually repayable in US dollars. Total external debt includes public, publicly guaranteed, and private long-term debt.

Deciduous (of plants, trees, a forest etc) dropping their leaves in the winter or in the dry season.

Decolonization The transfer of government from a colonial power to the people of the COLONY at the time of political independence.

Deforestation The felling of trees and clearing of forested land, which is then converted to other uses.

Delayed runoff See RUNOFF.

Delta A large accumulation of sediment, often fan-shaped, deposited where a river enters the sea or a lake. The flow of the river slows down on entering calmer waters and it is not able to transport the sediment it carries. Often the flow of the river splits into many channels, known as distributaries, creating new routes for the water and its load.

Democracy A form of government in which policy is made by the people (direct democracy) or on their behalf (indirect democracy). Indirect democracy usually takes the form of competition among political parties at elections.

Desert A very ARID area with less than 25 cm (10 in) rainfall a year. In hot deserts the rate of evaporation is greater than the rate of PRECIPITATION, and there is little vegetation.

Desertification The creation of desert-like conditions usually caused by a combination of overgrazing, soil EROSION, prolonged DROUGHT and climate change.

Developed country Any country characterized by high standards of living and a sophisticated economy, particularly in comparison to DEVELOPING COUNTRIES. A number of indicators can be used to measure a country's wealth and material well-being: for example, the GROSS NATIONAL PRODUCT, the PER CAPITA consumption of energy, the number of doctors per head of population and the average life expectancy.

Developing country Any country that is characterized by low standards of living and a SUBSISTENCE economy. Sometimes called THIRD WORLD countries, they include most of Africa, Asia and Central and South America.

Dictator A leader who concentrates the power of the STATE in his or her own hands.

Divide see WATERSHED.

Dominant species The most numerous or prevailing SPECIES in a community of plants or animals.

Dormancy A period during which the metabolic activity of a plant or animal is reduced to such an extent that it can withstand difficult environmental conditions such as cold or drought.

Drought An extended period in which rainfall is substantially lower than average and the water supply is insufficient to meet demand.

EC See EUROPEAN COMMUNITY

Ecology (1) The study of the interactions of living organisms with each other and with their ENVIRONMENT. (2) The study of the structure and functions of nature.

Ecosystem A community of plants and animals and the ENVIRONMENT in which they live and react with each other.

Effluent Any liquid waste discharged into the ENVIRONMENT as a byproduct of industry, agriculture or sewage treatment.

Emission A substance discharged into the air in the form of gases and suspended particles, from automobile engines and industrial smokestacks, for example.

Empire (1) A political organization of STATES and territories in which one dominates the rest. (2) The territory that constitutes such a group of states.

Endangered species A SPECIES whose population has dropped to such low levels that its continued survival is insecure.

Endemic species A SPECIES that is native to one specific area, and is therefore often said to be characteristic of that area.

Environment (1) The external conditions – climate, geology and other living things – that influence the life of individual organisms or ECOSYSTEMS. (2) The surroundings in which all animals and plants live and interact with each other.

Erosion The process by which exposed land surfaces are broken down into smaller particles or worn away by water, wind or ice.

Ethnic group A group of people sharing a social or cultural identity based on language, religion, customs and/or common descent or kinship.

European Community (EC) an alliance of western European nations formed to agree common policies in the areas of trade, aid, agriculture and economics. The six founder members in 1957 were France, West Germany, Belgium, Holland, Luxembourg and Italy. A further three – Britain, Ireland and Denmark – joined in 1973, Greece in 1981 and Spain and Portugal in 1986. East Germany became a member when it was reunited with West Germany in 1990.

Evolution The process by which SPECIES develop their appearance, form and behavior through the process of NATURAL SELECTION, and by which new species or varieties are formed.

Exotic (of an animal or plant) Not native to an area but established after being introduced from elsewhere, often for commercial or decorative purposes.

Exports Goods and services sold to other countries, bringing in foreign exchange.

Extinction The loss of a local population of a particular SPECIES or even the entire species. It may be natural or be caused by human activity.

Family A taxonomic term for a group of related plants or animals. For example, the family Felidae (cat family) includes the lion, the tiger and all the smaller cats. Most families contain several GENERA, and families are grouped together into orders. See CLASSIFICATION.

Famine An acute shortage of food leading to widespread malnutrition and starvation.

Fault A fracture or crack in the Earth along which there has been movement of the rock masses.

Fauna The general term for the animals that live in a particular region.

Feudalism (1) A type of society in which landlords collect dues from the agricultural producers in return for military protection. (2) A hierarchical society of mutual obligations that preceded CAPITALISM in Europe.

First World A term sometimes used to describe the advanced industrial countries.

Fjord A steep-sided inlet formed when a glaciated U-shaped valley is drowned by the sea. See GLACIATION.

Flora (1) The general term for the plant life of a particular region. (2) A book that lists and describes the plants of a given area.

Fossil fuel Any fuel, such as coal, oil and NATURAL GAS, formed beneath the Earth's surface under conditions of heat and pressure from organisms that died millions of years ago.

Free trade A system of international trade in which goods and services are exchanged without TARIFFS, QUOTAS or other restrictions.

GATT The General Agreement on Tariffs and Trade, a treaty that governs world imports and exports. Its aim is to promote FREE TRADE, but at the moment many countries impose TARIFF barriers to favor their own industries and agricultural produce.

GDP See GROSS DOMESTIC PRODUCT.

Genus (pl. **genera**) A level of biological CLASSIFICATION of organisms in which closely related SPECIES are grouped. For example, dogs, wolves, jackels and coyotes are all grouped together in the genus *canis*.

Ghetto A slum area in a city that is occupied by an ETHNIC minority. The word originally referred to the part of a city in medieval Europe to which Jews were restricted by law.

Glaciation (1) The process of GLACIER and ice sheet growth. (2) The effect of these on the landscape.

Glacier A mass of ice formed by the compaction and freezing of snow and which shows evidence of past or present movement.

Global warming The increase in the average temperature of the Earth that is believed to be caused by the GREENHOUSE EFFECT.

GNP See GROSS NATIONAL PRODUCT.

Greenhouse effect The effect of certain gases in the ATMOSPHERE, such as carbon dioxide and METHANE, in absorbing solar heat radiated back from the surface of the Earth and preventing its escape into space. Without these gases the Earth would be too cold for living things, but the burning of FOSSIL FUELS for industry and transportation has caused atmospheric levels of these gases to increase, and this is believed to be a cause of GLOBAL WARMING.

Green Revolution The introduction of high-yielding varieties of seeds (especially rice and wheat) and modern agricultural techniques to increase agricultural production in DEVELOPING COUNTRIES. It began in the early 1960s.

Gross Domestic Product (GDP) The total value of a country's annual output of goods and services, with allowances being made for depreciation. Growth in GDP is usually expressed in constant prices, to offset the effects of inflation. GDP is a very useful guide to the level of economic activity in a country.

Gross National Product (GNP) A country's GROSS DOMESTIC PRODUCT plus income from abroad.

Groundwater Water that has percolated into the ground from the Earth's surface, filling pores, cracks and fissures. An impermeable layer of rock prevents it from moving deeper so that the lower levels become saturated. The upper limit of saturation is known as the WATER TABLE.

Growing season The period of the year when the average temperature is high enough for plants to grow. It is longest at low latitudes and altitudes. Most plants can grow when the temperature exceeds 5°C (42°F).

Habitat The external ENVIRONMENT to which an animal or plant is adapted and in which it prefers to live, usually defined in terms of vegetation, climate or altitude – eg grassland habitat.

Hard currency A currency used by international traders because they think it is safe from devaluation.

Hardwood Any timber from broadleaf trees such as oak, ash and beech. Hardwoods are generally stronger and less likely to rot than wood from cone-bearing trees, which is known as SOFTWOOD.

Hinduism A body of religious practices, originating in India in the 2nd millennium BC, that emphasizes ways of living rather than ways of thought. Its beliefs and practices are based on the Vedas and other scriptures and are closely intertwined with the culture of the people of India.

HIV (Human Immunodeficiency Virus) See AIDS.

Hunter–gatherers People who obtain their food requirements by hunting wild animals and gathering the berries and fruits from wild plants.

Hurricane A tropical CYCLONE, usually found in the Caribbean and western North Atlantic.

Hybrid An animal or plant that is the offspring of two genetically different individuals. Hybrid crops are often grown because they give higher yields and are more resistant to disease.

Ice age A long period of geological time in which the temperature of the Earth falls and snow and ice sheets are present throughout the year in mid and high latitudes. There have been many ice ages in the Earth's history.

Igneous rock Rock formed when magma (molten material within the Earth's crust) cools and solidifies.

Imperialism The process whereby one country forces its rule on another country, frequently in order to establish an EMPIRE.

Imports Goods and services purchased from other countries.

Import substitution industry Any industry that has been set up (mainly in THIRD WORLD countries) to manufacture products that used to be imported. Import substitution industries are normally simple ones with an immediate local market such as the manufacture of cigarettes, soap and textiles. They are protected during their start-up phase by high TARIFFS on foreign rivals.

Indigenous peoples The original inhabitants of a region, generally leading a traditional way of life.

Islam A religion based on the revelations of God to the prophet Muhammed in the 7th century AD, which are contained in the Qu'ran. Islam is widely practiced throughout North Africa, the Indian Subcontinent, the Middle East and parts of Southeast Asia.

Judaism A religion founded in 2000 BC among the ancient Hebrews and practiced by Jews; it is monotheistic (believing in a single God) and its main beliefs are contained in the BIBLE.

Jute (*Corchorus capsularis* or *C. olitorius*) A fiber crop cultivated in Asia, used to make ropes, sacks, hessian, carpet backing and tarpaulin.

Labor force The economically active population,

including the armed forces and the unemployed. Full-time homemakers and unpaid caregivers are not included.

Leaching The process by which water washes nutrients and minerals downward from one layer of soil to another, or into streams.

Left-wing A general term to denote antiestablishment political views, specifically used as a label for socialist or communist parties. See COMMUNISM, SOCIALISM.

Legislature The branch of government responsible for enacting laws.

Limestone A sedimentary rock formed under the sea and consisting mainly of calcium carbonate. It is used as a building stone and in the manufacture of cement.

Literacy Usually defined as the ability to read and write a simple sentence.

Low income economy The poorest countries in the world, where the average PER CAPITA income was between $610 and $2,565 in 1990.

Mammal A vertebrate animal belonging to the CLASS Mammalia, having a four-chambered heart, fur or hair, and feeding its young on milk secreted by the mammae (nipples). With the exception of monotremes, mammals do not lay eggs, but give birth to live young.

Mangrove A dense forest of shrubs and trees growing on tidal coastal mudflats and estuaries throughout the tropics.

Maquis The typical vegetation of the Mediterranean coast, consisting of aromatic shrubs, laurel, myrtle, rock rose, broom and small trees such as olive, fig and holm oak.

Maritime climate A generally moist climate, determined mainly by proximity to the sea. The sea heats up and cools down more slowly than the land, reducing variations in temperature so that the local climate is more equable than farther inland.

Market economy An economy in which most economic activities are transacted by private individuals and firms in largely unregulated markets.

Marxism The system of thought derived from the 19th-century political theorist Karl Marx, in which politics is interpreted as a struggle between economic CLASSES. It promotes communal ownership of property when it is practiced, so is popularly known as COMMUNISM.

Mediterranean climate Any climate similar to that of the Mediterranean region: wet winters and hot, dry summers.

Methane A gas produced by decomposing organic matter that burns without releasing pollutants and can be used as an energy source. Excessive methane production from vast amounts of animal manure is believed to contribute to the GREENHOUSE EFFECT.

Migrant workers Part of the LABOR FORCE which has come from another country, or another part of the same country, looking for temporary employment.

Monetarism An economic philosophy that sees inflation as the main menace to economic growth and proposes a direct relationship between the rate of growth of the money supply of a country and its subsequent rate of inflation.

Monsoon (1) The wind systems in the TROPICS that reverse their direction according to the seasons; when they blow onshore they bring heavy rainfall. (2) The rain caused by these winds.

Montane The zone at middle altitudes on the slopes of mountains, below the ALPINE zone.

Nation A community that believes it consists of a single people, based upon historical and cultural criteria and sharing a common territory. Sometimes used interchangeably with STATE.

Nationalism An ideology that assumes all NATIONS should have their own STATE, a NATION-STATE, in their own territory, the national homeland.

Nation-State A STATE in which the inhabitants all belong to one NATION. Most states claim to be nation-states; in practice almost all of them include minority groups.

Natural gas A FOSSIL FUEL in the form of a flammable gas that occurs naturally in the Earth. It is often found in association with deposits of petroleum.

Natural resources RESOURCES created by the Earth's natural processes including mineral deposits, FOSSIL FUELS, soil, air, water, plants and animals. Most natural resources are harvested by people for use in agriculture, industry and economic activities.

Natural selection The process by which organisms not well suited to their ENVIRONMENT are eliminated by predation, parasitism, competition, etc, and those that are well suited survive to breed and pass on their genes to the next generation.

Nomad A member of a (usually pastoral) people that moves seasonally from one place to another in search of food, water or pasture for their animals. See PASTORALIST.

Nonrenewable resource A NATURAL RESOURCE that is present in the Earth's makeup in finite amounts (coal, oil etc) and cannot be replaced once reserves are exhausted.

OECD (Organization for Economic Cooperation and Development) An organization set up in 1961 to promote the economic growth of its (now 24) rich member countries.

One-party system A political system in which there is no competition to the government PARTY at elections (eg communist and military regimes) and all but the government party is banned.

OPEC The Organization of Petroleum Exporting Countries, a cartel that represents the interests of 11 of the chief petroleum exporting countries. It is able to exercise a degree of control over the price of their product.

Ozone layer A band of enriched oxygen or ozone found in the upper ATMOSPHERE. It absorbs harmful ultraviolet radiation from the Sun. The heat this creates provides a cap for the earth's weather systems.

Pangea The supercontinent that was composed of all the present-day continents and therefore included both Gondwanaland and Laurasia. It existed between 250 and 200 million years ago. See also CONTINENTAL DRIFT.

Parasite An organism that lives on or in another organism of a different SPECIES and derives nutrients from it, giving nothing beneficial in return.

Parliamentary democracy A political system in which the LEGISLATURE (parliament) is elected by all the adult members of the population and the government is formed by the PARTY that commands a majority in the parliament.

Party An organized group seeking political power to implement an agreed set of policies.

Pastoralist A person following a way of life based on tending herds of animals such as sheep, cattle, goats or camels; often NOMADIC, it involves moving the herds according to the natural availability of pasture and water.

Peat Soil formed by an accumulation of plant material incompletely decomposed due to low temperature and lack of oxygen, usually as a result of WATERLOGGING.

Per capita Per head.

Permafrost Soil and rock that remains permanently frozen, typically in the POLAR REGIONS. A layer of soil at the surface may melt in summer, but the water that is released is unable to drain away through the frozen subsoil and refreezes in colder conditions.

Pesticide Any chemical substance used to control the pests that can damage crops, such as insects and rodents. Often used as a general term for herbicides, insecticides and fungicides.

pH A measurement on the scale 0–14 of the acidity or alkalinity of a substance.

Plateau A large area of level, elevated land. When bordered by steep slopes it is called a tableland.

Polar regions The regions that lie within the lines of latitude known as the ARCTIC and Antarctic circles, respectively 66°32′ north and south of the Equator. At this latitude the sun does not set in midsummer nor rise in midwinter.

Polder An area of level land at or below sea level obtained by land reclamation. It is normally used for agriculture.

Poverty line A measure of deprivation that varies from country to country. In LOW-INCOME ECONOMIES the poverty referred to is an absolute poverty, where a certain percentage of the population lacks sufficient food to eat and resources to provide for shelter. In the advanced industrial world people are often considered to be in poverty if they earn less than 60 percent of the average wage. Their basic needs will be met by local welfare systems but they suffer poverty relative to their compatriots.

Prairie The flat grassland in the interior of North America between 30°N and 55°N, much of which has been plowed and is used to grow cereal crops.

Precipitation Moisture that reaches the Earth from the ATMOSPHERE, including mist, dew, rain, sleet, snow and hail.

Predator An animal that feeds on another animal (the PREY).

President A head of state, elected in some countries directly by the voters and in others by members of the LEGISLATURE. In some political systems the president is chief executive, in others the office is largely ceremonial.

Prey An animal that a PREDATOR hunts and kills for food.

Productivity (1) A measure of economic output in relation to the quantity of economic inputs (labor, machines, land, etc) needed for production. (2) The amount of weight (or energy) gained by an individual, a SPECIES or an ECOSYSTEM per unit of area per unit of time.

Quota A limit imposed on the amount of a product that can be imported in a given time.

Radioactivity The emission of alpha-, beta- and gamma particles from atomic nuclei. This is greatest when the atom is split, as in a nuclear reactor. Prolonged exposure to radioactive material can cause damage to living tissue, leading to cancers and ultimately death.

Rainforest Forest where there is abundant rainfall all year round and no dry season. The term is often associated with tropical rainforests, where growth is lush and very rapid, but there are also rainforests in TEMPERATE ZONES. Rainforests probably contain half of all the Earth's plant and animal species.

Refuge A place where a SPECIES of plant or animal has survived after formerly occupying a much larger area. For example, mountain tops are refuges for ARCTIC species left behind as the GLACIERS retreated at the end of the last ICE AGE.

Resource Any material, source of information or skill that is of economic value to industry and business.

Roman empire An EMPIRE founded in the year 27 BC from the Roman Republic, which began about 500 BC in present-day Italy. At its height it controlled the Mediterranean, large parts of western Europe and the Middle East. In the 5th century it divided, the eastern half becoming the Byzantine empire.

Runoff Water produced by rainfall or melting snow that flows across the land surface into streams and rivers. Delayed runoff is water that soaks into the ground and later emerges on the surface as springs.

Salinization The accumulation of soluble salts near or at the surface of soil, caused by an arid climate. Salinization can also occur when water used for irrigation evaporates; eventually the land becomes so salty that it is worthless for cultivation.

Savanna A HABITAT of open grassland with scattered trees in tropical and subtropical areas. There is a marked dry season and too little rain to support large areas of forest.

Second World A term sometimes used to describe the developed socialist countries (including the former Soviet Union and former Soviet bloc).

Semiarid land Any area between an ARID desert and a more fertile region where there is sufficient moisture to support a little more vegetation than can survive in the DESERT. Also called semidesert.

Separatism A political movement in a STATE that supports the secession of a particular minority group, within a defined territory, from that state.

Service industries Industries that supply services to customers or to other sectors of the economy; typically banking, transport, insurance, education, healthcare, retailing and distribution.

Shanty town An area of very poor housing consisting of ramshackle huts and other simple dwellings often made from waste materials and with inadequate services.

Shifting cultivation A method of farming prevalent in tropical areas in which a piece of land is cleared and cultivated until its fertility is diminished. The farmer then abandons the land, which restores itself naturally.

Slash-and-burn farming A method of farming in tropical areas where the vegetation cover is cut and burned to fertilize the land before crops are planted. Often a feature of SHIFTING CULTIVATION.

Socialism An economic system and political ideology based upon the principle of equality between people, the redistribution of wealth and property and equal access to benefits such as healthcare and education.

Softwood The wood from coniferous trees.

Solar energy The radiant energy produced by the Sun that powers all the Earth's natural processes. It can be captured and used to provide domestic heating or converted to produce electrical energy.

Specialization (in natural history) The evolutionary development of a SPECIES, leading to narrow limits of tolerance and a restricted role (or niche) in the community.

Species The basic unit of CLASSIFICATION of plants and animals. Species are grouped into GENERA and variations may be categorized into SUBSPECIES in descending order of hierarchy.

State The primary political unit of the modern world, usually defined by its possession of sovereignty over a territory and its people.

Steppe An open grassy plain with few trees or shrubs. Steppe is characterized by low and sporadic rainfall, and experiences wide variations in temperature during the year.

Subsistence A term applied to systems in which producers can supply their own needs for food, shelter, etc but have little or no surplus to trade.

Subspecies A rank in the CLASSIFICATION of plants and animals between SPECIES and variety. It is often used to denote a geographical variation of a species.

Subtropical The climatic zone between the TROPICS and TEMPERATE ZONES. There are marked seasonal changes of temperature but it is never very cold.

Succession The development and maturation of an ECOSYSTEM, through changes in the types and abundance of SPECIES. When it reaches maturity it stabilizes in a climax.

Sustainability The concept of using the Earth's NATURAL RESOURCES to improve people's lives without diminishing the ability of the Earth to support life today and in the future.

Tableland See PLATEAU.

Taiga The Russian name given to the CONIFEROUS FOREST and PEATland belt that stretches around the world in the northern hemisphere, south of the TUNDRA and north of the DECIDUOUS forests and grasslands.

Tariff A tax imposed on imported goods or services.

Taxonomy The scientific CLASSIFICATION of organisms.

Temperate zone Any one of the climatic zones in mid latitudes, with a mild climate. They cover areas between the warm TROPICS and cold POLAR REGIONS.

Terrestrial (of a plant, animal etc) spending its entire life cycle on the land.

Third World A term first used to refer to ex-COLONIES that were neither fully capitalist (FIRST WORLD) nor fully socialist (SECOND WORLD). Now used to refer to the poorer, less industrialized countries of the developing world.

Tribe A group of people united by a common language, religion, customs and/or descent and kinship; often used to describe the social groups of peoples who have no developed STATE or government and whose social organization is based on ancestry and extended family systems.

Tropics The area of the Earth lying between the Tropic of Cancer (23°30′ N) and the Tropic of Capricorn (23°30′ S). They mark the lines of latitude farthest from the Equator where the Sun is still found directly overhead at midday in midsummer.

Tundra The level, treeless land lying in the very cold northern regions of Europe, Asia and North America, where winters are long and cold and the ground beneath the surface is permanently frozen. See also PERMAFROST.

Upper-middle-income economy Any country where average PER CAPITA income was between $2,566 and $7,619 in 1990.

Urbanization (1) The process by which the proportion of a country's population living in towns or cities grows, while the rural population diminishes. (2) The process of city formation and growth.

Water table The uppermost level of underground rock that is permanently saturated with GROUNDWATER.

Waterlogging The complete saturation of land by water.

Watershed The boundary line dividing two river systems. It is also known as a water-parting or divide, particularly in the United States, where the word watershed refers to a river basin (the area drained by a river and its tributaries).

Welfare State A social and economic system based on STATE provision of, and responsibility for, such things as healthcare, pensions and unemployment benefit. These services are financed by general contributions from the working population, and access is intended to be equally available to all, free of charge. It originated in Britain at the start of the 20th century and became widespread in Europe after World War II.

Wetlands A HABITAT that is waterlogged all or enough of the time to support vegetation adapted to these conditions.

INDEX

Page numbers in **bold** refer to extended treatment of topic; in *italics* to captions, maps or tables

A

Abies 355
Acer 355
acid rain 359, 418
adaptation
in animals 346–347; in plants **357**, **360**
age distribution *385*
agriculture *304*, **314**, *315*, 362–369
agricultural zones *363*; climate and environment 362, 365, 369; economic aspects 380, *381*; environmental issues 416, 419, 421; exports 362, 364, *365*, 369; farm organization 365, 366, 367; fishing *362*, 363, 365; forestry 362, 363, 365, 368–369, *368*, *369*; food processing 370; fruit and vegetables 363, 365, *365*, 367; livestock 365; loss of land 334, 335; origins 362–363; role of government 366–367; staple crops 363, 365, 367
agrochemicals 366
see also fertilizers, pesticides
agroforestry *see* forestry industry, forests
Agropyron 355
air pollution 417, 418, 419
control 420–421
Alaska (USA) 301, 302
Alberta (Canada) 300, 301, 308, 314, 316, 364
Alectoria 357
algae *356*, 357
Algonquin Provincial Park (Canada) 336
Amerindian peoples *see* Native-Americans
Ammassalik *320*
Andropogon 355
animal life **302–305**, *304*, **344–351**, **352**, *352*
adaptation to cold 346–347; breeding programs 348, 349; camouflage 346; communication 349; extinction 348; migration 344–345
Antarctica 326
antelope, Pronghorn 347
apomictic plants 360
Appalachian Mountains 299, 324, 325
apples 365, *365*
aquaculture
see also fish farming
architecture 402–403, *402*
Arctic 301–302, *303*, 305, 306–307, *306*, 320–321
Canadian frontiers **413**; environmental issues 417, 418, 419, *419*, 421, **422**, *422*; habitats 334, 335, 337, 340–341, *343*, *343*; physical geography 324, *325*, 326–327, **327**, **330**; plant life **360**, *361*; settlement **401**; wildlife 344–347
Arctic Environmental Protection Strategy 421
art 391, 392, *395*
Artemisia 355
asbestos 371
aspen 355, 356
Athabasca glacier 329

B

atmosphere 332
see also greenhouse effect
aurorae **332**, *332*
Australia 365
automobile industry 373, *374*
avens, mountain 354, *354*, 358

badlands 328
Baffin, William 306
Baffin Island 302, 306, 326, 327, *327*
Balaenoptera 347
balance of trade 381, 382
Banff (Canada) *310*
Banff National Park (Canada) *328*, 338
Bangladesh 422
basswood 355
beach, raised 326, *327*
bear 346
Grizzly 349; Polar *343*, 344, 345, *345*, 346, 350, *419*
beaver 348, 350
beef production 365
Bell, Alexander Graham 376
Bell Canada 376
beluga *347*
Betula 355, *356*
Biosphere Reserves 336
birch *356*
white 355, 359
bison
North American 347, 348; Plains 348; Wood 348
blueberry 358, *358*
bobcat 350
bog *see* peatlands
boom–bust economic pattern 381, 382–383
boreal forest *see* coniferous forest
Boston (USA) 400
Bouteloua 355
breeding programs 348, 349
British colonial influence 305, 307, 308–309, 311, 313, 380, 393, 398, 406, 408
British Columbia 301, 308, *310*, 314, 315, *315*, 316, 318, 375, 384
Brown, Barnum 300
Bruce Peninsula National Park (Canada) 337
Buffalo (USA) 400
buffalo, North American *see* bison
Bush, George *410*

C

Cabot, John 306, 307, 406
cactus 355
Calgary (Canada) 309, *315*, 318, 399
Caltha 356
camouflage in animals 346
Canada **298–321**
agriculture *304*, **314**, *315*, **362–369**; economy **314–319**, **380–387**; environment **298–305**; environmental issues **416–423**, *417*; exploration 303, *305*, 306–307, *306*, 309, 321; film industry **319**, *319*; fishing and forestry **314–316**, *315*, *316*; fur

trade 304, 307, **308–309**, *309*, 316; government 305, **311–312**, **408–414**, *409*, *411*, *412*, *413*, *414*; habitats **334–341**, *334*, *335*, *337*, *338*, *339*, *340*; health and welfare 319; history 303, **305–310**; industry and resources **316**, **370–379**, *370*; landscape **298–302**; media 318; Mounties 311, *311*; people **388–396**; physical geography **324–329**, *325*, *328*, *332*; settlement **398–407**; society **305–313**, *308*, *313*; trade **316**; transport and communications **316**, **318**, *319*, **376–377**, *376*; vegetation and wildlife **302–305**, *304*, *309*, **344–351**, **354–361**
Canadian Shield 298, 299, 309, 316, 324, *325*
captive breeding programs 348, 349
Carex 355, *356*
caribou 344–345, 346
Cartier, Jacques *305*, 307
Cassiope 354, *361*
Catholicism *see* Roman Catholicism
Catlin, George 336
cattail *356*
cattle 348
domestic 365; *see also* beef production, dairying
cedar, red 358, 359
cement industry 374
cereals *see individual crops*
Champlain, Samuel de 307
cheetah 347
chemicals in the environment 418, 419, 421
chernozem soil 363
Chicago (USA) 318
China 364
chipmunks 346, *351*
Chrétien, Jean *410*, 411
Christianity *see* Protestantism, Roman Catholicism
Cladonia 356, *357*
clam 345
climate 302
and environment 362, *365*, 369; and plants **357**
climatic change 324, 422, *422*, 359
coal 371
Coast Ranges (Canada) 301, 302, 324
cod 345
cold, adaptation to 346–347, **357**
Cold War 413
colonialism 388–389, 394
Columbia icefield 328, 329
Columbus, Christopher 406
combine harvester *see* mechanization of farms
Commonwealth 380
communications industry **376–377**, *376*
computer industry *see* electrical, electronics and computer industry
coniferous forest 334, *337*, *340*
conifers 355, 356, 357, *359*
conservation groups and organizations 337, 339
Conservative Party (Canada) *see* Progressive Conservative Party
constitution of Canada 390
construction industry *374*
Cook, Frederick Albert 303
cooperative protection **337**

copper **378**, *378*
Corallorhiza 357
corn *see* maize
Cornus 358
Cornwallis Island (Canada) 422
crafts 373, *373*, *395*
crane
Sandhill 348; Whooping 348
crustaceans 345
cushion plant 354, 360

D

dairying *365*
daisy 360
Davis, John 306
Dawson City (Canada) *309*, *401*
de Gaulle, Charles 310
debt 383
deer 348
deforestation 338, 339, *339*, 358
replanting schemes 420; *see also* forestry industry
Delphinapterus 347
Denmark *413*
depopulation, rural 367
depression *see* Great Depression
desert, cold 326–327
Detroit (USA) 400
Dinosaur Provincial Park (Alberta) **300**, *300*
Distant Early Warning (DEW) Line 413
dogwood 358
dolphin, Bottle-nosed *347*
drought 334
Dryas 354
dryland farming *362*, 364
duck, Long-tailed 348

E

eagle, Bald 349
earthflow 329
EC *see* European Community
ecological reserves 337
economy **314–319**, **380–387**
age distribution 385; balance of trade 381, 382; boom–bust economic pattern 381, 382–383; colonization 380; debt 383; economic activity 398–399, 403; economic history 380–381; economic policy 383; education 384–385; environmental protection **383**; ethnic groups 383, *384*, **385**; exports 380, 381, 382, 386; gross domestic product 381, *381*; healthcare 385; imports 386; industrialization 380; inflation *381*; labor 386, 387; life expectancy 385; migration 385; poverty and wealth 384, *385*; recession 381, 382; taxation 383, 385; trade unions *386*, 387; unemployment 381, 384, 385; United States, trade with 380–381, 382, *382*, 383, 386–387; welfare system 383, 384–385
Edmonton (Canada) *391*, 399, 400, 403
education 384–385

Edward VII, King of Britain 311
Egede, Hans 320
electrical, electronics and computer industry 373, **376–377**, *376*
elk/moose 346, 349, *352*, *352*
Ellesmere Island (Canada) 302, 303, 326, 327
Ellesmere National Park (Canada) 339
elm, white 355
energy resources *370*, 371, *373*, *373*, *374*, *373*, **418**
environment **298–305**
environmental impact analysis 420
environmental issues **416–423**, *417*
    acid rain 418; agriculture 416, 419, 421; air pollution 417, 418, 419; chemicals 418, 419, 421; energy sources **418;** environmental legislation 421; European settlement 416; forests and deforestation 418, 419; global warming, effect of **422;** government policies 418, 419, 420–421; hunting 417, *417*, 421; indigenous peoples 416, 417, 418, 420, 421; industrialization 417, 418; marine pollution 419; mineral extraction 417; pollution control 420–421; pressure groups 420; public attitudes 420–421; regreening schemes 420; sewage and sanitation 419, 421, *421*; soil erosion 419; species loss 419; transboundary pollution 418; transportation 416; urbanization 417; waste and recycling 419, *419*, 421; water management 421, *421*; water pollution 416, 417, 418–419, 421; wilderness 417, 418
environmental protection **383**
Erie, Lake *328*
Erik the Red 321
Eriksson, Leif 305, 321
ermine 346, 350
erosion
    glacial 324–325; of soil 419; water *328*, *328*
Erythronium 358
Eschrichtius 347
Eskimo *see* Inuit people
ethnic groups 383, *384*, **385**, 388, **392–393**, *393*
    see also separatism
ethnic neighborhoods *402*, **403**, 404–405
European colonialism 388
European Community (EC) 382
European settlement 362, 363, *364*, 368, 416
eustasy 327
exploration 303, *305*, 306–307, *306*, 309, 321
extinct animals 348

F

family farms 365
farm organization 365, 366, 367
farming *see* agriculture
Fathom Five Provincial Park (Canada) 336
federal systems of government **410**
fertility of soil 364

fertilizers 365
film industry 319, *319*
fir
    alpine 355; Douglas 355, 358
fires 334, 356
fisher 350, *351*
fishing industry 316, *316*, 337, 345, *362*, 363, 365, 373, 380, 384
fjords 326, 330
flag of Canada 389, 392
flowers *see* horticulture
fodder crops 365, 367
food crops *see individual crops*
food preserving 362
forestry industry **314–315**, *315*, 338, 339, 358, **362–363**, 365, **368–370**, *368*, *369*, *370*, 371, 373, **375**, 380, *382*, 383
forests
    coniferous 334, *337*, *340*; deforestation 338, 339, *339*, 358; environmental issues 418, 419; replanting schemes 420; temperate rain- 334, *335*, 339, *339*
Fort William (Thunder Bay) 308, 318, *319*
fossils 328
fox
    Arctic 344, 346, 350, *350*, ; Gray 350; Red 350; Swift 349
Fram 303, *303*
France *see* French colonial influence
Franklin, John 306, *306*, 307, 309
Fraser river and valley 308, 314
Free Trade Agreement (FTA) (1989) 382, **386–387**, *386*, 410, 411–412
free trade *see* trade
freeze–thaw 327
French colonial influence 305, 307, 310, 313, 321, 362, 398, 406, 408, 414
French language 393
French-Canadian separatism 408, *408*, *409*, **414**, *414*
Frobisher, Martin 306
fruit and vegetables 363, **365**, *365*, 367
    see also individual crops
fur and skin industry 304, 307, **308–309**, *309*, 316, 348, **350–351**, 370, *373*, 380, 385

G

gas *see* natural gas
Gaultheria 358
GDP *see* gross domestic product
General Motors 374
George VI, King of Britain 350
glacial periods *see* ice ages
glaciation 324, 328–330, *330*, *330*, *331*
    see also erosion
Glacier National Park (USA) 336
glaciers 329, **330**, *330*, 331
    table of world's ice sheets and glaciers *330; see also* glaciation
global warming 417, **422**, *422*
    see also climatic change, greenhouse effect
goeduck 345
gold 371
Gold Rushes 309, *309*,
goldenrod 358

goose, Canada 344
government 305, **311–312**, 338–339, **408–414**, *409*, *411*, *412*, *413*, *414*
    environmental policies 418, 419, 420–421; industrial policies 372–373, 374–375; settlement policies 401–402
grain *see individual crops*
grass
    big bluestem 355; blue grama 355; wheat 355
grassland 336
    see also prairies
Great Britain *see* United Kingdom
Great Lakes 299, 302, 304, 307, 314, 317, 318, 324, 325
Great Plains 299, 301, 302, 324, 362, 363
greenhouse effect 327, 330
    see also global warming
greenhouse gases 422
Greenland 305, 306, **320–321**, *320*, 388, *413*, 422
    habitats 334, 335, 337; physical geography 324, *325*, 326, 327, 330, 331
Greenland National Park 337
Grierson, John **319**, *319*
gross domestic product 381, *381*
Gulf of Saint Lawrence 299, 317, *339*
gullying 328
Gunnbjørn, Mount (Greenland) 320
gymnosperms *see* conifers

H

habitats **334–341**, *334*, *335*, *337*, *338*, *339*, *340*
    destruction 349
Haida people 339
halibut 345
Halifax (Canada) 398
hare 348
    Snowshoe 346
health and welfare 319, 383, 384–385
Hearne, Samuel 309
heather, Arctic white 354
hemlock 358
    eastern 355; western 355, 358, *359*
hemp 369
Henson, Matthew 303
history of Canada 303, **305–310**, 398–399, 406
Hong Kong 393
hoodoos 328, *328*
horticulture 365
housing **393**, 403, *403*
Hudson, Henry 303, 306, 307
Hudson Bay 298, 302, 308, 318, 324
Hudson's Bay Company 307, **308–309**, 350, 396
Hull (Canada) 401
hunter–gatherers 362, 394
hunting 340
    animals 348, 350–351; environmental issues 417, *417*, 421; restrictions 337; traditional 339, *340*, 341
Huron, Lake 317
Hutterite community **391**
hydroelectric power (HEP) 338, 371, 374, **418**
Hylocomium 356

I

ice ages 330
ice caps 326
ice environment **343**
ice sheets **330**
    table of world's ice sheets and glaciers *330; see also* glaciation, isostasy
ice shelves 330
icebergs 330, *331*
immigration 388–389, 391, 392–393, 401, 403
indigenous peoples 339, 340–341, 388, **394–395**, *395*, 398, 401, 403, 408
    environmental issues 416, 417, 418, 420, 421; *see also* Native-Americans, Inuit people
industrialization 335, 403, 417, 418
industry and resources **316**, **370–379**, *370*
    agriculture and food 370; automobiles 373, *374*; communications **376–377**, *376;* construction 374; crafts 373, *373*; electrical and electronics 373, **376–377**, *376*; energy 370, 371, *373*, *373*, *374*, *373*; forestry and paper 370, *370*, 371, 373, **375;** fur 370, *373*; government policy 372–373, 374–375; labor 373, 374; manufacturing *370*, 372–374; metals and minerals 370–371, 374, **378**, *378*; tourism 373; trade with USA 371–372; transportation 374
International Biological Program 337
International Peace Park 336
Inuit people *306*, 339, 340–341, *362*, **385**, 388, 394, 395, 408, 417, *417*, 419, 421
Inuvialuit people 341
iron ore 371–372
Iroquois people 388, 394
irrigation *see* water management
Islands Protection Society 339
isostasy 327

J

jackpine 355
Jakobshavn (Greenland) 320
    glacier *331*
Japan
    automobiles 373; energy 371
Jasper National Park (Canada) 338
juniper, dwarf 356
Juniperus 356

K

Karlsefni, Thorfinn 305
Kelsey, Henry 309
Kicking Horse river *299*
King, Mackenzie 319
Kingston (Canada) 398, 402
Klondike *299*, 309, *309*
Kluane National Park (Canada) 337
Kootenay National Park (Canada) 336

Korea 382
Korean War (1950–53) 309
Kutchin people 395

L

labor 386, 387
  in industry 373, 374
Labrador 298, 302, 306
lakes, postglacial 324, *325*
lamprey, sea **346**
land
  loss to agriculture 334, 335;
  ownership 339; pressure on 366,
  367
landscape **298–302**
landslides 329
languages 388, 390, 393, 404–405
Larix 355, *356*
layering 360
Ledum 356
legislation 336, 421
lemming, Arctic/Norway 344
Lesage, Jean 414, *414*
Lévesque, René 414, *414*
Liberal Party (Canada) 410, 411,
  414, *414*
lichen *356*, 357
  old man's beard 357; reindeer 357
life expectancy *385*
lily, trout 358
lithospheric plates *see* plate, North
  American
livestock 365
lobster 345
Logan, Mount 301
logging *see* deforestation, forestry
London (Canada) 398
lousewort 354
lynx 346, 348, 350

M

McClintock, Francis *306*, 307
McClure, Robert 306
Mackenzie delta 324, 326
Mackenzie river and valley 301, 302,
  316, 318
MacMillan Bloedel 375
McSkimming, Robert 395
maize *364*, 365
Man and Biosphere Program
  (UNESCO) *see* Biosphere
  Reserves
Manitoba (Canada) *304*, 308, 314,
  316, 364
manufacturing industry *370*,
  372–374
maple 358
  red 355; sugar 355, 358, *358*
marigold, marsh *356*
marine pollution 419
Maritime Provinces **406**, *406*
market gardening *see* horticulture
marmot, Vancouver Island 349
marten 350
mass movement *see* landslides
mechanization of farms 365, 366
media **318**
medicinal plants 359
Meech Lake Accord (Canada) 393,
  409, 414

Megaptera 347
mesa 328
metals and minerals 335, 337, 338,
  339, 340, 370–371, 374, 378, *378*,
  380, 381, 417
Métis people 309, 313, 388, 394
Mexico 382, 386–387
Mid-Canada Line 413
migration, animal 344–345
minerals *see* metals and minerals
mink 350
mire *see* peatlands
Mississippi river 307, *328*
mixed farming 363, 365
Mohawk people *395*
molybdenum 371
Moneses 355
Monodon 347
Monster Houses **393**
Montreal (Canada) 299, *302*, 307,
  308, *313*, 318, 388, 392, 398, 400,
  401, 402, *402*, 403, 404–405, *404*
moose/elk 346, 349, **352**, *352*
moraines 329, 330
moss, feather 356
  see also Sphagnum
motor vehicles *see* automobile
  industry
Mount Revelstoke National Park
  (Canada) 336
Mounties *see* Royal Canadian
  Mounted Police
mudflow 329
Mulroney, Brian 409, *410*, 411
multiculturalism 392–393, *393*
muskrat 349

N

NAFTA *see* North American Free
  Trade Agreement
Nansen, Fridtjof **303**
narwhal *347*
National Film Board of Canada **319**,
  319
national parks 337–339, *337*, *338*,
  339, *339*, **340–341**, *340*
Native-Americans 388, **394–395**,
  408, 414
NATO *see* North Atlantic Treaty
  Organization
natural gas 371, 373
nature reserves *see* Biosphere
  Reserves
New Brunswick 299, 307, 308, 316
New Democratic Party (Canada)
  410, *411*
New Zealand 365
Newfoundland (Canada) 299, 307,
  308, 316, 318, 321, 406
Niagara Falls 299, 317, *328*
Niagara peninsula 363, 367
nickel 371
NORAD *see* North American
  Defense Agreement
North–South dialog 413
North American Defense
  Agreement (NORAD) 412, *412*,
  413
North American Free Trade
  Agreement (NAFTA) 382, **386–387**
North Atlantic Treaty Organization
  (NATO) 309, 412
  membership 413, *413*

North Pole 302, **303**
northern lights **332**, *332*
Northern Telecom 376
Northern Yukon National Park
  (Canada) 339, **340–341**, *340*
Northwest Passage **306–307**, 308
Northwest Territories (Canada) 308,
  309, 311, 312, 315, 316, 318, 394
Nova Scotia 299, 307, 308, 313, 318
Novatel *376*
nuclear power 371

O

oak 355
  white 358
oceans and seas 343
octopus, Giant 345
Official Language Act (Canada) 409
oil, petroleum and gas industry 335,
  337, 338, 339, 340, 343, 371, **373**,
  373, 381, 421
oilseed rape 365, 367
Ontario (Canada) 299, 302, 308, 314,
  315, 316, 372
Ontario, Lake 317, *328*
Ontario Natural Heritage League
  (Canada) 337
Opuntia 355
orchid, coral-root 357
Ottawa (Canada) 398, 401
Oxycoccus 358
Oxyria 354, *361*

P

pack ice 330
Panama Canal 307
paper and pulp industry 358, 383
Paris, Treaty of (1763) 307
parks *see* national parks
part-time farming 366
Parti Québécois (PQ) 411, 414, *414*
patterned ground 327
PCBs *see* polychlorinated biphenyls
Pearson, Lester 413
Peary, Robert **303**, *303*
peatlands 334, *356*
Pedicularis 354
Peggy's Cove *316*
pelicans 349
peoples and cultures **388–396**
  art 391, 392; colonialism 388–389,
  394; constitution 390; ethnic
  groups 388, **392–393**, *393*; flag
  389, 392; immigration 388–389,
  391, 392–393; indigenous peoples
  388, **394–395**, *395*; languages 388,
  390, 393; Mounties **396**, *396*;
  multiculturalism 392–393, *393*;
  sport 390, *391*; USA, influence of
  389, 390–391, 393
permafrost 327, *419*, 421
pesticides 366
petrochemical industry **373**
petroleum *see* oil, petroleum and
  gas industry
Philippines 393
physical geography **324–329**, *325*,
  328, *332*
Picea 354, 355, *359*
pig, domestic 365

pine 354, 357
  jack- 355; lodgepole 355;
  Monterey 355, 358; white 355,
  358, *359*
pingos *326*, 327
Pinus 354, 355, *359*
pitcher plant *356*, 358
plankton 345
plant life 302–304, **354–361**
  adaptation **357**, **360**; breeding
  367; in culture and ritual **359**; in
  medicine 359; *see also* vegetation
  and wildlife
plate, North American 324
Pleurozium 356
plover, Lesser golden 344
Poa 360
Poland 393
Polar Bear Pass 337
Polar Bear Provincial Park 336
polar regions *see* Arctic
Polar Sea incident **413**
pollution 349, 359, 416, 417,
  418–419, 421
  air 417, 418, 419; control 420–421;
  marine 419, *339*; transboundary
  418; *see also* acid rain
polychlorinated biphenyls (PCBs)
  419, 421
population 398, 399, *399*, 400, 403
  loss 367; pressure 335
Populus 355
porcupines *351*
potatoes 365
poultry 365
prairies 334, *334*, 355, 359, 364
  farming changes **367**; *see also*
  grassland
predator–prey relationships 347
preserving food *362*
pressure groups, environmental 420
price controls 366
Prince Edward Island 299, 307, 308,
  313, 314
Prince George (Canada) 399, 400
Prince Rupert (Canada)[A] 308, 318
Progressive Conservative Party
  (Canada) 410, 411
pronghorn 347
protection of animals 351
protectionism 372
Protestantism 392
provincial government (Canada)
  411, *411*
Pseudotsuga 355
ptarmigan, Rock 346
public attitudes to the environment
  420–421

Q

Quebec City (Canada) 398, *398*, 400,
  401, 402
Quebec province (Canada) 299, 305,
  305, 307, *307*, 308, 310, 312, 313,
  315, 316, 319
  economy 383, 384, *384*; people
  388, 389, *389*, 392, 393, 394
Quebec separatism *384*, 393, 408,
  408, 409, **414**, *414*
Quebec–Ontario corridor 372–373
Queen Charlotte Islands (Canada)
  301
Queen's Channel (Canada) *306*
Quercus 355, 358

R

raccoon 348
railroads 364, *366*, 374
rainforests, temperate 355, 358
  see also forests
Ramsar Sites 336
Ranunculus 354
rat, musk- 349
rattlesnake 344
recycling *see* waste and recycling
Red Deer river *328*
Regina (Canada) 399, 403
regreening schemes 420
reintroduced animal species 349
religion *see individual faiths*
religion and plants **359**
reserves *see* national parks
resettlement schemes 366
Resolute Bay (Canada) 422
Riel, Louis 309
Riel Rebellion 311
ritual use of plants **359**
river, transportation 369, *369*
road building 338
Rocky Mountains *299*, 301, 310, 314
  agriculture 363, 365, 368; physical
  geography 324, 328, *328*, 329, 330
Roman Catholicism 388, 392, 414
Rosaceae 360
roses 360
Royal Canadian Mounted Police
  311, *311*, **396**, *396*
rural depopulation 367
rural settlements 399–400
rural–urban migration 398
rye *364*, 367

S

Saint Basile le Grand toxic cloud
  (Canada) 421
Saint Helens, Mount (USA) 324
Saint Jean Vianney (Canada) **329**
Saint John (Canada) 398
Saint John's (Canada) 398, 400, 402,
  406
Saint Lawrence, Gulf of 299, 317,
  339
Saint Lawrence Lowlands 314, 316
Saint Lawrence river and Seaway
  307, 308, 317, *317*, 318, 324, 325,
  329, 404
Saint Pierre and Miquelon 307, 316,
  321
Salix 354
salmon, Pacific 349
saprophytes 357
Sarracenia 356, 358
Saskatchewan (Canada) *305*, 307,
  308, 316, 364
satellites *376*, 377
Saxifraga 354, 360, 361
saxifrage
  nodding 360; purple 354, 358,
  360, 354
sea and river transportation 369,
  369
sea-level change 330
seal 344, 346
  Common/Harbor 345; Harp *339*,
  345, **349**, 350, *351*; Hooded 350;
  Ringed 345

sedge 355, *356*
seeds 360
Selkirk, Lord 308
Selkirk Mountains 330
separatism *384*, 408, *408*, 409, **414**,
  414
service sector 382
settlement **398–407**
  architecture 402–403, *402*;
  economic activity 398–399, 403;
  ethnic neighborhoods 402, *403*,
  404–405; government policies
  401–402; history 398–399, 406;
  housing 403, *403*; immigration
  362, 401, 403; indigenous peoples
  398, 401, 403; industrialization
  403; languages 404–405; Maritime
  Provinces *406*, *406*; population
  398, 399, *399*, 400, 403; rural
  settlements 399–400; rural–urban
  migration 398; suburbs 403, *403*;
  transportation 403; urban growth
  398, *399*, 401–403
Seven Oaks Massacre (1816) 308
sewage and sanitation 419, 421, *421*
sheep, domestic 365
shield area 324, *325*
silage 365
society **305–313**, *308*, *313*
soil
  chernozem 363; erosion 359, 419;
  fertility 364
Solidago 358
sorrel, alpine 354, 360, *361*
South Korea 382
South Moresby National Park
  (Canada) *339*, *339*
Soviet Union, former *see* Union of
  Soviet Socialist Republics
soybean 365
Spar Aerospace 377
specialization in farming 365, *365*
species, animal
  protected 351; reintroduced 349
Sphagnum 356, *356*, 359
spider plant *361*
sport 390, *391*
spruce 354, 357, 358, 359
  black 356; black and white 355;
  Engelmann 355; red 355
staple crops 363, 365, 367
Stauning's Alps *331*
stoat 346, 350
suburbs 403, *403*
Sudbury (Canada) 399
Superior, Lake 317, 324
sweet corn *see* maize

T

tamarack 355, *356*
taxation 383, 385
tea, Labrador 356, *356*, 357
telecommunications industry
  376–377, *376*
temperate rainforest 334, *335*, 339,
  339
  see also forests
tern, Arctic 344
terraces 326
thermokarst 327
Third World, overseas aid to *412*,
  413
Thuja 359

Thunder Bay (Great Lakes) 308, 318,
  319
Tilia 355
timber industry 358, 380, *382*, 383
  see also forestry industry
tobacco 365
Toronto (Canada) 313, 318, 393, *393*,
  398, 400, *400*, 401, 402, *402*, 403,
  405
tourism 385
  disturbance by 338; economic
  value 338, 373
trade **316**
  free **386–387**, *386*
trade unions 386, 387
transboundary pollution 418
transportation and communications
  316, **318**, *319*, 368, 374, 403, 416
  railroads 364, *366*; sea and rivers
  369, *369*
trees adapting to cold **357**
triticale 367
Trudeau, Pierre Elliott *408*, 409, 411,
  413
Tsuga 355, *359*
tundra 324, *326*, 327, 334, *336*, *340*,
  354, *354*, 359, 360
turnstone, Ruddy 344, *344*
Tursiops 347
Typha 356

U

UK *see* United Kingdom
Ulmus 355
unemployment 381, 384, 385
Union of Soviet Socialist Republics
  (former USSR) 364
United Kingdom (UK) 362, 410
  see also British colonial influence
United Nations (UN)
  membership 413; peacekeeping
  role *412*
United States of America (USA)
  336, 390, *409*
  agriculture 362, 369; emigration
  from Canada 388; free market
  trading 382, **386–387**, *386*;
  influence in Canada 310, *313*, 389,
  389, 390–391, 393; trade with
  Canada 371–372; transboundary
  pollution 418
uranium 371
urban growth 398, *399*, 401–403
urbanization 417
USA *see* United States of America
Usnea 357
USSR, former *see* Union of Soviet
  Socialist Republics

V

Vaccinium 358
valley, U-shaped *331*
Vancouver (Canada) 392, 393, 398,
  399, 400, 402, 403, *403*
Vancouver Island (Canada) 301,
  308, 318
vegetation and wildlife **302–305**,
  304, 309, **344–351**, **354–361**
Victoria (Canada) 308, *310*, 400
Vietnam 393

W

walrus 344, *348*
waste and recycling 419, *419*, 421
water pollution 416, 417, 418–419,
  421
water resources, management of
  366, 421, *421*
waterfalls *328*
Waterton Lakes National Park
  (Canada) 336, 338
weathering *see* erosion
welfare *see* health and welfare
wetlands, prairie 334
  see also peatlands, Ramsar Sites
whale 347
  Blue *347*; Fin *347*; Gray *347*;
  Humpback *347*; Minke *347*;
  White *347*
wheat 362–367, *362*, *363*, *366*, 380,
  381
wheatear 344
Whitehorse (Canada) 400, 401
wilderness management 417, 418
wildlife **304–305**, *304*, **344–351**, **352**,
  352
willow 354
  creeping 360
Windsor (Canada) 400
Winnipeg (Canada) *304*, 309, 392,
  399, 403
wintergreen 355, 358
wolf, Gray 346, 347, 348
Wolfe, James 307, *307*
wolverine 350
Wood Buffalo National Park
  (Canada) 336
World Heritage Sites 336
World War I 389
World Wide Fund for Nature
  (WWF) 337

Y

Yellowknife (Canada) 400
Yoho National Park (Canada) 336
Yukon Native Brotherhood 395
Yukon river *300*, *309*
Yukon Territory (Canada) 301, 308,
  309, 311, 312, 315, 316, 394

Z

zinc 371

Acknowledgments

CONTRIBUTORS

General Advisory Editor
Professor Peter Haggett, University of Bristol, UK

COUNTRY PROFILES

Advisory Editor
Dr W. Robert Wightman, University of Western Ontario, Canada

Writers
Asgard Publishing Services:
Philip Gardner
Allan Scott
Michael Scott Rohan
Andrew Shackleton

REGIONAL PROFILES

Advisory Editors
Professor Ken J. Gregory, Goldsmith's College, London, UK
Physical Geography

Robert Burton, Huntingdon, UK
Habitats and their Conservation, Animal Life

Professor D.M. Moore, University of Reading, UK
Plant Life

Dr John Tarrant, University of East Anglia, UK
Agriculture

Dr Ian Hamilton, London School of Economics, UK
Industry

Dr Stuart Corbridge, University of Cambridge, UK
Economy

Dr Alisdair Rogers, University of Oxford, UK
Peoples and Cultures

Professor John Rennie Short, Syracuse University, USA
Cities

Dr Peter Taylor, University of Newcastle upon Tyne, UK
Government

Dr Michael Williams, University of Oxford, UK
Environmental Issues

Writers
Dr Michael J. Clark, University of Southampton, UK
Physical Geography, Environmental Issues

Dr D. Scott Slocombe, Wilfred Laurier University, Waterloo, Canada   *Habitats and their Conservation*

Professor J. Gordon Nelson, Wilfred Laurier University, Waterloo, Canada   *Habitats and their Conservation*

Dr Karen Burke da Silva, McGill University, Canada
Animal Life

Dr Jack da Silva, McGill University, Canada
Animal Life

Dr R.E. Longton, University of Reading, UK
Plant Life

Dr Guy M. Robinson, University of Edinburgh, UK
Agriculture

Dr Roger Hayter, Simon Fraser University, British Columbia, Canada   *Industry*

Dr Simon Milne, McGill University, Canada
Economy

Professor David Ley, University of British Columbia, Vancouver, Canada   *Peoples and Cultures*

Professor John Mercer, Syracuse University, USA
Cities

Professor Colin Williams, Staffordshire University, UK
Government

Editorial Director: Graham Bateman
Project Editors: Susan Kennedy, Candida Hunt
Series Editors: Victoria Egan, Fiona Mullan
Art Editor: Steve McCurdy
Chief Designer: Chris Munday
Cartographic Manager: Olive Pearson
Cartographic Editor: Sarah Phibbs
Picture Reasearch Managers: Thérèse Maitland, Jo Rapley, Alison Renney, Leanda Shrimpton
Typesetting: Brian Blackmore, Niki Moores
Production: Clive Sparling, Aleeta Cliff

Further reading

Barbour, M.G. and Billings, W.D. (eds.) *North American Terrestrial Vegetation* (Cambridge University Press, Cambridge, 1990)
Bone, R.M. *The Geography of the Canadian North* (Oxford University Press, Toronto, 1992)
Bowler, I.R. (ed.) *The Geography of Agriculture in Developed Market Economies* (Wiley, New York, 1992)
Burgess, M. (ed.) *Canadian Federalism* (Pinter, New York, 1990)
Fitzharris T. and Livingstone, J.A. *Canada: a Natural History* (Viking Penguin, New York, 1988)
Hall, S. *The Fourth World: the Heritage of the Arctic and its Destruction* (Alfred A. Knopf, New York, 1987)
Hayter, R. and Wilde, P.D. (eds.) *Industrial Transformation and Challenge in Australia and Canada* (Carleton University Press, Ottawa, 1990)
Herberg, E. *Ethnic Groups in Canada: Acculturation and Transition* (Nelson, Toronto, 1989)
Miles, H. and Salisbury, M. *Kingdom of the Ice Bear: a Portrait of the Arctic* (BBC, London, 1985)

Stonehouse, B. *Polar Ecology* (Chapman and Hall, New York, 1989)
Sugden, D. *Arctic and Antarctic* (Blackwell, Oxford, 1982)
Trenhaile, A.S. *The Geomorphology of Canada* (Oxford University Press, Toronto, 1990)
Yeates, M. *The North American City* 4th edn. (Harper and Row, New York, 1990)